Andaman Coast

Andrew Spooner & Lana Willocks

Credits

Travel 915.93 SPO 2012

Footprint credits
Editor: Jo Williams
Production and layout: Emma Bryers
Maps: Kevin Feeney

Managing Director: Andy Riddle
Commercial Director: Patrick Dawson
Publisher: Alan Murphy
Publishing Managers: Felicity Laughton,
Jo Williams, Nicola Gibbs
Marketing and Partnerships Director:
Liz Harper
Marketing Executive: Liz Eyles
Trade Product Manager: Diane McEntee
Account Managers: Paul Bew, Tania Ross
Advertising: Renu Sibal, Elizabeth Taylor
Trade Product Co-ordinator: Kirsty Holmes

Photography credits
Front cover: Dreamstime
Back cover: Shutterstock

Printed and bound in the United States
of America

Publishing information
Footprint *Focus Andaman Coast*
1st edition
© Footprint Handbooks Ltd
August 2012

ISBN: 978 1 908206 78 7
CIP DATA: A catalogue record for this book
is available from the British Library

® Footprint Handbooks and the Footprint
mark are a registered trademark of
Footprint Handbooks Ltd

Published by Footprint
6 Riverside Court
Lower Bristol Road
Bath BA2 3DZ, UK
T +44 (0)1225 469141
F +44 (0)1225 469461
footprinttravelguides.com

Distributed in the USA by Globe Pequot
Press, Guilford, Connecticut

Every effort has been made to ensure that
the facts in this guidebook are accurate.
However, travellers should still obtain advice
from consulates, airlines, etc, about travel
and visa requirements before travelling.
The authors and publishers cannot accept
responsibility for any loss, injury or
inconvenience however caused.

The content of Footprint *Focus Andaman
Coast* has been taken directly from
Footprint's *Thailand Handbook* which
was researched and written by
Andrew Spooner.

Contents

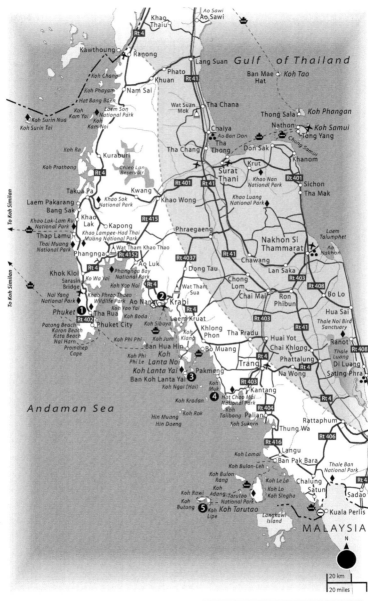

The Andaman coast presents a startling cultural mosaic, from Ranong's cheroot-smoking Burmese in the north to the south's strident Muslims, along with the numerous Chao Le sea gypsies and Chinese traders. On Ranong's rain-drenched islands, bare-knuckle boxing matches between Burmese and Thai re-enact an age-old rivalry, while a growing separatist movement continues to spread through the hotly contested deep South, parts of which were Malaysia a little over a century ago. Meanwhile, indigenous sea gypsies persist in animist practices, including offerings of human hair to the spirits of the treacherous Andaman.

Travellers will find many pleasures along this coast, from the Similan islands' world-famous diving sites, including Richelieu Rock, to Phuket's beaches: katoey paradise Patong and jetset Pansea. Further down the coast are Phangnga's sea cave paintings and the magical floating fishing village of Koh Panyi. Off Krabi – where giant prehistoric human skulls were found – are eerie towering limestone karsts revered by climbers. Further south are Koh Lanta's white-sand, coral-rimmed beaches and the brooding ex-prison island of Tarutao. The latter offers dense and terrifying untouched jungle populated by wild boar, barking deer and poisonous snakes. The Adang-Rawi archipelago's tiny islands – unreachable during the monsoon – provide homes for pythons and hornbills, while, only metres off shore, snorkellers can find untouched sea life, including shoals of barracuda. Finally, the whole of the coast is dotted with island retreats with no electricity or cars, among them Koh Muk, close to the Emerald Cave, and the tropical idyll of Koh Bulon-Leh.

Planning your trip

Getting to Thailand

Air

The majority of visitors arrive in Thailand through Bangkok's **Suvarnabhumi International Airport**, which opened in 2006 but has been plagued with problems. The city's old airport, Don Muang, has been re-opened to help cope with the overflow. Chiang Mai in the north and Phuket in the south also have international airports. More than 35 airlines and charter companies fly to Bangkok. **THAI** is the national carrier. Fares inflate by up to 50% during high season.

Flights from Europe The approximate flight time from London to Bangkok (non-stop) is 12 hours. From London Heathrow, airlines offering non-stop flights include **Qantas**, **British Airways**, **THAI** and **Eva Air**. You can easily connect to Thailand from the UK via most other European capitals. **Finnair** flies daily from Helsinki, **KLM** via Amsterdam and **Lufthansa** via Frankfurt. **SAS** flies from Copenhagen and **Swiss Air** from Zurich. Further afield, **Etihad** flies via Abu Dhabi, **Gulf Air** via Bahrain and **Qatar** via Muscat and Doha. Non-direct flights can work out much cheaper, so if you want a bargain, shop around. **Finnair**, www.finnair.com, often offers some of the cheapest fares. It is also possible to fly direct to Chiang Mai from Dusseldorf, Frankfurt and Munich in Germany, and to Phuket from Dusseldorf and Munich.

Flights from the USA and Canada The approximate flight time from Los Angeles to Bangkok is 21 hours. There are one-stop flights from Los Angeles on **THAI** and two-stops on **Delta**; one-stop flights from San Francisco on **Northwest** and **United** and two-stops on **Delta**; and one-stop flights from Vancouver on **Canadian**. THAI have now started a non-stop flight from New York to Bangkok, which takes 16 hours.

Flights from Australasia There are flights from Sydney and Melbourne (approximately nine hours) daily with **Qantas** and **THAI**. There is also a choice of other flights with **British Airways**, **Alitalia**, **Lufthansa** and **Lauda Air**, which are less frequent. There are flights from Perth with **THAI** and **Qantas**. From Auckland, **Air New Zealand**, **THAI** and **British Airways** fly to Bangkok.

Flights from Asia THAI, **Air India** and **Indian Airlines**, Air Lanka, THAI and **Cathay Pacific** fly from Colombo. From Dhaka, there are flights with **Biman Bangladesh Airlines** and **THAI**. **PIA** and THAI fly from Karachi. **Balkan** flies from Male. **Royal Nepal Airlines** and THAI fly from Kathmandu. It is also possible to fly to Chiang Mai from Kunming (China) and Singapore and to Phuket from Hong Kong, Kuala Lumpur, Penang, Singapore, Taipei and Tokyo. Numerous airlines fly from Hong Kong, Tokyo, Manila, Kuala Lumpur, Singapore and Jakarta to Bangkok. There are daily connections from Singapore and Kuala Lumpur to Hat Yai and from Singapore and Hong Kong to Koh Samui. It is also possible to fly to Phuket from Hong Kong, Kuala Lumpur, Penang, Singapore, Taipei and Tokyo.

There has been a massive proliferation of budget airlines in Southeast Asia with Bangkok becoming one of the primary hubs. There are cheap fares available to/from Laos, Cambodia, Singapore, China, Macau, Maldives, Hong Kong and Malaysia. The pick of the bunch is Air

Don't miss...

1 **Phuket's Vegetarian Festival**, page 47.
2 **Rai Leh**, page 101.
3 **Ban Koh Lanta Yai**, page 123.
4 **The Emerald Cave**, page 140.
5 **Koh Lipe**, page 152.

Numbers relate to map on page 4.

Asia (www.airasia.com) which runs various routes to neighbouring countries. Bangkok has a concentration of tour companies specializing in Indochina and Burma and is a good place to arrange a visa (although most of these countries now issue visas on arrival).

Flights from the Middle East Etihad, flies from Abu Dhabi, **Gulf Air** flies from Bahrain, and **Egyptair** from Cairo.

Road
The main road access is from **Malaysia**. The principal land border crossings are near Betong in Yala Province, from Sungei Golok in Narathiwat Province and at Padang Besar, where the railway line crosses the border. In April 1994 the Friendship Bridge linking Nong Khai with **Laos** opened and became the first bridge across the Mekong River. In addition to the Nong Khai/Friendship Bridge crossing, it is also possible to enter Thailand from Laos at the following places: Pakse to Chongmek (near Ubon Ratchathani); Savannakhet to Mukdahan; Thakhek to Nakhon Phanom; and Ban Houei Xai to Chiang Khong. At present only the crossing at Chiang Khong now requires travellers to cross the Mekong by boat and even there a new bridge is now being built.

Border crossings with **Burma** (**Myanmar**) have been in a state of flux ever since the first – at Mae Sai in the north – opened in 1992. Officially you're only allowed to fly into Burma from Thailand. Depending on the state of relations between Burma and Thailand, and on security conditions in the borderland regions, restrictions on travel are lifted and re-imposed at a day's notice. This applies to the crossing at Mae Sai in the north, Saam Ong in the west and at Mae Sot in the northwest. Sometimes, only Thai passport holders are permitted to cross. If foreigners are permitted to enter Burma it is usually only for forays into the immediate vicinity and sometimes only for day trips.

Crossing the border into **Cambodia** has also become much easier; visas are available at nearly all entry points and there are both sea and land routes.

Boat
No regular, scheduled cruise liners sail to Thailand any longer but it is sometimes possible to enter the country on a **freighter**, arriving at Khlong Toey Port in Bangkok. The *Bangkok Post* publishes weekly shipping details on ships leaving the kingdom.

There are frequent **passenger ferries** from Pak Bara, near Satun, in southern Thailand to Perlis and Langkawi Island, both in **Malaysia**. The passenger and car ferries at Ta Ba, near the town of Tak Bai, south of Narathiwat, make for a fast border crossing to Pengkalan Kubor in Malaysia. An alternative is to hitch a lift on a yacht from Phuket (Thailand) or from Penang (Malaysia). Check at the respective yacht clubs for information.

Rail

Regular services link Singapore and Bangkok, via Kuala Lumpur, Butterworth and the major southern Thai towns. Express air-conditioned trains take two days from Singapore, 34 hours from Kuala Lumpur, 24 hours from Butterworth. The **Magic Arrow Express** leaves Singapore on Sunday, Tuesday and Thursday. An additional train from Butterworth departs at 1420, arriving Bangkok 1210 the next day. The train from Bangkok to Butterworth departs 1420, arriving Butterworth 1255. See www.ktmb.com.my for a timetable for trains between Thailand and Malaysia. All tickets should be booked in advance. **Orient-Express Hotels**, which operates the *Venice Simplon Orient-Express* also runs the luxury *Eastern & Oriental Express* between Bangkok, Kuala Lumpur and Singapore. The air-conditioned train runs once a week from Singapore to Bangkok and back. This locomotive extravaganza departs from Bangkok on Sunday and returns from Singapore every Thursday. The journey takes 45 hours (three nights, two days) to cover the 2000-km one-way trip. Passengers can disembark at Hua Hin, Butterworth (Penang) and Kuala Lumpur. Reservations can be made at **Orient-Express Hotels**, T020-7921400, www.orient-express.com. **Orient-Express Hotels** also has agents in Bangkok (T02-2168661), Singapore (32-01 Shaw Towers, Beach Road, T3923500) and Kuala Lumpur to handle reservations, as well as sales offices in Australia, Japan, USA, France and Germany. See the website for details.

Transport in Thailand

Air

The budget airline boom has finally arrived in Thailand with carriers now offering cheap flights all over the country. As routes can change at very short notice, we would recommend travellers check the different airlines' websites to see what is available; nearly all major towns and cities and tourist destinations are served. **Air Asia** (www.airasia. com), **Bangkok Airways**, and **Nok Air** (www.nokair.com) are currently the major players in this market offering dirt cheap flights – but only if you book online and in advance. **Thai Airways** (THAI) is the national flag carrier and is also by far the largest domestic airline. Although it has had a relatively turbulent few years and standards have declined since the halcyon days of the late 1980s, it is still okay.

THAI flies to several destinations in Thailand. Its head office is found at 89 Vibhavadi Rangsit Road, Jompol, Jatujak, Bangkok 10900, T02-2451000, www.thaiair.com. It is better to book flights through a local office or travel agent displaying the THAI logo. Often THAI domestic fares are cheaper when booked with a credit card over the phone than via their website.

Bangkok Airways head office is at 99 Mu 14, Vibhavadirangsit Rd, Chom Phon, Chatuchak, Bangkok 10900, T02-265 5678 (ext 1771 for reservations centre), www.bangkokair.com.

Road

Bicycle The advice below is collated from travellers who have bicycled through Thailand and is meant to provide a general guideline for those intending to tour the country by bicycle (which is becoming more and more common).

Bicycle type Touring, hybrid or mountain bikes are fine for most roads and tracks in Thailand. Spares are readily available and even small towns have bicycle repair shops where it is often possible to borrow larger tools such as vices. Mountain bikes have made an impact, so accessories for these are also widely available. Components made of more unusual materials – such as titanium and rarer composites – are harder to find.

Attitudes to cyclists It is still comparatively rare to see foreigners cycling in Thailand, so expect to be an object of interest. Be aware that bicyclists give way to everything and everyone! Cars and buses often travel along the hard shoulder; be very wary, especially on main roads. Avoid cycling at night.

Useful equipment Basic tool kit – although there always seems to be help near at hand, and local workshops seem to be able to improvise a solution to just about any problem – including a puncture repair kit, spare tubes, spare tyre and pump. Also take a good map of the area, bungee cords, first-aid kit and water filter. Cover up well, including a hat, and take sunscreen and mosquito repellent.

Bicycle hire Guesthouses and specialized outlets hire out touring and mountain bikes. Expect to pay ฿80-150 per day.

Transporting your bicycle Bikes can be taken on trains, but check the security in the guards' van. Buses are used to taking bicycles (but the more expensive air-conditioned tour buses may prove reluctant), and most carry them for free, although some drivers may ask for a surcharge. Many international airlines take bicycles free of charge, provided they are not boxed. Check your carrier's policy before checking in.

Bus Private and state-run buses leave Bangkok for every town in Thailand; it is an extensive network and a cheap way to travel. The government bus company is called **Bor Kor Sor**, and every town in Thailand will have a **BKS** terminal. There are small stop-in-every-town local buses plus the faster long-distance buses (*rot duan* – express; or *rot air* – air-conditioned). **Air-conditioned buses** come in two grades: *chan nung* (first class, blue colour) and *chan song* (second class, orange colour). *Chan song* have more seats but less elbow and leg room, and will not offer hostess, food and drink services, or a toilet. *Chan nung* buses will have all of these as well as a maximum of 42 seats (adjustable to 70° recline). For longer/overnight journeys, air-conditioned de luxe (sometimes known as *rot tour*, officially Standard 1A buses, also blue like the *chan rung*) or VIP buses, stewardess service is provided with food and drink supplied en route and more leg room plus constant Thai music or videos. There should be no more than 24 seats (adjustable to 135° recline). The best luxury/VIP bus company in the country is Nakhonchai Air, which operates from its own hub near the Mo Chit main bus terminal, but its routing is limited to Bangkok–Chiang Mai and Bangkok–Khon Kaen. Many fares include meals at roadside restaurants, so keep hold of your ticket. If you're travelling on an overnight air-conditioned bus bring a light sweater and some earplugs – both the volume of the entertainment system and cooling system are likely to be turned up full blast.

The local buses are slower and cramped but worth it for those wishing to sample local life. The seats at the very back are reserved for monks, so be ready to move if necessary.

Private tour buses Many tour companies operate bus services in Thailand; travel agents in Bangkok will supply information. These buses are seldom more comfortable than the state buses but are usually more expensive. Overnight trips usually involve a meal stop (included in price of ticket) and stewardess service for drinks and snacks. They often leave from outside the company office, which may not be located at the central bus station. Some may also be dangerous, particularly those offered from 'backpacker' areas like Khao San Road. Our recommendation is that travellers take buses from the main bus terminals.

Car hire There are two schools of thought on car hire in Thailand: one, that under no circumstances should *farangs* (foreigners) drive themselves; and second, that hiring a car is one of the best ways of seeing the country and reaching the more inaccessible sights.

Increasing numbers of visitors are hiring their own cars and internationally respected car hire firms are expanding their operations (such as **Hertz** and **Avis**). Roads and service stations are generally excellent. Driving is on the left-hand side of the road.

Car hire The average cost of hiring a car from a reputable firm is ฿1000-2000 per day, ฿6000-10,000 per week, or ฿20,000-30,000 per month. Some companies automatically include insurance; for others it must be specifically requested and a surcharge is added. An international driver's licence, or a UK, US, French, German, Australian, New Zealand, Singapore or Hong Kong licence is required. The lower age limit is 20 years (higher for some firms). Addresses of car hire firms are included in the sections on the main tourist destinations. If the mere thought of competing with Thai drivers is terrifying, an option is to hire a chauffeur along with the car. For this service an extra ฿300-500 per day is usually charged, more at weekends and if an overnight stay is included. Note that local car hire firms are cheaper although the cars are likely to be less well maintained and will have tens of thousands of kilometres on the clock.

Safety There are a few points that should be kept in mind: accidents in Thailand are often horrific. If involved in an accident, and they occur with great frequency, you – as a foreigner – are likely to be found the guilty party and expected to meet the costs. Ensure the cost of hire includes insurance cover. Many local residents recommend that if a foreigner is involved in an accident, they should not stop but drive on to the nearest police station – if possible, of course.

Hitchhiking Thai people rarely hitchhike and tourists who try could find themselves waiting for a long time at the roadside. It is sometimes possible to wave down vehicles at the more popular beach resorts.

Motorbike Hiring a motorbike has long been a popular way for visitors to explore the local area. Off the main roads and in quieter areas it can be an enjoyable and cheap way to see the country. Some travellers are now not just hiring motorbikes to explore a local area, but are touring the entire country by motorcycle. It is the cheapest way to be independent of public transport, but the risks rise accordingly (see below).

Motorbike hire Rental is mostly confined to holiday resorts and prices vary from place to place; ฿150-300 per day is usual for a 100-150cc machine. Often licences do not have to be shown and insurance will not be available. Riding in shorts and flip-flops is dangerous – a foot injury is easily acquired even at low speeds and broken toes are a nightmare to heal – always wear shoes. Borrow a helmet or, if you're planning to ride a motorbike on more than one occasion, consider buying one – decent helmets can be found for ฿1500 and are better than the 'salad bowls' usually offered by hire companies.

Safety In most areas of Thailand it is compulsory to wear a helmet and while this law is not always enforced there are now periodic checks everywhere – even on remote roads. Fines are usually ฿300; if you have an accident without a helmet the price could be much higher. Thousands of Thais are killed in motorcycle accidents each year and large numbers of tourists also suffer injuries (Koh Samui has been said to have the highest death rate anywhere in the world). Expect anything larger than you to ignore your presence on the road. Be extremely wary and drive defensively.

Motorbike taxi These are becoming increasingly popular, and are the cheapest, quickest and most dangerous way to get from 'A' to 'B'. They are usually used for short rides down *sois* or to better local transport points. Riders wear coloured vests (sometimes numbered) and tend to congregate at key intersections or outside shopping centres for example. Agree a price before boarding – expect to pay ฿10 upwards for a short *soi* hop.

Songthaew ('two rows') *Songthaews* are pick-up trucks fitted with two benches and can be found in many upcountry towns. They normally run fixed routes, with set fares, but can often be hired and used as a taxi service (agree a price before setting out). To let the driver know you want to stop, press the electric buzzers or tap the side of the vehicle with a coin.

Taxi Standard air-conditioned taxis are found in very few Thai towns with the majority in the capital. In Bangkok all taxis have meters. Most Bangkok taxis will also take you on long-distance journeys either for an agreed fee or with the meter running. In the south of Thailand, shared long-distance taxis are common.

Tuk-tuks These come in the form of pedal or motorized machines. Fares should be negotiated and agreed before setting off. It will not take long to discover what is a reasonable price, but don't expect to pay the same as a Thai. Drivers are a useful source of local information and will know most places of interest, plus hotels and restaurants (and sometimes their prices). In Bangkok, and most other towns, these vehicles are a motorized, gas-powered scooter. Pedal-powered *saamlors* (meaning 'three wheels') were outlawed in Bangkok a few years ago and they are now gradually being replaced by the noisier motorized version throughout the country.

Boat
The waterways of Thailand are extensive. However, most people limit their water travel to trips around Bangkok or to Ayutthaya. *Hang-yaaws* (long-tailed boats) are a common form of water travel and are motorized, fast and fun.

Sea travel On the Andaman Coast there are services to and from Phuket, Koh Phi Phi, Krabi, Koh Lanta, the islands off Trang and from Ban Pak Bara and Koh Tarutao National Park. Note that services become irregular and are suspended during certain times of year because of the wet season and rough seas. Each section details information on the months that will affect regular boat services.

Maps
Although maps of Thailand and Southeast Asia are available locally, it is sometimes useful to buy one prior to departure in order to plan routes and itineraries.

Regional maps Bartholomew *Southeast Asia* (1:5,800,000); ITM (International Travel Maps) *Southeast Asia* (1:6,000,000); Nelles *Southeast Asia* (1:4,000,000); Hildebrand *Thailand, Burma, Malaysia and Singapore* (1:2,800,000).

Country maps Bartholomew *Thailand* (1:1,500,000); ITM (International Travel Maps) *Thailand* (1:1,000,000); Nelles *Thailand* (1:1,500,000).

Road maps The best (and cheapest) road maps are available locally and can be easily picked up from a petrol station. They are especially handy because they often give place names in Thai and English and therefore can help when you are trying to get somewhere (but no one understands you!). Michelin also produces a good book or road maps for the country.

Other maps Tactical Pilotage Charts (TPC, US Airforce) (1:500,000); Operational Navigational Charts (ONC, US Airforce) (1:500,000). Both of these are good at showing relief features, which are good for planning treks but less useful for roads, towns and facilities.

Map shops in the UK The best selection is available from **Stanfords**, 12-14 Long Acre, Covent Garden, London, T020-78361321, www.stanfords.co.uk, or 29 Corn Street, Bristol, and 39 Spring Gardens, Manchester. Recommended. Also recommended is **McCarta**, 15 Highbury Place, London, T020-73541616.

Where to stay in Thailand

Thailand has a large selection of hotels, including some of the best in the world. Standards outside of the usual tourist areas have improved immensely over recent years and while such places might not be geared to Western tastes they offer some of the best-value accommodation in the country. Due to its popularity with backpackers, Thailand also has many small guesthouses, serving Western food and catering to the foibles of foreigners. These are concentrated in the main tourist areas.

Hotels and guesthouses
Hotels and guesthouses are listed under eight categories, according to the average price of a double/twin room for one night. It should be noted that many hotels will have a range of rooms, some with air conditioning (a/c) and attached bathroom facilities, others with just a fan and shared facilities. Prices can therefore vary a great deal. If a hotel entry lists 'some a/c', then these rooms are likely to be in the upper part of the range, perhaps even in the next range. Few hotels in Thailand provide breakfast in the price of the room. A service charge of 10% and government tax of 7% will usually be added to the bill in the more expensive hotels (categories **$$$$-$$**). Ask whether the quoted price includes tax when checking in. Prices in Bangkok are inflated.

During the off-season, hotels and guesthouses in tourist destinations may halve their room rates so it is always worthwhile bargaining or asking whether there is a special price. Given the fierce competition among hotels, it is even worth trying during the peak season. Over-building has meant that there is a glut of rooms in some towns and hotels are desperate for business.

Until 10 years ago, most guesthouses offered shared facilities with cold-water showers and squat toilets. Levels of cleanliness were also less than pristine. Nowadays, Western toilet imperialism is making inroads into Thai culture and many of the better-run guesthouses will have good, clean toilets with sit-down facilities and, sometimes, hot water. Some are even quite stylish in their bathroom facilities. Fans are the norm in most guesthouses although, again, to cash in on the buying power of backpackers with more disposable income more and more offer air-conditioned rooms as well. Check that mosquito nets are provided.

Security is a problem, particularly in beach resort areas where flimsy bungalows offer easy access to thieves. Keep valuables with the office for safekeeping (although there are regular cases of people losing valuables that have been left in 'safekeeping') or on your person when you go out. Guesthouses can be tremendous value for money. With limited overheads, family labour and using local foods they can cut their rates in a way that larger hotels with armies of staff, imported food and expensive facilities simply cannot.

Price codes

Where to stay

$$$$	over US$100	**$$$**	US$46-100
$$	US$20-45	**$**	under US$20

Prices include taxes and service charge, but not meals. They are based on a double room, except in the **$** range, where prices are almost always per person.

Restaurants

$$$	over US$12	**$$**	US$6-12	**$**	under US$6

Prices refer to the cost of a two-course meal, not including drinks.

Camping and national park accommodation

It is possible to camp in Thailand and **national parks** are becoming much better at providing campsites and associated facilities. Most parks will have public toilets with basic facilities. Some parks also offer bungalows; these fall into our **$$** accommodation category but because they can often accommodate large groups their per person cost is less than this. The more popular parks will often also have privately run accommodation including sophisticated resorts, sometimes within the park boundaries. For reservations at any of the national parks contact: **Reservation Office** ① *National Parks Division, Royal Forestry Department, 61 Phanhonyothin Rd, Ladyao, Jatujak, Bangkok, T02-56142923. The official website, www.dnp.go.th/parkreserve, is excellent for making online bookings.* Alternatively, you can phone the park offices listed in the relevant sections of this guide. **Beaches** are considered public property – anybody can camp on them for free.

In terms of what to bring and wear, bear in mind that at night at high elevations, even in muggy Thailand, it can be cold. In the north it can fall to close to freezing during the cooler months. So make sure you have a thick coat and a warm sleeping bag. During the day, long trousers (to avoid scratches), sturdy shoes (if you are thinking of trekking any distance), and a hat are recommended. In the evening, long-sleeved shirts (to keep the mosquitoes at bay) are required. If you are camping, remember that while the more popular parks have tents for hire, the rest – and this means most – do not. Bring your own torch, camp stove, fuel and toilet paper.

Food and drink in Thailand

Thai food, for long an exotic cuisine distant from the average northerner's mind and tongue, has become an international success story. The Thai government, recognizing the marketing potential of their food, has instituted a plan called 'Global Thai' to boost the profile of Thai food worldwide as a means of attracting more people to visit its country of origin. Thai food has become, in short, one of Thailand's most effective advertisements.

Thai food is an intermingling of Tai, Chinese and, to a lesser extent, Indian cuisines. This helps to explain why restaurants produce dishes that must be some of the (spicy) hottest in the world, as well as others that are rather bland. *Larb* (traditionally raw – but now more frequently cooked – chopped beef mixed with rice, herbs and spices) is a traditional 'Tai' dish; *pla priaw waan* (whole fish with soy and ginger) is Chinese in origin; while *gaeng mussaman* (beef 'Muslim' curry) was brought to Thailand by Muslim immigrants. Even satay, paraded by most restaurants as a Thai dish, was introduced from Malaysia and Indonesia (which themselves adopted it from Arab traders during the Middle Ages).

Despite these various influences, Thai cooking is distinctive. Thais have managed to combine the best of each tradition, adapting elements to fit their own preferences. Remarkably, considering how ubiquitous it is in Thai cooking, the chilli pepper is a New World fruit and was not introduced into Thailand until the late 16th century (along with the pineapple and the papaya).

A Thai meal is based around rice, and many wealthy Bangkokians own farms upcountry where they cultivate their favourite variety. When a Thai asks another Thai whether he has eaten he will ask, literally, whether he has 'eaten rice' (*kin khao*). Similarly, the accompanying dishes are referred to as food 'with the rice'. There are two main types of rice – 'sticky' or glutinous (*khao niaw*) and non-glutinous (*khao jao*). Sticky rice is usually used to make sweets (desserts) although it is the staple in the northeastern region and parts of the north. *Khao jao* is standard white rice.

In addition to rice, a meal usually consists of a soup like *tom yam kung* (prawn soup), *kaeng* (a curry) and *krueng kieng* (a number of side dishes). Thai food is spicy, and aromatic herbs and grasses (like lemongrass, coriander, tamarind and ginger) are used to give a distinctive flavour. *Nam pla* (fish sauce made from fermented fish and used as a condiment) and *nam prik* (*nam pla*, chillies, garlic, sugar, shrimps and lime juice) are two condiments that are taken with almost all meals. *Nam pla* is made from steeping fish, usually anchovies, in brine for long periods and then bottling the peatish-coloured liquor produced. Chillies deserve a special mention because most Thais like their food HOT! Some chillies are fairly mild; others – like the tiny, red *prik khii nuu* ('mouse shit pepper') – are fiendishly hot.

Isaan food – from the northeast of Thailand – is also distinctive, very similar to Lao cuisine and very popular. Most of the labourers and service staff come from Isaan, particularly in Bangkok, and you won't have to go far to find a rickety street stall selling sticky rice, aromatic *kai yang* (grilled chicken) and fiery *som tam* (papaya salad). *Pla ra* (fermented fish) is one of Isaan's most famous dishes but is usually found only in the most authentic Isaan dishes, its salty, pungent flavour being too much for effete Bangkokians.

Due to Thailand's large Chinese population (or at least Thais with Chinese roots), there are also many Chinese-style restaurants whose cuisine is variously 'Thai-ified'. Many of the snacks available on the streets show this mixture of Thai and Chinese, not to mention Arab and Malay. *Bah jang*, for example, are small pyramids of leaves stuffed with sticky rice, Chinese sausage, salted eggs, pork and dried shrimp. They were reputedly first created for the Chinese dragon boat festival but are now available 12 months a year – for around ฿20.

To sample Thai food it is best to go in a group to a restaurant and order a range of dishes. To eat alone is regarded as slightly strange. However, there are a number of 'one-dish' meals like fried rice and *phat thai* (fried noodles) and restaurants will also usually provide *raat khao* ('over rice'), which is a dish like a curry served on a bed of rice for a single person.

Strict non-fish-eating **vegetarians** and **vegans** are in for a tough time. Nearly every cooked meal you will eat in Thailand will be liberally doused in *nam pla* or cooked with shrimp paste. At more expensive and upmarket international restaurants you'll probably be able to find something suitable – in the rural areas, you'll be eating fruit, fried eggs and rice, though not all at once. There are a network of Taoist restaurants offering more strict veggie fare throughout the country – look out for yellow flags with red Chinese lettering. Also asking for 'mai sai nam pla' (no *nam pla* please)– when ordering what should be veggie food might keep the fish sauce out of harm's reach.

Restaurants

It is possible to get a tasty and nutritious meal almost anywhere – and at any time – in Thailand. Thais eat out a great deal so that most towns have a range of places. Starting at the top, in pecuniary terms at any rate, the more sophisticated restaurants are usually air-conditioned, and sometimes attached to a hotel. In places like Bangkok and Chiang Mai they may be Western in style and atmosphere. In towns less frequented by foreigners they are likely to be rather more functional – although the food will be just as good. In addition to these more upmarket restaurants are a whole range of places from **noodle shops** to **curry houses** and **seafood restaurants**. Many small restaurants have no menus. But often the speciality of the house will be clear – roasted, honeyed ducks hanging in the window, crab and fish laid out on crushed ice outside. Away from the main tourist spots, 'Western' breakfasts are commonly unavailable, so be prepared to eat Thai-style (noodle or rice soup or fried rice). Yet, the quality of much Thai food can be mixed, with many Thai restaurants and street stalls using huge amounts of sugar, MSG and oil in their cooking.

Towards the bottom of the scale are **stalls and food carts**. These tend to congregate at particular places in town – often in the evening, from dusk – although they can be found just about anywhere: outside the local provincial offices, along a cul-de-sac, or under a conveniently placed shady tree. Stall holders will tend to specialize in either noodles, rice dishes, fruit drinks, sweets and so on. Hot meals are usually prepared to order. While stall food may be cheap – a meal costs only around ฿15-20 – they are frequented by people from all walks of life. A well-heeled businessman in a suit is just as likely to be seen bent over a bowl of noodles at a rickety table on a busy street corner as a construction worker.

A popular innovation over the last 10 years or so has been the *suan a-haan* or **garden restaurant**. These are often on the edge of towns, with tables set in gardens, sometimes with bamboo furniture and ponds. Another type of restaurant worth a mention is the **Thai-style coffee shop**. These are sometimes attached to hotels in provincial towns and feature hostesses dressed in Imelda-esque or skimpy spangly costumes. The hostesses, when they are not crooning to the house band, sit with customers, laugh at their jokes and assiduously make sure that their glasses are always full.

In the north, *khantoke* dining is de rigueur – or so one might imagine from the number of restaurants offering it. It is a northern Thai tradition, when people sit on the floor to eat at low tables, often to the accompaniment of traditional music and dance.

Tourist centres also provide good European, American and Japanese food at reasonable prices. Bangkok boasts some superb restaurants. Less expensive Western **fast-food** restaurants can also be found, including **McDonald's** and **Kentucky Fried Chicken**.

The etiquette of eating

The Thai philosophy on eating is 'often', and most Thais will snack their way through the day. Eating is a relaxed, communal affair and it is not necessary to get too worked up about etiquette. Dishes are placed in the middle of the table where diners can help themselves. In a restaurant rice is usually spooned out by a waiter or waitress – and it is considered good manners to start a meal with a spoon of rice. While food is eaten with a spoon and fork, the fork is only used to manoeuvre food onto the spoon. Because most food is prepared in bite-sized pieces it is not usually necessary to use a knife. At noodle stalls chopsticks and china soup spoons are used while in the northeast most people – at least at home – use their fingers. Sticky rice is compressed into a ball using the ends of the fingers and then dipped in the other dishes. Thais will not pile their plates with food but take several small portions from the dishes arranged on a table. It is also considered good manners when invited out to leave some food on your plate, as well as on the serving dishes on the table. This demonstrates the generosity of the host.

Drink
Water in nearly every single restaurant and street stall now comes from large bottles of purified water but if you're unsure, buy your own.

Coffee is consumed throughout Thailand. In stalls and restaurants, coffee comes with a glass of Chinese tea. Soft drinks are widely available too. Many roadside stalls prepare fresh fruit juices in liquidizers while hotels produce all the usual cocktails.

Major brands of **spirits** are served in most hotels and bars, although not always off the tourist path. The most popular spirit among Thais is Mekhong – local cane whisky – which can be drunk straight or with mixers such as Coca-Cola. However, due to its hangover-inducing properties, more sophisticated Thais prefer Johnny Walker or an equivalent brand.

Beer drinking is spreading fast. The most popular local beer is Singha beer brewed by Boon Rawd. Singha, Chang and Heineken are the three most popular beers in Thailand. Leo and Cheers are agreeable budget options although they are seldom sold in restaurants. Beer is relatively expensive in Thai terms as it is heavily taxed by the government. It is a high status drink, so the burgeoning middle class, especially the young, are turning to beer in preference to traditional, local whiskies – which explains why brewers are so keen to set up shop in this traditionally non-beer drinking country. Some pubs and bars also sell beer on tap – which is known as *bier sot*, 'fresh' beer.

Thais are fast developing a penchant for **wine**. Imported wines are expensive by international standards but Thailand now has six wineries, mainly in the northeastern region around Nakhon Ratchasima.

Essentials A-Z

Accident and emergency
Emergency services Police: T191, T123. **Tourist police**: T1155. **Fire**: T199. Ambulance: T02-2551134-6. **Tourist Assistance Centre**: Rachdamnern Nok Av, Bangkok, T02-356 0655.

Calling one of the emergency numbers will not usually be very productive as few operators speak English. It is better to call the tourist police or have a hotel employee or other English-speaking Thai telephone for you. For more intractable problems contact your embassy or consulate.

Customs and duty free
Customs
Non-residents can bring in unlimited foreign and Thai currency although amounts exceeding US$10,000 must be declared. Maximum amount permitted to take out of Thailand is ฿50,000 per person.

Prohibited items
All narcotics; obscene literature, pornography; firearms (except with a permit from the Police Department or local registration office); and some species of plants and animals (for more information contact the **Royal Forestry Department**, Phahonyothin Rd, Bangkok, T02-561 0777).

Duty free
500 g of cigars/cigarettes (or 200 cigarettes) and one litre of wine or spirits.

Export restrictions
No Buddha or Bodhisattva images or fragments should be taken out of Thailand, except for worshipping by Buddhists, for cultural exchanges or for research. However, it is obvious that many people do – you only have to look in the antique shops to see the abundance for sale. A licence should be obtained from the Department of Fine Arts, Na Prathat Rd, Bangkok, T02-224 1370, from **Chiang Mai National Museum**, T02-221308, or from the **Songkhla National Museum**, Songkhla, T02-311728. 5-days' notice is needed; take 2 passport photos of the object and photocopies of your passport.

VAT refunds
Most of the major department stores have a VAT refund desk. Go to them on your day of purchase with receipts and ask them to complete VAT refund form, which you then present, with purchased goods, at appropriate desk in any international airport in Thailand. They'll give you another form that you exchange for cash in the departure lounge. You'll need to spend at least ฿4000 to qualify for a refund.

Disabled travellers
Disabled travellers will find Thailand a challenge. The difficulties that even the able bodied encounter in crossing roads when pedestrian crossings are either non-existent or ignored by most motorists are amplified for the disabled. Cracked pavements, high curbs and lack of ramps add to the problems for even the most wheelchair savvy. Buses and taxis are not designed for disabled access either and there are relatively few hotels and restaurants that are wheelchair-friendly. This is particularly true of cheaper and older establishments. This is not to suggest that travel in Thailand is impossible for the disabled. On the plus side, you will find Thais to be extremely helpful and because taxis and tuk-tuks are cheap it is usually not necessary to rely on buses. The **Global Access – Disabled Travel Network** website, www.globalaccess.news.com, is useful. Another informative site, with lots of advice on how to travel with specific disabilities, plus listings and links,

belongs to the **Society for Accessible Travel and Hospitality**, www.sath.org. Another site, www.access-able.com has a specific section for travel in Thailand.

Electricity
Voltage is 220 volts (50 cycles). Most first- and tourist-class hotels have outlets for shavers and hairdryers. Adaptors are recommended, as almost all sockets are 2-pronged.

Embassies and consulates
Thai embassies worldwide
www.thaiembassy.org is a useful resource.

Gay and lesbian travellers
On the surface, Thailand is incredibly tolerant of homosexuals and lesbians. In Bangkok and other major cities there's an openness that can make even San Francisco look tame. It is for this reason that Thailand's gay scene has flourished and, more particularly, has grown in line with international tourism. However, overt public displays of affection are still frowned upon. Attitudes in the more traditional rural areas, particularly the Muslim regions, are far more conservative than in the cities. By exercising a degree of cultural sensitivity any visit should be hassle free.

Several of the free tourist magazines distributed through hotels and restaurants in Bangkok and Phuket provide information on the gay and lesbian scene, including bars and meeting points. The essential website before you get there is **www. utopia-asia.com** which provides good material on where to go, current events, and background information on the Thai gay scene in Bangkok and beyond. **Utopia tours** at Tarntawan Palace Hotel, 119/5-10 Suriwong Rd, T02-634 0273, www.utopia-tours.com, provides tours for gay and lesbian visitors. There's also a map of gay Bangkok. Gay clubs are listed in *Bangkok Metro* magazine (www.bkkmetro. co.th) and include **DJ Station** (by far the most famous Bangkok gay club) and its sister club

Freeman Dance Arena, 60/18-21 Silom Rd, www.dj-station.com. The main centres of activity in Bangkok are Silom Rd sois 2 and 4 and Sukhumvit Soi 23. There is also a gay scene on Phuket. See also the Thai section of **www.fridae.com**, one of Asia's most comprehensive gay sites.

Health
Hospitals/medical services are listed in the Directory sections of each chapter.

Staying healthy in Thailand is straight-forward. With the following advice and precautions you should keep as healthy as you do at home. Most visitors return home having experienced no problems at all beyond an upset stomach. However, in Thailand the health risks, especially in the tropical areas, are different from those encountered in Europe or the USA. It also depends on how you travel and where. The country has a mainly tropical climate; nevertheless the acquisition of true tropical disease by the visitor is probably conditioned as much by the rural nature and standard of hygiene of the surroundings than by the climate. Malaria is common in certain areas, particularly in the jungle. There is an obvious difference in health risks between the business traveller who tends to stay in international class hotels in the large cities and the backpacker trekking through the rural areas. There are no hard and fast rules to follow; you will often have to make your own judgement on the healthiness or otherwise of your surroundings. Check with your doctor on the status of Avian flu before you go. At the time of writing, Thailand was clear of bird flu.

Before you go
Ideally, you should see your GP/practice nurse or travel clinic at least 6 weeks before your departure for general advice on travel risks, malaria and recommended vaccinations. Your local pharmacist can also be a good source of readily accessible advice. Make sure you have travel insurance, get a

dental check (especially if you are going to be away for more than a month), know your own blood group and if you suffer a long-term condition such as diabetes or epilepsy make sure someone knows or that you have a **Medic Alert** bracelet/necklace with this information on it.

Recommended vaccinations
No vaccinations are specifically required for Thailand unless coming from an infected area, but tuberculosis, rabies, Japanese B encephalitis and hepatitis B are commonly recommended. The final decision, however, should be based on a consultation with your GP or travel clinic. You should also confirm that your primary courses and boosters are up to date (diphtheria, tetanus, poliomyelitis, hepatitis A, typhoid).

A yellow fever certificate is required by visitors who have been in an infected area in the 10 days before arrival. Those without a vaccination certificate will be vaccinated and kept in quarantine for 6 days, or deported.

Useful websites
www.nathnac.org National Travel Health Network and Centre.
www.who.int World Health Organization.
www.fitfortravel.scot.nhs.uk Fit for Travel. This site from Scotland provides a quick A-Z of vaccine and travel health advice requirements for each country.

Books
Dawood R, editor. *Travellers' health* (3rd edition, Oxford University Press, 2002). *Expedition Medicine* (The Royal Geographic Society) Editors David Warrell and Sarah Anderson ISBN 1 86197 040-4.

Internet
Apart from a few remote islands Thailand has an excellent internet network. Tourist areas tend to be well catered for with numerous internet shops offering a connection for between ฿30-90 per hr. Some guesthouses and hotels have free wireless while the more expensive ones charge extortionate rates of up ฿1000 per day. You might also be able to pick up wireless for free from office blocks, etc. The cheapest internet options tend to be the small games rooms run primarily for Thai kids who eagerly play online games, usually ฿10-20 per hr, or by using your web-enabled mobile phone with a local simcard – see Mobiles, page 24.

Insurance
Always take out travel insurance before you set off and read the small print carefully. Check that the policy covers any activities that you may end up doing. Also check exactly what your medical cover includes, ie ambulance, helicopter rescue or emergency flights back home. And check the payment protocol; you may have to cough up first (literally) before the insurance company reimburses you. It is always best to dig out all the receipts for expensive personal effects like jewellery or cameras. Take photos of these items and note down all serial numbers. You are advised to shop around. **STA Travel** and other reputable student travel organizations offer good-value policies. Young travellers from North America can try the **International Student Insurance Service** (ISIS), which is available through STA Travel, T1-800-7814040, www.sta-travel.com. Other recommended travel insurance companies in North America include: **Travel Guard**, T1-800-8261300, www.noelgroup.com; **Access America**, T1-800-2848300; **Travel Insurance Services**, T1-800-9371387; and **Travel Assistance International**, T1-800-821 2828. Older travellers should note that some companies will not cover people over 65 years old, or may charge higher premiums. The best policies for older travellers (UK) are offered by **Age Concern**, T0845-601 2234.

If diving in Thailand, it's worth noting that there are no air evacuation services, and hyperbaric services can charge as much as US$800 per hr so good dive insurance is imperative. It is inexpensive and well worth it in case of a problem, real or perceived. Many general travel insurance policies will not cover diving. Contact **DAN (the Divers' Alert Network)** for more information, www.diversalertnetwork.org; **DAN Europe**, www.daneurope.org; or **DAN South East Asia Pacific**, www.danseap.org.

Language

English is reasonably widely spoken and is taught to all school children. Off the tourist trail, making yourself understood becomes more difficult. It is handy to buy a Thai/ English road atlas of the country (most petrol stations sell them) – you can then point to destinations.

The Thai language is tonal and, strictly speaking, monosyllabic. There are 5 tones: high, low, rising, falling and mid-tone. These are used to distinguish between words which would otherwise be identical. For example: *mai* (low tone, new), *mai* (rising, silk), *mai* (mid-tone, burn), *mai* (high tone, question indicator), and *mai* (falling tone, negative indicator). Not surprisingly, many visitors find it hard to hear the different tones, and it is difficult to make much progress during a short visit. The tonal nature of the language also explains why so much of Thai humour is based around homonyms – and especially when *farangs* (foreigners) say what they do not mean. Although tones make Thai a challenge for foreign visitors, other aspects of the language are easier to grasp: there are no marked plurals in nouns, no marked tenses in verbs, no definite or indefinite articles, and no affixes or suffixes.

Visitors may well experience 2 oddities of the Thai language being reflected in the way that Thais speak English. An 'l' or 'r' at the end of a word in Thai becomes an 'n', while an 's' becomes a 't'. So some Thais refer to the 'Shell' Oil Company as 'Shen', a name like 'Les' becomes 'Let', while 'cheque bill' becomes 'cheque bin'. It is also impossible to

have 2 consonants after one another in Thai. If it occurs, a Thai will automatically insert a vowel (even though it is not written). So the soft drink 'Sprite' becomes 'Sa-prite', and the English word 'start', 'sa-tart'.

Despite Thai being a difficult language to pick up, it is worth trying to learn a few words, even if your visit to Thailand is short. Thais generally feel honoured that a *farang* is bothering to learn their language, and will be patient and helpful. If they laugh at some of your pronunciations do not be put off – it is not meant to be critical.

Media
Newspapers and magazines

There are 2 major English-language dailies – the *Bangkok Post* (www.bangkok post.net) and *The Nation* (www.nation multimedia.com), although journalistic standards in both newspapers are very low and they have a long-standing reputation of distorting the news. There are a number of Thai-language dailies and weeklies, as well as Chinese-language newspapers. The local papers are sometimes scandalously colourful, with gruesome pictures of traffic accidents and murder victims.

International newspapers are available in Bangkok.

Television and radio

CNN and BBC are available in most mid- or upper-range hotels. Local cable networks will sometimes provide English language films, while a full satellite package will give you English football and various movie and other channels. Programme listings are available in *The Nation* and *Bangkok Post*.

Short wave radio frequencies are **BBC**, London, Southeast Asian service 3915, 6195, 9570, 9740, 11750, 11955, 15360; Singapore service 88.9MHz; East Asian service 5995, 6195, 7180, 9740, 11715, 11750, 11945, 11955, 15140, 15280, 15360, 17830, 21715. **Voice of America** (VoA, Washington), Southeast Asian service 1143, 1575, 7120, 9760, 9770, 15185, 15425;

Indonesian service 6110, 11760, 15425. **Radio Beijing**, Southeast Asian service (English) 11600, 11660. **Radio Japan** (Tokyo), Southeast Asian service (English) 11815, 17810, 21610. For information on Asian radio and television broadcasts.

Internet
Recent events in Thailand have exposed the vested interests hiding in the background of papers such as *The Nation* and they are no longer reliable news sources. See our list of websites on page 25.

Money
Currency
Exchange rates: for up-to-the-minute exchange rates visit www.xe.com.

The unit of Thai currency is the **baht** (฿), which is divided into 100 **satang**. Notes in circulation include ฿20 (green), ฿50 (blue), ฿100 (red), ฿500 (purple) and ฿1000 (orange and grey). Coins include 25 satang and 50 satang, and ฿1, ฿2, ฿5, and ฿10. The 2 smaller coins are disappearing from circulation and the 25 satang coin, equivalent to the princely sum of US$0.003, is rarely found. The colloquial term for 25 satang is saleng.

Exchange
It is best to change money at banks or money changers which give better rates than hotels. The exchange booths at Bangkok airport have some of the best rates available. There is no black market. First-class hotels have 24-hr money changers. Indonesian rupiah, Nepalese rupees, Burmese kyat, Vietnamese dong, Lao kip and Cambodian riels cannot be exchanged for baht at Thai banks. (Money changers will sometimes exchange kyat, dong, kip and riel and it can be a good idea to buy the currencies in Bangkok before departure for these countries as the black-market rate often applies.) There is a charge of ฿23 per cheque when changing **traveller's cheques** (passport required) so it works out cheaper

to travel with large denomination traveller's cheques (or avoid them altogether).

Credit and debit cards
Plastic is increasingly used in Thailand and just about every town of any size will have a bank with an ATM. Visa and MasterCard are the most widely taken credit cards, and cash cards with the Cirrus logo can also be used to withdraw cash at many banks. Generally speaking, AMEX can be used at branches of the **Bangkok Bank**; JCB at **Siam Commercial Bank**; MasterCard at **Siam Commercial** and **Bangkok Bank**; and Visa at **Thai Farmers' Bank** and **Bangkok Bank**. Most larger hotels and more expensive restaurants take credit cards as well. Because Thailand has embraced the ATM with such exuberance, many foreign visitors no longer bother with traveller's cheques or cash and rely entirely on plastic. Even so, a small stash of US dollars cash can come in handy in a sticky situation.

Notification of credit card loss: **American Express**, SP Building, 388 Phahonyothin Rd, Bangkok 10400, T02-2735544; **Diners Club**, Dusit Thani Building, Rama IV Rd, T02-233 5644, T02-238 3660; **JCB**, T02-256 1361, T02-2561351; **Visa** and **MasterCard**, Thai Farmers Bank Building, Phahonyothin Rd, T02-251 6333, T02-273 1199.

Cost of living
One of the key pledges of the Yingluck Shinawatra government elected in 2011 was to increase the minimum wage to ฿300 a day (US$10). By mid-2012, despite complaints by many of the richest individuals and companies in Thailand, this was coming into force. The average salary of a civil servant is around US$250 a month. Of course, Thailand's middle classes – and especially those engaged in business in Bangkok – will earn far more than this. Thailand has appalling wealth distribution yet Thai society is remarkably cohesive. A simple but good meal out will cost ฿60; the rental of a modern house in a provincial city will cost perhaps ฿4000 a month.

Cost of travelling

Visitors staying in the best hotels and eating in hotel restaurants will probably spend at least ฿2000 per day, conceivably much much more. Tourists staying in cheaper a/c accommodation and eating in local restaurants will probably spend about ฿600-900 per day. Backpackers staying in fan-cooled guesthouses and eating cheaply, should be able to live on ฿300 per day. In Bangkok, expect to pay 20-30% more.

Opening hours

Hours of business Banks: Mon-Fri 0830-1530. Exchange: daily 0830-2200 in Bangkok, Pattaya, Phuket and Chiang Mai. In other towns opening hours are usually shorter. Government offices: Mon-Fri 0830-1200, 1300-1630. Shops: 0830-1700, larger shops: 1000-1900 or 2100. Tourist offices: 0830-1630.

Safety

In general, Thailand is a safe country to visit. The vast majority of visitors to Thailand will not experience any physical threat what so ever. However, there have been some widely publicized murders of foreign tourists in recent years and the country does have a very high murder rate. It is best to avoid any situation where violence can occur – what would be a simple punch-up or pushing bout in the West can quickly escalate in Thailand to extreme violence. This is mostly due to loss of face. Getting drunk with Thais can be a risky business – Westerners visiting the country for short periods won't be versed in the intricacies of Thai social interaction and may commit unwitting and terrible faux pas. A general rule of thumb if confronted with a situation is to appear conciliatory and offer a way for the other party to back out gracefully. It should be noted that even some police officers in Thailand represent a threat – at least 3 young Western travellers have been shot and murdered by drunken Thai policemen in the last few years. Confidence tricksters, touts, all operate, particularly in more popular tourist centres. Robbery is also a threat; it ranges from pick-pocketing to the drugging (and subsequent robbing) of bus and train passengers. Watchfulness and simple common sense should be employed. Women travelling alone should be careful. Always lock hotel rooms and place valuables in a safe deposit if available (if not, take them with you).

Areas to avoid

The UK Foreign and Commonwealth Office (www.fco.gov.uk/travel) advises against all but essential travel to the 4 provinces of **Yala**, **Pattani**, **Narathiwat** and **Songkhla** on the Thai-Malay border. The US State Department (www.travel.state.gov) does the same. These areas are the main base of Thailand's Muslim minority and are currently home to a slow-burning separatist insurgency. Car bomb explosions, shootings and other acts of politically motivated violence are weekly, often daily occurences.

In light of events between Mar and May 2010, when political protests throughout Thailand resulted in the deaths of over 90 people, including several foreigners, and injuries to over 2200 people, it is also recommended that you avoid all political demonstrations, no matter how benign or carnival-like they seem.

If you do get any problems contact the tourist police rather than the ordinary police – they will speak English and are used to helping resolve any disputes, issues, etc. The country's health infrastructure, especially in provincial capitals and tourist destinations, is good.

For background information on staying healthy, see page 18. The UK's Foreign and Commonwealth Office's 'Know Before You Go' campaign, www.fco.gov.uk/travel, offers some advice.

Foreign and Commonwealth Office (**FCO**), T0845-850 2829, www.fco.gov.uk/travel. The UK Foreign and Commonwealth Office's travel warning section.

US State Department, www.travel.state. gov/travel_warnings.html. The US State Department updates travel advisories on its 'Travel Warnings and Consular Information Sheets'. It also has a hotline for American travellers, T202-647-5225.

Bribery
The way to make your way in life, for some people in Thailand, is through the strategic offering of gifts. A Chulalongkorn University report recently estimated that it 'costs' ฿10 million to become Bangkok Police Chief. Apparently this can be recouped in just 2 years of hard graft. Although bribing officials is by no means recommended, resident *farangs* report that they often resort to such gifts to avoid the time and hassle involved in filling in the forms and making the requisite visit to a police station for a minor traffic offence. As a visitor, it's best to play it straight.

Drugs and prostitution
Many prostitutes and drug dealers are in league with the police and may find it more profitable to report you than to take your custom (or they may try to do both). They receive a reward from the police, and the police in turn receive a bonus for the detective work. Note that foreigners on buses may be searched for drugs. Sentences for possession of illegal drugs vary from a fine or one year in jail for marijuana up to life imprisonment or execution for possession or smuggling of heroin. The death penalty is usually commuted.

Prisons
Thai prisons are very grim. Most foreigners are held in 2 Bangkok prisons – Khlong Prem and Bangkwang. One resident who visits overseas prisoners in jail wrote to us saying: "You cannot over-estimate the horrors! Khlong Prem has 7000 prisoners, 5 to a cell, with not enough room to stretch out, no recreation, one meal a day (an egg on Sundays) … ". One hundred prisoners

in a dormitory is not uncommon, and prisoners on Death Row have waist chains and ankle fetters permanently welded on.

Tourist police
In 1982 the government set up a special arm of the police to deal with the demands of the tourist industry – the tourist police. Now, there is no important tourist destination that doesn't have a tourist police office. The Thai police have come in for a great deal of scrutiny over recent years, although most policemen are honest and only too happy to help the luckless visitor. **Tourist Police**, Bangkok, T02-2815051 or T02-2216206. Daily 0800-2400.

Traffic
Perhaps the greatest danger is from the traffic – especially if you are attempting to drive yourself. More foreign visitors are killed or injured in traffic accidents than in any other way. Thai drivers have a 'devil may care' attitude towards the highway code, and there are many horrific accidents. Be very careful when crossing the road – just because there is a pedestrian crossing, do not expect drivers to stop. Be particularly wary when driving or riding a motorcycle (see page 9).

Student travellers
Anyone in full-time education is entitled to an **International Student Identity Card** (ISIC). These are issued by student travel offices and travel agencies across the world and offer special rates on all forms of transport and other concessions and services. The ISIC head office is: **ISIC Association**, Box 9048, 1000 Copenhagen, Denmark, T45-3393 9303. Students are eligible for discounts at some museums but the use of student cards is not widespread so don't expect to save a fortune.

Tax
Airport tax is now included in the price of a ticket. For VAT refunds, see Customs and duty free, page 17.

Telephone → *Country code +66.*
From Bangkok there is direct dialling to most countries. To call overseas, you first need to dial the international direct dial (IDD) access code, which is 001, followed by the country code. Outside Bangkok, it's best to go to a local telephone exchange if calling internationally.

Local area codes vary according to province. Individual area codes are listed through the book; the code can be found at the front of the telephone directory.

Calls from a telephone box cost ฿1. All telephone numbers marked in the text with a prefix 'B' are Bangkok numbers.

Directory enquiries
For domestic long-distance calls including Malaysia and Vientiane (Laos): T101 (free), Greater Bangkok BMA T183, international calls T02-2350030-5, although hotel operators will invariably help make the call if asked.

Mobiles
Quite simply the cheapest and most convenient form of telephony in Thailand is the mobile/cell phone. Mobiles are common and increasingly popular – reflecting the difficulties of getting a landline as well as a desire to be contactable at all times and places. Coverage is good except in some border areas.

Sim cards and top-up vouchers for all major networks are available from every single 7-11 store in the country. You will need a sim-free, unlocked phone but you can pick up basic, second-hand phones for A600 from most local markets. Unfortunately for smart-phone users, most of Thailand has yet to acquire 3G, although cheap GPRS packages are available from all providers and coverage is pretty good.

AIS and *Happy D Prompt* sim cards and top ups are available throughout the country and cost ฿200 with domestic call charges from ฿3 per min and international calls from ฿8 per min. This is a very good

deal and much cheaper than either phone boxes or hotels.

Internet
GPRS data deals are also incredible cheap – the AIS network offers 100 hrs of mobile internet connection for ฿300 per month. Speeds are slow though the network is perfectly adequate for text emails, basic web-browsing and social sites such as Facebook.

Time
GMT plus 7 hrs.

Tipping
Tipping is generally unnecessary. However, a 10% service charge is now expected on room, food and drinks bills in the smarter hotels as well as for any personal service. Increasingly, the more expensive restaurants add a 10% service charge; others expect a small tip.

Tour operators
UK
Asean Explorer, PO Box 82, 37 High St, Alderney, GY9 3DG, T01481-823417, www.asean-explorer.com. Holidays for adventurers and golfers in Thailand.
Buffalo Tours, the Old Church, 89b Quicks Rd, Wimbeldon, London SW19 1EX, T020-8545 2830, www.buffalotours.com. Arrange tours throughout Southeast Asia. Also has offices in Bangkok and Phuket.
Exodus Travels, 9 Weir Rd, London, T020-9500039, T020-8673 0859, www.exodus.co.uk. Small group travel for walking and trekking holidays, adventure tours and more.
Magic of the Orient, 14 Frederick Pl, Bristol, BS8 1AS, T0117-3116050, www.magicofthe orient.com. Tailor-made holidays to the region. Established in 1989 the company's philosophy is to deliver first-class service from knowledgeable staff at good value.
Silk Steps, Compass House, Rowdens Rd, Wells, Somerset, BA5 1TU, T01749-685162, www.silk steps.co.uk. Tailor-made and group travel.

STA Travel, 33 Bedford St, Covent Garden, London, WC2E 9ED, T0871-468 0612, www.statravel.co.uk. Specialists in low-cost student/youth flights and tours, also good for student IDs and insurance.
Symbiosis Expedition Planning, Holly House, Whilton, Daventry, Northamptonshire, T0845-1232844, www.symbiosis-travel.com. Specialists in tailor-made and small group adventure holidays for those concerned about the impact of tourism on environments.
Trans Indus, 75 St Mary's Rd and the Old Fire Station, Ealing, London, W5 5RW, T020-8566 2729, www.transindus.co.uk. Tours to Thailand and other Southeast Asian countries.

North America
Nine Dragons Travel & Tours, 1476 Orange Grove Rd, Charleston, SC 29407, USA, T1317-281 3895, www.nine-dragons.com. Guided and individually customized tours.
STA Travel, 920 Westwood Blvd, Los Angeles, CA 90024, T1-310-824 1574, www.statravel.com.

Thailand
Luxury Travel Thailand, c/o East West Siam, 40/83 Intramara Soi 8, Suthisan Rd, Samseannai, Payathai, Bangkok 104000, T66-266007, www.luxurytravelvietnam.com. Asain specialist in luxury privately guided and fully bespoke holidays in Vietnam, Laos, Cambodia, Myanmar and Thailand.

Tourist information
Tourist Authority of Thailand (TAT), 1600 New Phetburi Rd, Makkasan, Ratchathewi, T02-2505500, www.tourismthailand.org; also at 4 Rachdamnern Nok Av (intersection with Chakrapatdipong Rd), Mon-Fri 0830-1630; in addition there are 2 counters at Suvarnabhumi Airport, in the Arrivals halls of Domestic and International Terminals, T02-134 0040, T02-134 0041, 0800-2400. Local offices are found in most major tourist destinations in the country. Most offices

open daily 0830-1630. TAT offices are a useful source of local information, often providing maps of the town, listings of hotels/guesthouses and information on local tourist attractions. The website is a useful first stop and is generally well regarded.

Tourism authorities abroad
Australia, Suite 2002, 2nd floor, 56 Pitt St, Sydney, NSW 2000, T9247-7549, www. thailand.net.au.
France, 90 Ave des Champs Elysées, 75008 Paris, T5353-4700, tatpar@wanadoo.fr.
Germany, Bethmannstr 58, D-60311, Frankfurt/Main 1, T69-1381390, tatfra@t-online.de.
Hong Kong, 401 Fairmont House, 8 Cotton Tree Drive, Central, T2868-0732. tathkg@hk.super.net.
Italy, 4th floor, Via Barberini 68, 00187 Roma, T06-487 3479.
Japan, Yurakucho Denki Building, South Tower 2F, Room 259, 1-7-1, Yurakucho, Chiyoda-ku, Tokyo 100-0006, T03-218 0337, tattky@criss cross.com.
Malaysia, c/o Royal Thai Embassy 206 Jalan Ampang, 50450 Kuala Lumpur, T26-23480, sawatdi@po.jaring.my.
Singapore, c/o Royal Thai Embassy, 370 Orchard Rd, Singapore 238870, T2357901, tatsin@mbox5.singnet.com.sg.
UK, 1st floor, 17-19 Cockspur St, Trafalgar Sq, London SW1Y 5BL, T0870-900 2007, www.tourismthailand.co.uk.
USA, 1st floor, 611 North Larchmont Blvd, Los Angeles, CA 90004, T461-9814, tatla@ix.netcom.com.

Useful websites
www.asiancorrespondent.com Regional news website featuring guest blogs on Thai politics by writers who dig deep rather than toe the line. A better source of unbiased analysis than either the *Bangkok Post* or *The Nation*.
www.bangkokpost.com Homepage for the country's most widely read English-language daily.

www.bk.asia-city.com The online version of Bangkok's weekly freebie BK Magazine offers instant access to the hipper side of city life, from upcoming events to comment, chat and lifestyle features.

www.fco.gov.uk/travel The UK Foreign and Commonwealth Office's travel warning section.

www.paknamweb.com Umbrella website for the Paknam Network, expat Richard Barrow's assorted websites and blogs covering all facets of Thai culture.

www.thaifolk.com Good site for Thai culture, from folk songs and handicrafts through to festivals like Loi Kratong, and Thai myths and legends. Information posted in both English and Thai – although the Thai version of the site is better.

www.thai-language.com An easy-to-use Thai-English online language resource with an excellent dictionary, thousands of audio clips, lessons and a forum.

www.tourismthailand.org A useful first stop.

www.travel.state.gov/travel The US State Department updates travel advisories on its Travel Warnings & Consular Information Sheets.

Visas and immigration

For the latest information on visas and tourist visa exemptions, see the consular information section of the **Thai Ministry of Foreign Affairs** website, www.mfa. go.th. Having relocated from its central location on Soi Suan Plu, the immigration department that deals with tourists is now on the outskirts: Immigration Bureau, Government Complex Chaeng Wattana, B Building, Floor 2 (South Zone), Chaengwattana Rd Soi 7, Laksi, Bangkok 10210, T02-141 9889, www.immigration. co.th. Mon-Fri 0830-1200, 1300-1630, closed Sat, Sun, official hols.

For tourists from 41 countries (basically all Western countries, plus some Arabic

and other Asian states – see www.mfa. go.th), Thai immigration authorities will issue a 30-day visa-exemption entry permit if you arrive by plane. If you enter at a land crossing from any neighbouring country, the permit is for 15 days.

Visas on arrival

Tourists from 28 countries (most of them developing countries) can apply for a 15-day visa on arrival at immigration checkpoints. Applicants must have an outbound (return) ticket and possess funds to meet living expenses of ฿10,000 per person or ฿20,000 per family. The application fee is ฿1000 and must be accompanied by a passport photo.

Tourist visas

These are valid for 60 days from date of entry and must be obtained from a Thai embassy before arrival in Thailand.

Visa extensions

These are obtainable from the Immigration Bureau (see above) for ฿1900. Applicants must bring 2 photocopies of their passport ID page and the page on which their tourist visa is stamped, together with a passport photograph. It is also advisable to dress neatly. Visas are issued by all Thai embassies and consulates. The length of time a visa is extended varies according to the office and the official.

Weights and measures

Thailand uses the metric system, although there are some traditional measures still in use, in particular the *rai*, which equals 0.16 ha. There are 4 *ngaan* in a *rai*. Other local measures include the krasorp (sack) which equals 25 kg and the *tang* which is 10-11 kg. However, for most purchases (for example fruit) the kilogram is the norm. Both kilos and kilometres are often referred to as lo – as in ki-lo.

Contents

Andaman Coast

Ranong to Khao Lak

A wild, untouched landscape begins to unfold, with waterfalls, lush rainforest and dense mountains all home to fantastical species like the largest flower in the world and insects the size of a man's hand. Ranong, on Route 4, is famous for both its hot springs and visa runs by expats and travellers who can cross the border into Burma by boat to renew their visas in a day. Like Mae Sot, its proximity to Burma fosters a border diaspora as Burmese workers – many illegal – hasten across, desperately searching for work in a country which traditionally has fought bitterly with the their own. In Ranong and the surrounding islands, the tribal Burmese clearly stand out with the men wearing sarongs and the women daubed with clay face paint smoking cheroots. There are often boxing competitions between the two nationalities which dramatically display another difference, between the fighting style of the highly ritualistic Thai muay and compared frenzied freeform Burmese style.

From Prathong Island near Takua Pa (south of Ranong), right down to Phuket, virtually the entire western coast of Phangnga province comprises great long sandy bays with the occasional peninsula or rocky headland. With the Thai Muang National Park to the south, the Khao Lak Lam Ru National Park bordering the Khao Lak area, and the Khao Sok National Park inland to the north, tourism operators along the coast of Phangnga are targeting those interested in 'getaway' and nature tours. Meanwhile Ranong's proximity to the Similan and Surin islands (the western coast resorts in Phangnga are also the closest departure points for the Similan Islands) makes it an ideal stopover for divers. Certainly, as the gateway to Richelieu Rock and the Mergul archipelago, it is hard to beat.

Ranong → *For listings, see pages 36-44.*

Surrounded by forested mountains, Ranong is a scenic place to stay for a day or two. It is a small and unpretentious provincial capital and an important administrative centre. Increasingly, it is being eyed up as a spa/hot spring location but is currently still more popular with Southeast Asian tourists than those from further afield. The free municipal hot springs just outside the town are a charming spot, where the area's varied population gather day and night to get warm, floppy and relaxed in the ever hot water. It offers an excellent way to watch all levels of Thai society at their most lethargic while warming yourself after one of the town's many thunderstorms. There are waterfalls here, one of which, Punyaban, can be seen from the road as you approach the town. It is also the jumping-off point for a number of beautiful islands in the Andaman Sea. There is a small tourist office on Kamlungsab Road.

Arriving in Ranong

From Bangkok, there are several bus departures daily, with the best air-conditioned buses departing roughly nine times a day. However, the road journey from the north is arduous (eight hours at least) and the last half is through hills, so is not good for travel-sickness sufferers. Consider taking the train from Bangkok to Chumphon and the bus from there (which takes the same time in total). The bus terminal is on Highway 4 on the edge of town, near the **Jansom Thara Hotel**; buses also stop in town on Ruangrat Road before the terminal. You can also reach Ranong by bus from Khao Lak, Phuket, Surat Thani and Krabi. There is an airport 20 km south of town; in early 2012, small budget airline **Happy Air** (www.happyair.co.th) was flying three times a week to Bangkok.

Background

The name Ranong is derived from *rae* (tin) *nong* (rich), and the town was established in the late 18th century by a family from Hokkien, China. Prosperous through its tin mines, Ranong relied heavily on slave labour. Indeed, when Khaw Soo Cheang, another Chinese émigré became governor of Ranong in the mid-1800s, he imported indentured Chinese labourers from Penang to work in the tin mines. The working conditions were so merciless that a popular Ranong saying at the time went: 'The Ranong pit is easy to get into, but it is impossible to get out of.' In 1876, when Khaw Soo Cheang went to China to pay an ancestral visit, 2000 Chinese labourers revolted but Kaw Soo Cheang, a self-made man from a poor background, was able to quell the mob on his return and was duly rewarded by the Thai monarch – Rama V – with the title of the rajah of Ranong. Today you can see the legacy of Kaw Soo Cheang with Ranong still boasting a predominantly Sino-Thai population and a number of attractive 19th-century Chinese-style houses.

Ranong province is the first southern province bordering the Indian Ocean and it is Thailand's rainiest (often in excess of 5000 mm per year), narrowest and least populated province. Kra Buri, 58 km north of Ranong, is the point where the Kra Isthmus is also at its narrowest, and there has been debate for centuries about the benefits of digging a canal across the isthmus, so linking the Gulf of Thailand with the Andaman Sea and short-cutting the long hike down the peninsula to Singapore and north through the Melaka Strait.

Places in Rangong

The town contains excellent geo-thermal mineral water springs (65°C) at **Wat Tapotharam** ① *2 km east of the town and behind the Jansom Thara Hotel, free.* To get there, walk or take a *songthaew* along Route 2; ask for 'bor nam rawn' (hot water well). Surrounded by dramatic forested hills, the spa water bubbles out of the ground hot enough to boil an egg and cools sufficiently to allow the city's residents to enjoy a free hot bath and take refuge in its cosy depths during Ranong's frequent thunderstorms. The valley also has a luxurious hot spring and health club, offering a jacuzzi, gym, steam room, sauna and massages from ฿300, but it lacks the natural setting and village green feel of the municipal springs across the road. Around the park are several seafood restaurants and food stands. The springs also provide the **Jansom Thara Hotel** with thermal water for hot baths and a giant jacuzzi. There is a small park with a cable bridge over the river, a tiny cave containing a small Buddhist shrine and a number of municipal bathing pools. The wat here contains a footprint of the Buddha. Continuing along Route 2 for another 6 km or so, the road reaches the old tin-mining village of **Hat Som Paen**. **Wat Som Paen** is worth a visit to see the numerous giant carp, protected because of their supposed magical qualities. Deep in the hills, a few kilometres further up the road, is Ranong canyon, where city folk escape to recline in pretty shalas above the water, swim or feed countless hungry catfish.

Port of Ranong lies 3 km from town. Each morning the dock seethes with activity as Thai and Burmese fishing boats unload their catches. Boats can be hired, at a pontoon next to the dock, to tour the bustling harbour and look across the Kra River estuary to the Burmese border (approximately ฿400). Border officials can be touchy so carry your passport. Ranong is an important point of contact between Burma and Thailand. Like Mae Sot, there are more intensive searches and check points as you leave the area. Do not be surprised if the military come onto your bus up to three or four times on the way out to check documents.

Laem Son National Park → *For listings, see pages 36-44.*

There are a number of notable beaches and islands in the neighbourhood of Ranong, many within the limits of the Laem Son National Park, such as Hat Bang Baen, Koh Khang Khao, Koh Khao Khwai, Koh Nam Noi, Koh Kam Yai, Koh Kam Tok, Koh Chang and Koh Phayam (pronounced pie-yam). The water here is warm and a pleasure to swim in, especially around the reefs. The park and the islands effectively lie at the outer limits of the Kra River estuary – so don't expect coral on all islands or excellent visibility. Mangroves fringe many of the islands and because of the high rainfall in the area the natural vegetation is tropical rainforest. While the islands may not have the best snorkelling and water, they hide some wonderfully white sand and secluded beaches and they do have good birdlife (there are around 138 bird species in the park). The best birdwatching months are December to February with many migrating birds and optimum weather conditions.

Arriving in Laem Son National Park

Laem Son National Park is 45 km south of Ranong. The park offices are at Hat Bang Baen (see below). Slow boats leave up to four times a day during high season to Koh Chang and Koh Phayam from the island pier (aka Sapaan Plaa pier) in Ranong at the end of Sapaan Plaa Rd. The cost is ฿150 and the journey takes one to two hours. The schedule in low season is less certain and you may have to wait some time in Ranong for a boat. There are also some speedboat connections in high season; these vary from year to year but there should be up to three departures a day. The price is likely to more than double that of the slow boat, but journey times are only 30 to 40 minutes. Other islands can be accessed via Hat Bang Baen (see below). For trips to Koh Surin and Koh Similan, see page 35.

Beaches and islands

Hat Bang Baen is an enormous, relatively untouched beach lined by forest, with lovely shells and fine sand. You can organize boat trips from here to nearby islands. These include **Koh Khang Khao** (25 minutes from Hat Bang Baen), where you'll find a small white-sand beach for sunbathing and rocks for picnics; **Koh Khao Khwai** (30 minutes from Khang Khao), another beautiful island boasting a long stretch of beach and azure water; **Koh Kam Yai** (15 minutes from Khao Khwai), which is all rocks and mountains, with just one short, quiet beach, and **Koh Kam Noi** (10 minutes from Kam Yai), which has only one small white-sand beach. To reach all these islands you will need to negotiate with the locals for boat transportation; prices fluctuate widely during the seasonal highs and lows. You may have to pay an entry fee here of ฿200. To get there take any bus heading to the south from Ranong and get off on the main route No. 4 road roughly 60 km south at Sam Nak. From there you might be able to find a pick-up, motorcycle or tuk tuk to take you to the beach – you are very likely to be overcharged. Alternatively you can call **Wasana Resort** (See Where to stay) who offer a free pick-up for their guests. Another option is to just rent a motorcycle in Ranong and make your own way.

Koh Chang Unlike the larger Koh Chang on Thailand's east coast, Ranong's tiny Koh Chang has more to offer birdwatchers than beach lovers, but is best known for its distinctly laid-back ambience. Commonly sighted birds are kites, sea eagles and the endearingly clumsy hornbill. And, in the forest along the coast, monkeys and deer can be spied – and heard. The beaches here are mediocre at best and grim at worst, with streaks of black and dubious grey-yellow sand. The island also hibernates from June to mid-October when the monsoon rains lash down with even locals shifting to the mainland, leaving Koh Chang almost empty. But what this island lacks in beach bounty, it makes up for in the chill-out stakes. While there is a burgeoning backpacker tourist industry replete with yoga and dive schools, beach bars and tattooists, the economy still depends on fishing and plantations of rubber, palm and cashew nut. Self-generated electricity remains sporadic and there is no sign of cars, with most people getting around on motorbikes through tracks to the beaches. But, while the beaches are never going to be used in an ice cream advert, the swimmable **Ao Yai** on the west coast is worth a visit. It's split in two by a strip of a lagoon. From Ao Yai you can see the thuggish silhouette of Burma's mountainous jungle-covered **St Matthew's Island**, which seems to take up most of the horizon. St Matthew's is a massive radar site with a direct satellite link to China. Koh Chang also sports a radar site, for the Thai navy.

Koh Phayam Buffered by Koh Similan, Koh Phayam, along with Koh Chang, were the only inhabited islands on the Ranong coastline not to suffer any deaths from the 2004 tsunami. Only on Koh Phayam would there be both Full Moon Parties – albeit low-key ones – and a Miss Cashew Nut Beauty Competition (held during the Cashew Nut Festival). Koh Phayam has no cars, and boasts only narrow rutted roads, which run through the nut plantations. There are, however, a series of small tracks around the island for walking, cycling or motorbiking to make a change from lounging on the long and curving white-sand beaches at Ao Yai 'Sunset Bay' or Ao Khao Kwai 'Buffalo Bay'. These days, Koh Phayam has become a quiet hit for the laid-back diving and snorkelling set, see What to do, page 43. This is partly because the island, sometimes called the 'muck divers playground', offers such offshore delights as flat worms, ascidians, sponges, soft corals, nudibranchs and a variety of sea horses. If you are not the diving sort, the island is also home to wonderfully diverse wildlife with hornbills, while further inland away from the white sandy beaches are monitor lizards, boar, deer, monkeys and snakes. There is also a tiny fishing village on the east coast of the island and a sea gypsy settlement to the west. As for locals, Koh Phayam is populated by Burmese and Thai, 200 and 300 respectively, and there are even a handful of full-time *farang* but, come May, this hardy bunch largely dribbles away.

Though still a relatively sleepy island, Koh Phayam's guesthouses, especially on Buffalo Bay, have developed steadily since the tsunami, flourishing as the Koh Surin, which are easily accessible from Phayam, become ever more popular. The effects of this development on the island's idyllic status is a cause of concern; there are already serious problems with sewage and rubbish from the ferries crossing between the islands and the mainland. Ecological awareness is therefore high on the island's agenda; recycling, solar power and conservative use of electricity are encouraged (bring a torch). It is possible to hire motorbikes (฿200 per day) but be warned that the roads are sometimes treacherous, narrow and uneven.

South of Ranong → *For listings, see pages 36-44.*

Kuraburi
Between Ranong and Takua Pa, the small town of Kuraburi offers some adequate accommodation for a stopover to break up the journey. You can visit the town's attractive beach 12 km to the north, or use Kuraburi as a base to explore the surrounding forests or before a boat journey to the Surin or Prathong islands. Surin boats leave from here daily at 0900 between mid-November and mid-May and cost ฿1500 for the slow boat (4½ hours). You should also be able to pick up a ride on a speedboat here; expect to pay up to ฿2000 per person each way, journey time 90 minutes. **Tom & Am Tour** on the main road in Kuraburi sell boat tickets and can arrange transfers to and from the pier.

Takuapa and around
Located about 25 km north of Khao Lak, Takuapa is an important transport hub if you are travelling between Khao Lak, Khao Sok, Phuket, Surat Thani and Ranong. There is little to do in the small town itself, apart from wait for a bus, but the nearby small fishing town of **Bang Nam Khem** is worth a visit if you do stop off here. Nam Khem suffered the largest number of Thai-national deaths in the 2004 tsunami, with an unknown total of maybe thousands of illegal Burmese migrants also dying here. A few years ago a **Tsunami Memorial Park** was created here and represents one of the only proper monuments to the tsunami dead anywhere on the Andaman coast. It consists of a large walk-through sculpture and a long black stone wave breaking onto a concrete wall. The inner wall of the wave is inscribed with the names of the lost. Despite its obscure location, the park is a tasteful and relaxing space to spend a couple of hours, located on a promontory with cooling sea breezes, plenty of shade and a decent beach at low tide. You can also find food and drink here. South of Nam Khem are some fantastic and almost completely unspoilt beaches, with at least one excellent place to stay available at the time of publication.

Khao Sok National Park
ⓘ *www.khaosok.com, entry ฿400.*
Arriving in the park The closest town to Khao Sok National Park is Takua Pa (see Where to stay, page 39) but companies from Phuket, Phangnga, Krabi and Surat Thani operate day and overnight tours. An overnight tour is the best way to explore the park. If you want to get into the forest, take an overnight tour into the park with an experienced

guide. Overnight stays by the lake, although spartan, are recommended, as the scenery is spectacular and the early morning calm is hard to beat. Tours are available from virtually all the guesthouses near the park (see Where to stay, page 38). Park rangers will also act as guides. Have a chat with your guide before you make up your mind to go so you can be sure you feel comfortable about the level of English (or other languages) they speak, familiarity with the park and knowledge of the environment and wildlife. Taking a guide is sensible as the treks take longer than a day and can be daunting, even for the more experienced walkers. Expect to pay from ฿1300 per person for a guide to take you on a day trek, and around ฿2500 per person for an overnight trip to the reservoir (this includes accommodation and all meals), plus the ฿400 to enter the park. Prices vary depending on how many people are in the group. If visiting the park independently, buses from Phuket to Surat Thani stop on the main road a couple of kilometres from the park entrance and hub of guesthouses. When you arrive at the stop, there will usually be a number of bungalow operators waiting to whisk you off to their establishment; you can otherwise walk or take transport into the park. If you decide to walk, take a small pack as it's quite a hike to some bungalows.

Landscape and wildlife Khao Sok National Park has limestone karst mountains (the tallest reaches more than 900 m), low mountains covered with evergreen forest, streams and waterfalls, and a large reservoir and dam. The impressive scenery alone would be a good enough reason to visit, but Khao Sok also has a high degree of endemism and an exceptionally large number of mammals, birds, reptiles and other fauna.

The list of 48 confirmed species of mammals include: wild elephants, tigers, barking deer, langur, macaques, civets, bears, gibbons and cloud leopards. Of the 184 confirmed bird species, perhaps the most dramatic include: the rhinoceros hornbill, great hornbill, Malayan peacock pheasant and crested serpent-eagle. The plants to be found here are also of interest. The orchids are best seen from late February to April. If you visit between December and February, the **rafflesia Kerri Meijer** is in flower. This parasitic flower (it depends on low-lying lianas) has an 80-cm bloom – the largest in the world – with a phenomenally pungent odour so that it can attract the highest number of pollinating insects. It also has no chlorophyll. Besides the astounding rafflesia, there are also at least two palms endemic to the Khao Sok area.

Around the park In the centre of the park is the **Rachabrapah Reservoir**. Near the dam there is a longhouse of sorts, and several houseboats. The best location for animal spotting is near the reservoir where grassland at the edge of the reservoir attracts animals.

In addition to camping, canoeing and walking tours, you can take elephant treks at Khao Sok. The routes taken must be outside the park, however, as elephant trekking is not permitted within the confines of the national park.

Like many of the wonders of nature in Thailand, Khao Sok does not come without a giant technological blot. In this case, it's a hydroelectric dam right next to Khao Sok that has formed a vast artificial lake that now comprises one border of the national park. This dam began in the 1980s and has since become the bane of the park, as it transformed hills and valleys into small islands, trapping the wildlife with rising tides. While there have been attempts to rescue the beleaguered wildlife, nothing has proved successful as yet. But Khao Sok is successfully capitalizing on its assets, including its association with the famous Canadian naturalist Thom Henley (see above).

Tsunami

Obliterating miles of picture-perfect coastline and killing thousands, the tsunami of Boxing Day 2004, left the world reeling in shock. Among the dead were countless Burmese, Mon and Karen intinerant workers without papers, while those who escaped the tsunami fled into the dense hills and rubber plantations of Phangnga or to Phuket or Ranong to evade repatriation.

In the wake of the disaster, the dearth of tourists compounded the horrors as small businesses suffered bankruptcy while traditional sea gypsies remained in limbo, unable to return to their former coastal homes because they lacked property deeds and also because they feared another wave. Since those early days, the tourist industry has been rebuilt, most famously Patong Beach which now boasts the cleanest sands in years.

Fortunately, many of the dive sites, including the Similan Islands, Ko Bon, Ko Tachai, Surin and Richelieu Rock received only superficial damage. And, while it will be some time before Khao Lak returns to a lucrative holiday strip, much of the Andaman remains gloriously lush with an abundance of accommodation and rare sights.

For many locals, however, the nightmare is not yet over. Along with the tsunami came the hired hench men of the nai toons or money barons who descended on villages that had been devastated by the waves, demanding property deeds from impoverished and often illiterate villagers. All up and down the coast from Laem Pon in Ban Nem Khem to Ban Sangka-oo on Koh Lanta and Kamala in Ranong, the same story was told of villagers who had been evicted and even barred from searching for the bodies of their loved ones in their former villages, following the tsunami. However, while many were loath to speak out for fear of losing compensation administered by corrupt local administrators, others fought back by refusing to move into new homes far from their original coastal sites. The oft-disparaged sea gypsies, in particular the Moken at Ban Tung Wa and Ban Tap Tawan in Phangnga, turned out to be the most united in their fight and successful, returning to their homes to rebuild rather than move into the small concrete bungalows far from the sea. At the time, Hon Klatalay, leader of the Ban Tung Wa community said: "We are one big family and we speak and move as one."

Khao Lak

A few years ago, before the infamous 2004 tsunami that killed 5000 and before the construction boom that followed it, Khao Lak was a sleepy beach town. Palms swayed, locals served up food and beer, and the almost empty beaches provided an idyllic backdrop. If you look closely enough, Khao Lak's original ambience can still be found, but it is certainly on the endangered list.

Khao Lak encompasses a range of beaches, coves and headlands spread out along a 10- to 15-km stretch of coast. There isn't actually a town officially called Khao Lak, but the main settlement is centred near busy **Nang Thong** beach. Here you'll find a run of generic four- to five-star resorts, with some, illegally, being built directly on the beach. **Bang Niang** is also fairly busy, with a similar run of resorts aimed at package tourists, whilst the beaches to the north (**Khuk Kak, Pakweeb** and **Bangsak**) get progressively quieter. It seems that, such was the rush to redevelop Khao Lak after the tsunami, there are now too many resorts competing for a small market share; how many will still be operating in five years' time is debatable. It is also worth noting that the Thai domestic market that existed pre-tsunami has now almost disappeared, because the superstitious Thais refuse to stay somewhere where the potential for malevolent ghosts and spirits is high.

Yet, despite having undergone all these dramatic changes in such a short period, the beaches here are still excellent and, if you find the right spot, you should be able to have an excellent beach holiday or short break here. Given its proximity to the Koh Similans, Khao Lak is now becoming something of a dive mecca, with a few excellent dive operators based here. The best way to get around is to rent a bicycle or small motorbike (฿150-250 per day). There are some songthaews available but they are notorious for fleecing tourists and are best avoided.

Koh Surin → *For listings, see pages 36-44.*

Five islands make up this marine national park, just south of the Burmese border, and 53 km off the mainland. The two main islands, **Koh Surin Tai** and **Koh Surin Nua** (South and North Surin respectively), are separated by a narrow strait which can be waded at low tide. Both islands are hilly, with few inhabitants; a small community of Chao Le fishermen live on Koh Surin Tai.

Visiting Koh Surin
Boats run by the national park leave from the pier at Ban Hin Lat, 1 km west of Kuraburi (4-5 hours, ฿1500). Long-tailed boats can be hired around Koh Surin. Various tour operators, agents, resorts and dive shops from both Phuket and Ranong organize their own speedboats, liveaboards and the like to visit Surin, with prices and travel times varying according to the distance and level of service provided. The national park office is at Ao Mae Yai, on the southwest side of Koh Surin Nua. Best time to visit is December to March. Koh Surin Tai may close to visitors during the full moon each March, when the Chao Le hold a festival.

Diving
The diving and snorkelling is good here, and the coral reefs are said to be the most diverse in Thailand. However, overfishing has led some people to maintain that diving is now better around the Similan Islands. Novices will still find the experience both exhilarating and enchanting.

There have been concerns expressed regarding the detrimental effects of tourism on several marine national parks, including the Surin Islands Marine National Park and, for a while, parts of the island have been closed to visitors. Everyone visiting the Surin should engage in the best diving/snorkelling practices and not touch or remove any wildlife or coral. A good website for information on snorkelling and diving in and around Surin is www.ko-surin-diving.com.

Koh Similan → *For listings, see pages 36-44.*

ⓘ *Vessels depart from Thap Lamu pier, 20 km north of Thai Muang (3-5 hrs) to the Similans, 40 km offshore. Boats also leave from Ao Chalong and Patong Beach, Phuket with Songserm Travel (T076-222570), Tue, Thu and Sat from Dec-Apr, 6-10 hrs. Boats also leave from Ranong. The best time to visit is Dec-Apr. The west monsoon makes the islands virtually inaccessible during the rest of the year; be warned that boats have been known to capsize at this time. Also, bear in mind that transport away from the islands is unpredictable and you might find yourself stranded here, rapidly running out of money. At the end of Mar/early Apr underwater visibility is not good, but this is the best time to see manta rays and whale sharks.*

The Similan Islands lying 80 km northwest of Phuket and 65 km west of Khao Lak are some of the most beautiful, unspoilt tropical idylls in Southeast Asia. The national park consists of nine islands (named by Malay fishermen, who referred to them as the 'Nine Islands' – *sembilan* is Malay for nine). The water surrounding the archipelago supports a wealth of marine life and is considered one of the best diving locations in the world, as well as a good place for anglers. A particular feature of the islands is the huge granite boulders. These same boulders litter the seabed and make for interesting peaks and caves for scuba divers. On the west side of the islands the currents have kept the boulders 'clean', while on the east, they have been buried by sand. The contrast between diving on the west and east coasts is defined by the boulders. On the west, currents sweep around these massive granite structures, some as large as houses, which can be swum around and through and many have fantastic colourful soft coral growing on them. A guide is essential on the west, as navigation can be tricky. The east is calmer, with hard coral gardens sloping from the surface down to 30-40 m. Navigation is straightforward here and can be done with a buddy, without the need for a guide.

Koh Miang, named after the king's daughter, houses the park office and some dormitory and camping accommodation. While water did sweep over Koh Miang, it is largely recovered and was the first place that Thailand's navy established a tsunami warning system. **Koh Hu Yong**, the southernmost island, is the most popular diving location.

Ranong to Khao Lak listings

For hotel and restaurant price codes and other relevant information, see pages 12-16.

◯ Where to stay

Ranong *p29*

$$$$-$$$ Jansom Hot Spa Hotel, 2/10 Petkasem Rd, T077-811 5103, www.jansom hotsparanong.net. In places, this is a slightly shabby spa hotel with charming pretensions of grandeur. However, there have been some improvements over the years, and the rooms remain a good deal, with bathtubs, linen, fridge and TV. The rooms, pool and a huge jacuzzi are all supplied with mineral water from the nearby hot springs. Breakfast included.

$$$-$$ Jansom Beach Resort, 135 Moo 5, 10 km from Ranong Town, T077-821611. Set in a scrub of jungle beside a poor excuse for a beach is a small block of 30 rooms, all with private balconies overlooking the Andaman Sea and Victoria Point (Burma). Rooms have rather low ceilings and are somewhat busy with furniture, but there's a pool and restaurant, and it's a great location. Popular during Chinese New Year and Songkran.

$$$-$$ Khao Nanghong Resort & Spa, 123/6 Moo 5, T077-831088, www.khaonang hongresort.com. A beachside boutique resort with large, airy, luxury thatched villas set in gardens overlooking Burma's Victoria Point. Stylish design, spa and a romantic restaurant with sea views.

$$$-$$ Royal Princess Ranong, 41/144 Tamua-ng Rd, T077-835240-44, www.dusit. com. A comfortable 4-star hotel (part of the long-established Dusit chain) with excellent service and good facilities, including a mineral spa, pool and babysitting services. One of the best hotels in Ranong but still very corporate.

$ Bangsan (TV Bar), 281 Ruangrat Rd, T077-811240. Super-cheap, very basic rooms with fan above the trendiest cocktail bar in town. Popular with the young Thai and backpacker crowd.

$ Dahla House, 323/5 Ruangrat Rd, T077-812959, dahla.siam2web.com. Nice, clean bungalows set in a private compound within easy walking distance of the town centre. All have en suite facilities with hot water. The owners are friendly and speak good English. They also have an internet cafe and sell very average food.

$ Rattanasin Hotel, 226 Ruangrat Rd, T077-811242. This is an old, atmospheric Chinese hotel slap bang in the town centre. There are creaking, steep staircases up to the en suite rooms, some with fan and some with a/c. Relatively clean, this place makes a reasonable budget option.

Hat Bang Baen *p31*

$$-$ Wasana Resort, T077-828209. This Dutch/Thai operation is on the left before the main park entrance. It has 10 smart concrete bungalows tastefully decorated, with Western toilets and verandas, arranged around a pleasant garden with a badminton net, ping-pong table, children's pool and good restaurant. The proprietors are helpful, friendly and arrange day trips.

Koh Chang *p31*

While Koh Chang has retained its reputation as a bit of a hippy hideaway, the number of guesthouses on the island has more than doubled over the past couple of years. Most are in the budget range. As Koh Chang is largely covered by rainforest, it is difficult to see many resorts from the boat because they are camouflaged in the foliage. The majority of the resorts (around 15) are at **Ao Yai beach** on the west side. There is also a smattering of secluded beachfront and cliffside operations in **Ao Tadaeng** and **Ao Siad** to the south. Many can be booked through travel agents in Ranong.

$$-$ Cashew Resort, T077-820116. The granddaddy of the resorts and the largest with a variety of bungalows, pool table, travel services, credit card facilities, money exchange and attached yoga

school. The resort has its own boat for fishing and trawling.

$$-$ Koh Chang Resort, T077-820176. Restaurant and sturdy wooden huts with attached bathrooms tucked among the trees. Snorkelling and fishing can be organized from here.

$ Contex Resort, Ao Yai, T077-820118. Popular, simple place run by a Thai family with around 15 bungalows and a decent restaurant on an idyllic beach at the northern tip of Ao Yai.

$ Sabai Yai T08-6278 4112 (mob). Swedish and Thai owned with good Western food, excellent service and well-kept rooms including dorms and bungalows. Home-baked bread.

$ Sunset, T077-820171. This small family-run operation has clean, airy bungalows and a friendly atmosphere.

Koh Phayam *p31*

Koh Phayam has around 30 guesthouses, with the most recent arrivals seen on **Ao Kao Kwai** (**Buffalo Bay**), which was previously the sleepier of the 2 large beaches.

$$$-$ Ao Yai Bungalows, Ao Yai, T077-821753, gilles_phatchara@hotmail.com. The original operation on this strip, this pretty, immaculately kept place in a secluded spot is run by a French/Thai couple, Gilles and Phatchara, who know the island intimately and have a range of wood and concrete bungalows on stilts. Some are surrounded by lovely gardens and set among pine and coconut trees. West facing, it makes for an ideal spot to watch the wildlife and the sunsets. Tasty restaurant.

$$-$ Baan Suan Kayoo Cottage, Ao Yai, T077-820133, www.gopayam.com. At the northern tip of the beach, with cottages and large restaurant set in a charming tropical garden – 'suan kayoo' means cashew nut garden in Thai. A choice of sturdy wooden superior en suite cottages with king-size beds and up-market interior or budget thatched cottages with attached Thai-style toilet. Mosquitoes can be a problem.

$$-$ Bamboo Bungalows, Ao Yai, T077-820012, www.bamboo-bungalows. com. A beach-side idyll and probably the most popular place on Ao Yai – booking is recommended during high season – although it is one of the few operations open year round. Bungalows range from new luxurious wooden villas with sprung mattresses, sofas, marble floors, sliding balcony doors and woven gables, through to pretty A-frame shell-covered bungalows. All have romantic outdoor bathrooms. There are also a few cheaper bamboo huts. The landscaped communal areas, large dining table, small yoga space, beach campfires and volleyball sessions create a community vibe. The excellent restaurant with huge portions and home-baked bread attracts visitors from neighbouring bungalows. Kayaks, surfboards and snorkelling equipment are available.

$$-$ Hornbill Hut, Ao Yai, T077-825543, hornbill_hut@yahoo.com. Fantastically friendly family-run place with a great reputation and several styles of basic bamboo bungalows with concrete bathrooms set among the trees, along with a few excellent-value concrete villas with high ceilings and windows which allow the sea breeze to whistle through. Recommended.

$$-$ Jansom Bungalow, Buffalo Bay, T077-8353179. A retreat set above Buffalo Bay with great views. It belongs to the **Jansom Beach Resort** in Ranong and has simple, clean wooden huts with vast tiled bathrooms and a traditional Thai outdoor restaurant overlooking the boulder-strewn expanse of sand.

$$-$ Uncle Red's, turn left from the Phayam village pier, over the small bridge. 4 basic but clean and well-kept en suite bungalows just over a bridge from the pier. An alternative option to the bigger beaches on a secluded strip of sand presided over by the picturesque wooden skeleton of a marooned boat. Close to the village shops and morning ferry off the island. The

similarly basic operation which has opened next door looks promising and there are plans to open a campsite with communal kitchen on the beach.

$$-$ Vijit Bungalows, Buffalo Bay, T077-834082, www.kohpayam-vijit.com. Another of the island's original operations, this place is popular and renowned for its laid-back ambience.

Kuraburi *p32*

$$-$ Boon Piya Resort, T08-1752 5457 (mob). Has 20 spotless modern a/c bungalows squeezed in next to the main road. Well decorated and with TVs.

$ Countryheart Riverside, next to the river, northside of the bridge, run by **Tom & Am Tour**, T08-6272 0588. Small, basic, cheap huts aimed at budget travellers. Rooms are simple, with cold-water bathrooms, the pricier ones have a/c. Quiet.

Khao Sok National Park *p32*

Tourism is well developed around Khao Sok, and visitors have a considerable choice in how they travel to the park and where they stay. There are several excellent bungalow operations near the park headquarters and new businesses sprout up every year. Be aware that colourful, deadly snakes occasionally invade the resorts and visitors should tread carefully.

$$$$ Thanyapura, 102 Moo 6, T076-336000, www.thanyapura.com. Super-luxurious, high-end resort, with stunning suites, villas and rooms set on a small hill overlooking the park. The rooms are elegant Thai-contemporary, done out with hardwoods and silks. Great views, nice swimming pool and wonderful organic food complete the picture.

$$$-$$ Khaosok Las Orquideas Resort, 343 Moo 6, T08-72693359 (mob), www. khao-sok-resort.com. Set up a drive on the road into the park, this small and beautifully tended guesthouse is the pride and joy of its friendly Spanish owner, Francisco. A set of small bungalows clings to a hillside, each one complete with marble flooring, views across the tree-tops and en suite bathrooms. The price includes an awesome breakfast and bicycle hire – a little bit more expensive than some of the other places here but with massive added value. Highly recommended.

$$$-$$ Art's Riverview Lodge, T08-6470 3234 (mob), artsriverviewlodge@yahoo. co.uk. Art's is long-running, stylish and popular, so book ahead. Its 30 rooms include substantial lodges with balconies overlooking the river and solid furniture; many have a spare bedroom and small dining room. There is no hot water. The restaurant is beside the river near a swimming hole with a rope providing endless entertainment. Impertinent monkeys congregate at sunset to be fed bananas by residents.

$$$-$$ Khao Sok Green Valley Resort, T077-395145. Run by the friendly Eit, this is a great little resort with 8 spotless bungalows, all with hot water and a/c. Recommended.

$$$-$$ Khao Sok River Lodge, T077-395165, reservation@phukettrekkingclub. com. This surprisingly cheap government-run resort was apparently forced to reduce its prices because of lack of interest. The 15 exclusive rooms are immaculately kept and stylishly fitted, with balconies overlooking the river, making it the area's best-value resort. An elevated bamboo walkway leads from the charming wooden restaurant to the more solid concrete bungalows. Villagers complain that, like that of many of the larger resorts, the construction led to the removal of so many large trees that it left the area exposed to flooding.

$$$-$$ Khao Sok Treehouse Resort, T08-99703353 (mob), khaosok_treehouse@ yahoo.com. Sandwiched between 2 rivers, the 8 treehouses offer a quirky night's sleep with huge trees crashing through their floors and ceilings. The rooms, which have fresh linen, hot water and bathrooms filled with plants, are slightly cramped compared with other Khao Sok rooms.

$$$-$$ Morning Mist Resort, T08-9971 8794 (mob). Spread next to the river with 16 bungalows of varying quality. The larger, more expensive rooms have hot water, fridges, flat concrete floors and a balcony with a bamboo boat hammock with the water rushing beneath. Some of the resort's paths are poorly lit at night.

$$$-$$ Our Jungle House, T08-9909 6814 (mob), ourjunglehouse@yahoo.de. At the end of bumpy track, this riverside resort run by a Thai/German couple offers some of Khao Sok's most comfortable rooms. The family bedroom has a neat mezzanine floor. The 12 polished teakwood bungalows are well spaced and tastefully decorated.

$$-$ Khao Sok Palmview Resort, 234 Moo 6, T08-6163 5478, www.khaosok-palmview.com. The local family that runs this collection of excellent budget bungalows is wonderfully friendly, and, consequently, this feels more like a homestay than a resort. Rooms are basic – fans and cold water in the cheaper ones – but the atmosphere is pleasingly soporific. The family also serves excellent and authentic Thai food. Recommend.

$$-$ Khao Sok Valley Lodge, T08-6283 9933 (mob), khaosok@hotmail.com. Has 5 basic, concrete-mounted, en suite bungalows. Although the rooms could do with a little more furniture, the English-speaking owner Bao is an expert on the park and leads tours using his park ranger father to enhance his trips, which cost between ฿300 and ฿2500.

$$-$ Nung House, 202 Moo 6 Klong Sok, T077-395147, T08-6283 1037 (mob), www.nunghouse.com. Popular with back-packers, Nung's 12 spacious and comfortable bungalows are good value, starting at just ฿150, and its restaurant is the place to meet trekking companions.

Takuapa and Baan Nam Khem
Accomodation is limited.

$$$$-$$ ThaiLife Homestay, 1/3 Moo 2, Bang Muang, T08-1812 0388, www.thailife

homestay.com. Just south of Baan Nam Khem the beach stretches out into a long slice of unspoilt white sand. Set back some 800 m from the sand, near the village of Bang Muang, is the **ThaiLife Homestay**: a collection of gorgeous, raised wooden villas, set around a pond, all with a/c, TV, hot showers and very comfy interiors. ThaiLife is the only resort on this entire stretch of beach, so it has a supremely relaxing vibe. It's also friendly and serves great food. It's slightly tricky to reach; you'll need either your own transport or an arrangement with ThaiLife to collect you from Khao Lak (฿400), Phuket town (฿2200) or the airport (฿1800). Recommended.

$$-$ Baanpoonyavee, just off main rd, 1 km south of the town centre, T08-1797 6559. Very nice clean rooms with tiled floors, a/c, fans and hot-water bathrooms, set in a quiet, private garden. You may need to walk to get here.

Khao Lak *p34*

Most of the accommodation in Khao Lak is now tailoured to suit the needs of north European package tourists. This means that large 4- and 5-star resorts have colonized almost the entirety of the beachfront in the busier areas of Nang Thong and Bang Niang. Nearly all of these resorts are of an excellent standard yet little differentiates them, and walk-in rates will be much higher than buying a package back home. We've picked the best of these, plus places catering to independent travellers, which are owned by local families. Prices out of season can be very low; the price ranges below reflect this.

$$$$ Meridien Khao Lak Beach and Spa Resort, 9/9 Moo 1, Khuk Kak, T076-427500, www.starwoodhotels.com. Huge, well-managed resort beside a beautiful stretch of sand about 8 km north of Khao Lak town. It has a superb kids' play area, complete with a scarily large teddy bear, and all the usual spa and swimming pool facilities you'd expect, plus a range of accommodation from standard rooms through to stunning villas complete with private pools. The food is also top-notch. Recommended – if you can afford it.

$$$$ Mukdara Beach Villa and Spa, T076-429999, www.mukdarabeach.com. The bungalows had to be rebuilt after the tsunami, but the 3-storey block survived the tragedy. It offers the services that would be expected considering the price tag of up to ฿26,000 per night. There are 6 restaurants and 148 rooms.

$$$$-$$$ Kantary Beach, 64/65 Moo 2, Khuk Kak, T076-584700, www.kantary collection.com. Of the numerous excellent mid-range and luxury resorts in Khao Lak, Kantary Beach, set on a quiet corner of Pakweeb Beach, is one of the best, and makes for a great choice for families, too. The contemporary designer rooms are massive – each comes with separate living area, sofa bed, mini-kitchen and balcony – but surprisingly affordable, and the 11 km of palm-fringed beach that front the resort is perfect for luxuriant tropical lazing. The resort serves excellent seafood and Thai grub, has a kids' play area, a huge pool and also rents out kayaks and mini-catamarans to guests.

$$$$-$$ Nangthong Bay Resort, T076-485088, www.nangthongbayresort.de. One of the first beachside resorts to reopen after the tsunami, this exclusive hotel has a pool, spotless seaside restaurant and superior beach bungalows with outdoor slate-fitted shower rooms. The rooms are elegant, if a little modern, characterless and squashed along the prized coastline.

$$$-$$ Father and Son Bungalow, just off main road, south of Khao Lak town, T076-48527, www.father-sonsiam.com. The friendly Nom family are planning to add to their 10 fan bungalows, which are spread around a charming, shaded garden where the road is barely audible. The more expensive en suite rooms are good value. They also run a locally renowned spa and massage service.

$$$-$$ Green Beach Resort, north end of Nang Thong beach, T076-485845, www.khaolakgreenbeachresort.com. Very friendly, slightly eccentric complex of 44 bungalows in a lovely secluded spot. The beach here is gorgeous, and the resort provides ample deck chairs and loungers for their patrons. Bungalows are wooden, with a/c or fan, all with mosquito nets and en suite. Most come with verandas as well. Good food in the restaurant.

$$$-$$ Jerung Guesthouse, 24 Moo 7, T076-485815, www.jerungguesthouse.com. Modern, family-run guesthouse on the main road in the centre of Khao Lak town. Great location for the nearby bars, food and shops but a bit of a walk from the beach. Try to get rooms at the back or it will be noisy. Stylish, simple rooms, with en suite, a/c, fan and free Wi-Fi. Also a good choice if you arrive at night.

$$$-$$ Khao Lak Banana Bungalow, 4/147 Moo 7, Khuk Kak, T076-485889, www.khaolakbanana.com. Friendly owners provide a range of cramped-together, eccentric collection of bungalows set back from the road at the end of a quiet soi. Range of quality and price. Small pool.

$$$-$$ Khao Lak Golden Place, 30/30 Moo 7, Soi Had Nang Thong, T076-485686, www.khaolakgoldenplace.com. Nice small hotel, set a short walk from Nang Thong beach. Contemporary, neat rooms, with cooling tiled floors and all the other facilities (a/c, en suite, TV, Wi-Fi) you'd expect. One of the cheapest and best options in this part of Khao Lak. Recommended.

$$$-$$ Khao Lak Palm Hill Resort and Spa, 4/135 Moo 7, Khuk Kak, T076-485138, www.khaolakpalmhill.com. Friendly, well-run small resort set on a back soi, 5 mins' walk from the beach. The rooms are large, cool affairs, all backing out onto a large pool. Decent food make this place one of the nicest away from the beach. Recommended.

$$$-$$ Krathom Khao Lak, T076-485149, krathom_khaolak@hotmail.com. Set in a lush garden that leads to the beach, the spacious a/c bungalows are considerably more comfortable than their bamboo, fan-cooled counterparts.

$$$-$$ Lake View Bungalows, 56/1 Moo2, T08-7890 7307, www.lakeviewbungalows. com. Set in an off-the-beaten track location down a small lane some 800 m from Khuk Kak beach, this friendly and engaging resort is perfect for those wanting peace and quiet. Bungalows are spread out amongst the trees and flowers and are nice enough, with the usual a/c and en suite facilities but no TV or Wi-Fi. Small restaurant/bar attached.

$$$-$$ Motive Cottage, 21/16 Moo 5, Khuk Kak, T076-486820, www.motivecottage resort.com. Elegant, minimalist rooms, each with their own little balcony, surround a bijou pool at this uplifting place. All rooms have a/c, en suite facilities and hot water. Set beside the main road, it's a 5-min walk from the beach. Recommended.

$$$-$$ Sweet Mango Bungalow, 6/25 Moo 5, Khuk Kak, about 800 m from Bang Neng beach, T08-4844 4041, www.sweet-mango-bungalow.com. Bungalows and rooms are set in gardens a short walk from the main road. Clean, en suite rooms, with a/c, cable TV etc, but no Wi-Fi.

$$$-$$ White Sand Bungalows, 28/2 Moo 2, T076-487580. Excellent little bungalow operation on Pakweeb Beach. Some of the neat and tidy bungalows – all en suite, with a/c, fans, hot water – are set right on the beach, while the rest are placed in a compound in the trees a short walk away. Has a bar and excellent restaurant attached, so you never need to leave. Recommended.

$$$-$ Thup Thong Guest House, Bang Niang Beach, 53/1 Moo 5, T076-486722, thupthong@gmail.com. One of the few buildings to survive the 2004 tsunami that obliterated most of Khao Lak, Thup Thong is also one of the only remaining budget, family-run places on a beachfront now dominated by self-replicating mid-range and luxury package-tourist resorts. The rooms in the guesthouse are basic, but clean, with a/c and fan and all en suite. The owners have now started to build a few brand-new, more stylish bungalows in land adjacent to the main property. There's also a small restaurant/bar plus a friendly welcome. Recommended for those on a budget.

$$ Khao Lak Youth Club, 5/55 Moo 7, Khuk Kak Beach, T076-485900. Owned by the same people as Tony's Lodge, this place offers a cluster of tiny bungalows crammed together on a slope overlooking a small shopping arcade. The rooms are nice enough, with hot water, a/c and cable TV. There's a dorm (A200) if you want company.

$$-$ The Sandy House, 57/5 Moo 5, T076-486224, krabidir.com/thesandyhouse. Small expat-run guesthouse very close to Bang Niang beach. It's one of the cheapest options in Khao Lak, with clean, basic rooms with fan or a/c and showers, but nothing special. If you'll be spending most of your time on the beach and are on a budget, this is a good option.

Koh Surin *p35*

$$$-$ National Park bungalows are available for ฿2000 a night; camping costs ฿300 in a rented tent. Call the park offices on T076-491378, T076-419028 for bookings, which are advised, or visit www.dnp.go.th for more details.

Koh Similan *p35*

$$$-$ Bungalows are now available on Koh Ba Ngu. Reservations can be made at the Similan National Park Office, Thai Muang, or at Tap Lamu Pier, T076-411 914. Camping may also be possible on Koh Ba Ngu. Bring your own tent. Visit www.dnp. go.th for more details.

🍴 Restaurants

Ranong *p29*

The markets on Ruangrat Rd offer some of the best eating opportunities in town with specials worth sampling including the roast pork and duck. Also worth seeking out for its famously delicious dahl lunches

is the Muslim roti shop (no English sign) on Rungruat Rd, opposite TV Bar and guesthouse. Look for the roti/pancake stand outside.

$$-$ Somboon Restaurant, opposite the Jansom Thara Hotel. Delicious Thai and Chinese seafood, much of which is displayed in tanks at the front.

$ D&D coffee, Ruangrat Rd. Where Ranong's café society congregates to discuss the day's issues, eat delicious Thai dishes over rice and sample a wide selection of good coffees.

$ J&T Food and Ice, also centrally located on Ruangrat Rd. Excellent range of delicious but very reasonably priced Thai food and ice creams; popular place with locals and visitors, friendly owners.

Koh Phayam *p31*

Most guesthouses have cheap restaurants and guests have been known to be asked to leave resorts during the high season if they fail to eat where they are staying. There are 3 other restaurants to bear in mind:

$ Middle Village, on the road to Ao Yai. Renowned for its excellent Isaan (northeastern Thai) dishes and rowdy karaoke nights.

$ Oscar's Bar, also in the village, turn right from the pier. Run by the infamously affable Englishman Richard, a self-proclaimed food buff who offers a wealth of information about the island and its politics. The bar serves great, unexpected Western and Thai dishes to a sociable crowd.

$ Pom's Restaurant, in the village by the pier. Its sign, "Thai food, cheap and delicious" sums it up.

Khao Lak *p34*

There are plenty of *farang* orientated restaurants on the main drag, though most of them aren't very special. Most resorts and guesthouses will also offer food of some kind.

$$$-$$ Pizzeria, main road, next to Siam Commercial Bank, T076-485271. Open

1200-2300. Passable pizzas, pasta and other Italian dishes.

$$ Discovery Cafe, main road near Nang Thong Beach, T08-1425 6236 (mob). Open 0930-midnight. Tasty cheeseburgers onoffer here along with some good Thai food.
$$ The Dome, north end opposite Town Plaza. Pies, beer, Thai and international food.
$$ La Dolce Vita, 4/10-11, Moo 7, Sawasdee Plaza, T076-485480. Wood-fired pizzas, Italian pasta and Argentinian grill.
$$ Sun Star Siam, 26/27 Moo 7, Khuk Kak, T076-485637. Friendly, homely Thai-Swiss run place serving up excellent Thai food.

⏱ What to do

Ranong *p29*
Diving
A-One-Diving, has branches at 256 Ruangrat Rd as well as a dive school on Koh Phayam (opposite the pier), www.a-one-diving.com, T077-832984. Organizes trips all over the Andaman Sea including the Similans, Surin and Burma.

Tour operators
Pon's Place Travel Agency, by the new market on Ruangrat Rd, T077 823344. Run by the affable Mr Pon who is an excellent source of information on the islands and areas surrounding Ranong and can help with tours, travel information, guesthouse/ hotel bookings, and car and bike rental.
Ranong Travel, 37 Ruangrat Rd. Probably a better source of information than the tourist information office. It can book bungalows on Koh Chang, arrange fishing trips and advise on visiting Burma.

Koh Phayam *p31*
Diving
A-One-Diving, see Ranong, above.

Khao Sok National Park *p32*
Tour operators
Khao Sok Track & Trail Travel, T08-1747 3030, www.khaosoktrackandtrail.info.

This very helpful tour operator and travel agency just by the gates of the park can arrange a variety of trekking tours, including canoeing, visits to the lake and overnight trips. They also have currency exchange and internet. Recommended.

Khao Lak *p34*
Diving
Diving operations, including live-aboard boats, day trips and courses, are still widely available from various operators, see page 72. Dive sites along the coast, including the Similan Islands, Koh Bon, Koh Tachai, Koh Surin and Richelieu Rock as well as the Mergui Archipelago, received minimal damage during the tsunami although there have been some changes around Island Number Nine in the Similans that you will need to check. The best way to enjoy the Surin Islands is to join one of the daily dive trips from coastal towns. The dive sites in the Mergui Archipelago were left unscathed while the islands escaped topside damage or destruction. Contrary to reports, there are still Moken sea gypsies living in the Mergui Archipelago.
Khao Lak Scuba Adventures, 13/47 Moo 7, Khuk Kak, T076-485602, www.khaolakscuba adventures.com. Well-run 5-star PADI dive resort located in central Khao Lak, offering all the usual PADI courses and live-aboard trips to the Koh Similans.
Sea Dragon, 9/1 Moo 7, T Khuk Kak, T076-420420, www.seadragondivecenter.com. A well-established operation organizing day trips or liveaboards to Richelieu Rock, Similan and Surin Islands. Teaches PADI dive courses. European-managed.

Koh Similan *p35*
Hotels and tour operators organize boat and dive trips and most dive companies in Phuket offer tours to the Similan Islands (see page 72). Although it is possible to visit the Similan Islands independently, it can be an expensive and/or time-consuming business; it is far easier to book

onto a tour. See also under Khao Lak, above, for further information.

Transport

Details of transport to and between the various islands along this part of the Andaman Coast is given in the main text, see page 29-36.

Ranong *p29*
Air
Several budget airlines have attempted to turn **Bangkok**–Ranong into a viable route but all have pulled out after a couple of years. In early 2012, **Happy Air** (www.happyair.co.th), which also flies under the name Ranong Air (www.ranongair.com), was running 5 flights in each direction a week, though reliability is questionable and flights may be cancelled at short notice.

Bus
The bus terminal is on the edge of town, Highway 4, near the **Jansom Thara Hotel**. There are regular a/c and non-a/c connections with **Bangkok**'s Southern bus terminal near the Thonburi railway station. Also connections with **Chumphon**, **Surat Thani** and **Phuket** (304 km south).

Kuraburi *p32*
Buses travelling between **Ranong** (2 hrs) and **Phuket** (4 hrs) pass through Kuraburi.

Khao Sok National Park *p32*
There are about 6 local buses daily from the bus shelter on the main road to both **Phuket** and **Surat Thani** – journey time is about 4 hrs to both. **Khao Sok Track & Trail Travel** (see What to do, above) run connecting minibuses and onward ticketing to a variety of destinations including the **Gulf Islands**, **Chiang Mai**, **Krabi**, **Trang** and even south to **Malaysia**.

Khao Lak *p34*
There are some a/c and non-a/c connections with the Southern terminal in **Bangkok** and connections to **Takuapa**, **Ranong**, **Kuraburi** and **Phuket**. Buses stop on the main road in Khao Lak town, near Nang Thong beach, though you should be able to get them to let you off on any part of the main road.

Phuket Island

Known as the 'Pearl of the Andaman', Phuket lies on Southern Thailand's west coast on the warm Andaman Sea and is connected to the mainland by a 700-m-long causeway. It is a fully developed resort island, with hundreds of hotels and restaurants, marinas, golf courses and some gorgeous beaches. As Thailand's largest island, about the same size as Singapore, there are still remnants of tropical rainforest and traditional life to be found inland and a few cultural attractions, including the thriving, often-overlooked Phuket City, where there's an emerging arts and dining scene and a push to restore its charming old Sino-Portuguese buildings.

Arriving in Phuket

Getting there

Phuket is nearly 900 km south of Bangkok but getting to the island is easy. Phuket International Airport is in the north of the island, about 30 km from Phuket City, but rather closer to many of the main beaches and hotels. There are international connections and multiple daily connections with Bangkok, as well as with Koh Samui, Chiang Mai and Hat Yai, and daily connections to Krabi. The municipal airport bus service to Phuket City (see www.airportbusphuket.com) has 12 departure times 0630-2045 and costs ฿85. It stops at eight destinations along the way and takes about an hour. From Ranong Rd in Phuket City you can catch other buses to the main beaches. Alternatively, shared minivans, metered yellow taxis or limousine taxis are available, the latter two options working out a lot more expensive. All have been known to make unscheduled stops at travel agents in the hope that you'll book a hotel or tour – politely decline any sales pitches and you should be on your way again soon.

As you leave the airport, hordes of limousine drivers will try and usher you into their vehicles. To get to the metered taxis, turn right as you exit the airport and walk down to the kiosk. Despite being metered, the taxis will usually insist you agree on the fare beforehand or levy a ฿100 surcharge. A taxi from the airport to Phuket City shouldn't cost more than ฿500, while a minivan service should cost about ฿150. Several resorts offer free transport from the airport; be sure to check when booking. Airport transfers can also be prearranged through most hotels, as well as operators like **Phuket Shuttle** ① *T08-9972 3300 www. phuketshuttle.com*, or **Hello Phuket Co** ① *www.hellophuket.net*.

Cheaper ways into Phuket City are either to walk or catch a *songthaew* the 5 km to the main north–south road, Route 402, and pick up a public bus or alternatively, walk out of the airport gate and wait for a motorcycle taxi dropping someone off (฿30), they cannot pick up fares at the airport itself. Buses take passengers to Patong, Kata and Karon beaches for ฿100, or by private taxi for ฿400.

The main **bus terminal** ① *Phangnga Rd, T076-211480*, is in Phuket City and there are regular connections with Bangkok (14 hours) as well as destinations in the south. In Bangkok, many buses for Phuket leave from Khaosan Rd. Be careful with these and

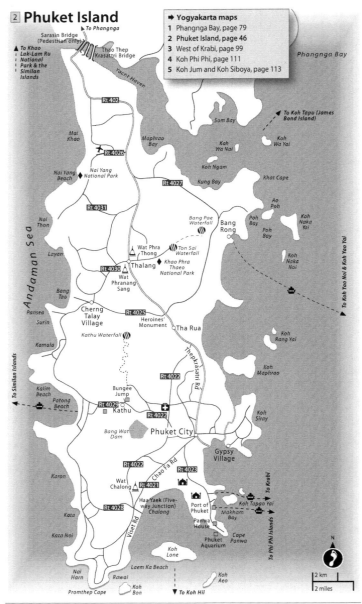

2 Phuket Island

➜ Yogyakarta maps
1 Phangnga Bay, page 79
2 Phuket Island, page 46
3 West of Krabi, page 99
4 Koh Phi Phi, page 111
5 Koh Jum and Koh Siboya, page 113

To Phangnga

Sarasin Bridge
(Pedestian only)

Thao Thep
Krasattri Bridge

To Khao
Lak-Lam Ru
National
Park & the
Similan
Islands

Yacnt Haven

Rt 402

Phangnga Bay

Mai Khao

Rt 4026

Maphrao
Bay

Som Bay

To Koh Tapu (James
Bond Island)

Koh
Wa Nai

Koh
Wa Yai

Nai Yang
Beach

Nai Yang
National Park

Koh Ngam

Khat Cape

Rt 4027

Kung Bay

Ao
Poh

Nai Thon

Rt 4031

Poh
Bay

Koh
Naka
Yai

Bang Pae
Waterfall

Bang
Rong

Poh
Bay

Layan

Wat Phra
Thong

Ton Sai
Waterfall

Koh
Naka
Noi

Andaman Sea

Bang
Tao

Rt 4030

Thalang

Khao Phra
Thaeo
National Park

To Koh Yao Noi & Koh Yao Yai

Wat
Phranang
Sang

Pansea

Surin

Cherng
Talay
Village

Rt 4025

Heroines'
Monument

Tha Rua

Kamala

Kathu Waterfall

Koh
Rang Yai

Thepkrasatri Rd

Koh
Maphrao

To Similan Islands

Rt 4022

Bungee
Jump

Kalim
Beach

Patong
Beach

Rt 4029

Kathu

Rt 4022

Koh
Siray

Bang Wat
Dam

Phuket City

Gypsy
Village

Karon

Rt 4022

Chao Fa Rd

Rt 4023

To Krabi

Wat
Chalong

Rt 4021

Koh Tapao Yai

Haa Yaek (Five-
way Junction)
Chalong

Port of
Phuket

Makham
Bay

Rt 4028

Viset Rd

To Phi Phi Islands

Panwa
House

Kata

Cape
Panwa

Phuket
Aquarium

Kata Noi

Koh
Lone

Nai Harn

Laem Ka Beach

Rawai

Koh
Aeo

N

Promthep Cape

Koh
Bon

To Koh Hil

2 km

2 miles

Phuket's Vegetarian Festival

The first four days of the Ngan Kin Jeh (Chinese Vegetarian Festival) are comparatively ordinary. It is during the last five days that events, for most foreigners, turn really weird. Each of the five Chinese temples or pagodas of Phuket City arranges a procession. Devotees show their commitment and the power of the gods by piercing their bodies with an array of objects apparently chosen by the gods. The processions end in a large field where razor ladders, cauldrons of boiling oil and pits of burning coals await the supplicants.

Tourists have tried to take part and ended up severely injured but locals say those successfully possessed by the spirits feel no pain, unless the gods leave them while the object is still embedded. Islanders insist the festival's real message is to eat healthy food and do good deeds but this is often hard to square with the image of people strolling down the street with a chair, model battleship, miniature Eiffel Tower or potted plant through their cheek.

On the ninth day, a crowd of thousands converge on Saphan Hin to the south of Phuket City and offerings are cast into the sea, thereby allowing the Nine Emperor Gods to return to their heavenly abode, and many of the participants to return home and eat a meal of meat.

The festival occurs in late September or early October and is determined by the Chinese lunar calendar.

don't economize as thieves have been known to board the Khaosan buses, which have a suspicious habit of 'breaking down'. Much better buses may be booked directly at Bangkok's Southern Bus Terminal. The southern railway line doesn't come to the island. However, it is possible to take a train to Phun Phin near Surat Thani and then catch a connecting bus (six hours). ➤➤ *See Transport, page 76, for further information.*

Getting around

Songthaew buses run from Phuket City to Patong, Kamala, Surin, Makham Bay, Nai Yang, Kata, Karon, Nai Harn, Rawai, Thalang and Chalong about every 30 minutes between 0600 and 1800 from the market on Ranong Road. Fares range from ฿25-35, to whatever the ticket collector thinks he can get away with. There are also numerous places to hire cars/ jeeps, for ฿900 a day, and motorbikes, for ฿200 a day, as well as tuk-tuks. Local buses stop around 1800; tuk-tuks take advantage of this so it is essential to know what constitutes a reasonable fare: travel within Phuket City shouldn't be more than about ฿100 and travel to Patong from Phuket City and vice versa should cost you about ฿450. Thanks to the power of the local tuk-tuk operators, metered taxis are not allowed to pick up passengers from anywhere in Phuket except at the airport or unless they are booked privately.

Best time to visit

The driest and sunniest months are November to April. May to October are wetter with more chance of overcast conditions, although daily sunshine still averages five to eight hours. August is when the monsoon begins and red flags appear to warn swimmers not to venture out because of powerful and sometimes fatal currents.

Tourist information

The **TAT office** ① *191 Thalang Rd, T076-212213, tatphket@tat.or.th, daily 0830-1630*, is good for specific local questions. The island's two weekly newspapers, *Phuket Gazette*, www. phuketgazette.net and The Phuket News, www.thephuketnews.com, are good sources of information, with quirky local human-interest stories, events calendars and community updates. Two independent expat-run blogs, Jamie's Phuket (www.jamie-monk.blogspot. com) and Phuket 101 (www.phuket101.blogspot.com) offer resort and restaurant reviews and insider's tips on things to do and see. For details of tour companies offering a range of excursions and tours, see What to do, page 71.

Background

Phuket was first 'discovered' by Arab and Indian navigators around the end of the ninth century. Always a rich island – known for its pearls, fish and fruits – Phuket proved irresistible to the Burmese, who carried out a surprise attack in 1785. The previous governor's young widow, Chan, and her sister, Mook, immediately disguised all the women of the town as men and had them pose as soldiers. Fearing the worst from the fierce-looking ranks, the Burmese retreated. Chan and Mook were honoured for their bravery and, today, on the road to the airport, you can see the Heroines' Monument to the two sisters. Much of Phuket's considerable wealth was derived from tin, and the island was dubbed 'Junk Ceylon' in the mid-16th century. In 1876, during the reign of King Rama III, Chinese workers flooded the island to work in the mines. The slave conditions that ensued later led to rebellion but conditions improved and, in 1907, modern tin-mining methods were introduced by Englishman Captain Edward Miles. Phuket Town became so wealthy that paved roads and cars appeared. These days, tourism is the big earner, with rubber, coconut and fisheries also contributing to the island's wealth. A third of the island's official 300,000 population now live in Phuket City. While around 30% of these are Chinese descendents, the rest are indigenous Thais, Sikhs, Hindus, Malay Muslims and Chao Le sea gypsies. In the December 2004 tsunami, Phuket's coastal areas suffered damage and loss of life, particularly on Patong and Kamala beaches, but the island made a relatively quick recovery and, aside from the tsunami towers that line its shores, there are no lingering signs of the destructive waves. Indeed, the island has weathered many storms over the past decade, including the global financial crisis and riots in Bangkok, and its visitor arrival numbers just keep rising. However, this tendency to focus on quantity rather than quality is putting Phuket at risk of becoming an overgrown, overblown mass tourism destination; many would argue that it already is. With its airport operating well beyond capacity, handling 8.4 million passengers in 2011, traffic jams and a strained infrastructure, some lament that the island is starting to resemble Bangkok with a beach.

Phuket City → *For listings, see pages 57-77.*

Phuket City was given city status in 2004, although most islanders still call it "Phuket Town". This upgrade came as a surprise to many who still regard it as a sleepy provincial hub, hardly big or bustling enough to merit the city crown. Treated largely as a stopover by divers en route to the Similan or Surin islands and beach junkies headed further up the coast, Phuket City is now anxious to revamp its image and pull in a more sophisticated crowd. So, in addition to its Sino-Portuguese architectural heritage, which is reminiscent of Georgetown in Malaysian Penang – a leftover of the wealthy Chinese tin barons of the

19th century – there is a burgeoning arts and literary scene. It seems to be working as, increasingly, the city's incomers include weary Bangkok urbanites hankering for a business by the sea and expat foodies attracted by the city's excellent restaurant reputation. But Phuket City is still small enough and swamped enough by the glory of the beaches, to be down the pecking order. Not that this matters to the old-timers who can still remember when the town was surrounded by virgin forest. This is, perhaps, the card up Phuket City's sleeve – a subtle confidence underneath the tourist glitter, especially in the old town, and a feeling that another chapter is unravelling in this prosperous settlement. A cooler, hipper Phuket could easily emerge if the arts scene gets beyond the cottage industry feel and allows itself to be injected by that incoming Bangkok and expat buzz. What will aid Phuket City is that it still has some grand old buildings left, which are rare in Thailand and a magnet for those with an eye for architecture. The push in recent years to restore and beautify these historical buildings and streets has certainly helped inject a sense of pride and culture into the Old Town.

At the end of the 19th century, Phuket Town, one of the richest settlements in the country, saw a flowering of Sino-Portuguese mansions built by tin-barons revelling in their wealth. In Old Phuket you'll still find houses and shops in styles similar to that of Penang and Macao and dating back 100 to 130 years. Featuring complex latticework, Mediterranean coloured ceramic tiles, high ceilings and gleaming wooden interiors, these architectural dreams, remain cool in the summer and free of damp during the monsoon. While the style is commonly called Sino-Portuguese, many were actually built by Italian workers who imported materials straight from their homeland. During the Old Phuket Town Festival, held each year after Chinese New Year, some of these houses are open to the public. The best examples are along Thalang, Yaowarat, Ranong, Phangnga, Krabi, Dibuk, Rassada, Soi Romanee and Damrong roads.

A particularly notable example of one of Phuket's finer older buildings is the **Government House**, which stood in as the 'American Embassy' in Phnom Penh in the classic film – *The Killing Fields*. Preservation orders have been placed on all buildings in Old Phuket. Among the finer ones are the **Chartered Bank THAI office** ① *Ranong Rd opposite the market*, and the **Sala Phuket** ① *Damrong Rd*. Less grand, but quietly elegant, are the turn-of-the-20th-century **shophouses** on, for example, Thalang Road. There has been considerable renovation of buildings on Dibuk, Thalang and Krabi roads but nearby there are still side streets with some lovely examples of traditional shophouses. **Soi Romanee**, the island's former red-light district, in particular is such a street with traditional merchant houses on both sides of the road, a few with fading paintwork on the walls. Some of the renovation has introduced smart new restaurants, cafés, art galleries and antique shops. Notably, **The Loft**, which sells expensive Southeast Asian antiques and Chinese porcelains and received an award for its efforts in conserving traditional architecture. At the same time there are still plenty of more traditional hardware stores, small tailors, stationery shops and the like, that clearly cater to the locals. Another sight worth visiting in the old town is the **Temple of the Serene Light** ① *Phangnga Rd, entrance is marked in English and Thai*. The narrow alleyway leading to it has been opened up, making the temple easier to spot from the street but destroying some of its mystery in the process. More than a century old, this is a small Taoist temple, filled with paintings and religious artefacts, that was rebuilt following a fire. It is the oldest Taoist temple in Phuket and is dedicated to the Goddess of Mercy. For more information on Phuket's past, The Old Town Foundation has opened a small museum on Phangnga Road, and a museum for the Baba Perkanen (Straits Chinese) culture is being developed at the former police station on Rassada Rd.

Ladyboys

Katoeys, transvestites or, as they tend to be known by farang in Thailand, 'ladyboys', are larger in number than one might expect. They are also part of a long tradition of transvestites in Southeast Asia. Many bars and clubs will have katoeys working for them, whether as bar 'girls' or in shows of one sort or another. They are often very beautiful and extraordinarily difficult, if not impossible, to tell apart from the real thing. In Bangkok there are also groups of katoeys who have been known to surround and pick-pocket farang men on the street – particularly on the Landmark side of Sukhumvit Road and along sois 5-11.

There are **night markets** on Ong Sim Phai and Tilok Uthit 1. These are excellent places to buy spicy rolls and other street foods on a nocturnal prowl through the old town. Khao Rang Viewpoint is a romantic spot atop a large hill in Phuket City. Although the view isn't quite as stunning as at Promthep Cape, Khao Rang is a cool place to watch over the whole of the city. There's also a fitness park up here if you feel like a bit of exercise. There are a few reasonable Thai restaurants around that offer the same great views. To reach Khao Rang, you need to make your way up the hill by either travelling from Yaowarat Road on to Soi Vachira, turning right at the end of the *soi* and following the hill up; or take the turn up to Khao Rang at the point where Thung Kha Road and Mae Luan Road meet.

A few kilometres south of Phuket City is **Phuket Zoo** ① *23/2 Moo 3, Soi Palai, Chao Fa Rd, T076-381227, www.phuketzoo.com*. There are regular elephant, monkey and crocodile shows here but the place screams 'tourist photo opportunity', and foreign visitors are covertly charged about four times the local price. Only recommended if you relish the thought of having your picture taken with a chained-up, heavily sedated white tiger.

Phuket's beaches and sights → *For listings, see pages 57-77.*

The gorgeous 3-km-long sweep of sand and coconut palms of Patong Beach (see below) that attracted backpackers in the 1970s is now a dim memory. Now the island's party central, Patong has a boisterous nightlife scene and the beach is crammed with speedboats, jet-skis and row upon row of rental sun loungers. For less hedonistic, smaller beaches that still have charm, go south of Patong. Here you will find the twin, horseshoe-shaped Karon and Kata beaches. **Karon Beach** is around half the size of Patong, less densely developed, and with a general atmosphere that is more laid-back and family friendly. **Kata Beach** is also popular with families, but its streets are like a mini-Patong, with hotels, restaurants and shops chaotically jostling for space.

At Phuket's southern end is **Nai Harn**, a pretty white beach favoured by Thais, with a small number of more expensive hotels and limited amenities. In the middle of this charming beach, the **Samnak Song Monastery** acts as an unexpected bodyguard against major developers, but the main road leading here, Sai Yuan, is under furious development.

The east coast of Phuket is only thinly developed from a tourist point of view. Much of it is rocky and the beaches that are to be found here do not compare with those on the west coast. There are some excellent hotels, but these are largely stand-alone establishments; don't expect a great wealth of facilities.

Kamala Beach, north of Patong, was severely affected by the 2004 tsunami, but it has now completely recovered and is one of the fastest-growing resort areas of Phuket. The next beach north is **Surin**, home to Phuket's first golf course more than 60 years ago, during the reign of King Rama VII. The course is now in disuse and serves as a public park and overflow car park. A growing beach club scene is turning Surin into a place to swill cocktails while looking fabulous.

Surin and **Bang Tao**, further north, are similar in that the resorts are widely spaced with no centre for shops. Bang Tao was formerly used for tin mining which turned the landscape into a desert. **Nai Ton** and **Layan** are small bays with exclusive resorts. Finally, at the northern end of the island, is **Nai Yang Beach** and the **Nai Yang National Park**, a 9-km casuarina-lined beach with a few resorts and some park bungalows.

Patong Beach

Patong began to metamorphose from a hippy paradise into a commercial centre during the 1970s. It is now a mass of neon signs advertising hotels, massage parlours, restaurants, straight bars, gay bars, nightclubs and the plain peculiar. While families may not be able to avoid vulgarity, they will be able to bypass ladyboys and devious side-street deals by choosing from a range of excellent family hotels. Patong tourists are a mixed lot – a Butlins overspill, shameless beer boys and plump retirees. Increasingly, Russians are also turning up, both for business and revelry.

Take Patong for what it is: an overdeveloped mass of cheap booze, expensive restaurants, mediocre beaches and odd characters. For a night out, it's fun, but otherwise, there's little point in basing your holiday around a stay in Patong. Many visitors to Phuket spend all of their time in Patong and then leave with a negative view of the island as a whole. Don't be one of them, there is so much more to Phuket.

Patong does, however, offer the widest selection of watersports on Phuket and, in spite of hotel development, it is still possible to snorkel on the reef at the southern end of the bay.

Driving towards Karon from Patong you will come to **Tri Trang Beach**, a charming little beach located in front of the Merlin Beach Resort. The area is spotless with very few disturbances but the water is full of rocks and not suitable for swimming during low tide. There is decent snorkelling here and few tourists ever make it out this way. From Tri Trang Beach it's possible to charter a long-tailed boat to picturesque **Freedom Beach**, you can't get to there by road, where the water and sand are beautiful.

Karon and Kata beaches

The horseshoe-shaped Karon and Kata beaches south of Patong are divided by a narrow rocky outcrop. Karon started tourist life as a haven for backpackers; it is now well developed, with a range of hotels and bungalows and a wide selection of restaurants. Though Russian visitors are starting to come here in larger numbers, the Karon scene is dominated by prosperous Scandinavians. Some places bear mini Swedish flags, and it is usually these establishments that are guaranteed to make you feel as if you never left the aeroplane. This can prove tedious and an air of predictability and safety pervades the beach. Karon's major drawback, physically, is the overly exposed beach despite its cosy curve. Nonetheless, there are good mid-range places to stay, and the slower pace of life here will appeal to many.

Kata consists of two beaches: **Kata Yai** (Big) and **Kata Noi** (Little), divided by a cliff. Both bays are picturesque with rocks along the edges and sweeping fine pale yellow sands in the centre. Descending a winding hill, Kata Noi comes as a pleasant surprise, offering an adorable little bay with a small and perfect beach. Although it is dominated by the **Katathani Phuket Beach Resort**, on the whole it feels much like a hidden seaside harbour, and even the tourist infrastructure of souvenir shops, guesthouses, laundries and restaurants are made up of a pleasant jumble of locally owned businesses. There are also cheapish bungalows here. The snorkelling is good at the south end of Kata Noi and around Koh Pu, the island in the middle of the bay that looks like a squashed bowler hat. Kata Yai, just the other side, is a sprawling mass of development: hotels, souvenir shops and roadside restaurants abound. It provides excellent facilities for the holidaymaker. including numerous options for watersports and mostly low-key nightlife choices down the rambling streets running inland from the coast. Despite this, the huge hotels on the beach overwhelm the bay with umbrellas and sunbeds spread across almost the entire beach. The beautifully painted and cared-for tour boats with their smart wooden benches and umbrellas are a far cry from the traditional fisherman's longboats, on which they are obviously modelled.

Nai Harn and Promthep Cape
Nai Harn, a small, gently sloping beach – home to the prestigious **Royal Phuket Yacht Club** – is one of the island's most beautiful locations, renowned for its spectacular sunsets. From Nai Harn it is possible to walk to **Promthep Cape**, the best place to view the sunset if you don't mind the crowds. Near the highest point there is a shrine covered in gold leaf and surrounded by wooden elephants.

Rawai → *14 km south of Phuket City.*
To the north of Promthep Cape, up the eastern side of the island, the first beach is Rawai, which was 'discovered' by King Rama VII in the 1920s. This crescent-shaped beach is now relatively developed although not to the same degree as Patong or Karon, being more popular with Thai and Southeast Asian tourists, particularly during Chinese New Year and Songkran. Many Thais go to Rawai for the cheap restaurants, although prices are going up. The bay is sheltered and it is safe to swim throughout the year, but the beach, although long and relatively peaceful, is rather dirty and rocky. Rawai is more of a jumping-off point for offshore trips to Koh Hae (Coral Island), Koh Bon and Koh Lone. At Rawai's northern end there is also a sea gypsy village, **Chao Le**.

Koh Kaew Pisadarn
① *Take a long-tailed boat from Rawai Beach; negotiate with one of the boat owners, take a picnic and arrange to be picked up.*
Koh Kaew Pisadarn can be seen from Promthep Cape and is a 15-minute boat ride from Rawai Beach. The island is the site of three footprints of the Buddha. Two are among the boulders and stone on the upper shore; the third is just below the low watermark. For many years important Buddhist festivals were celebrated here because of the island's supposed spiritual power and significance. Then, about 40 years ago, these religious pilgrimages stopped. Sam Fang, who researched a story on the island for the *Bangkok Post*, discovered a tragedy had occurred about that time. Some rowing boats en route to the island had sunk during a storm, which was blamed on a sea serpent that had become enraged by continual trespassing. Between 1952 and 1967, attempts to construct a Buddha on the island were continually thwarted by bad weather and high seas. The island quickly gained the reputation of being cursed. Only in 1994 were attempts at erecting a Buddha image renewed and, defying superstition, a 1.5-m-high concrete statue now stands on the northeastern side of the island, overlooking Promthep Cape. The statue, about a 10-minute walk along a laid path from the boat landing, is surrounded by two protective nagas that slither over the top of the encircling balustrade. Steps lead down to the footprints on the shore beneath the Buddha.

Laem Ka and Chalong beaches

The next beaches up the east coast and south of Phuket City are Laem Ka and Chalong. Ao Chalong is 1 km off the main road. There is not much here for the sun and sea worshipper: the beach is filthy and full of speedboats. From Chalong's long pier boats can be caught to the offshore islands for game fishing, snorkelling and scuba diving. There are also a few reasonable seafood restaurants from which you can watch the dozens of working and pleasure boats gather off the pier in the harbour. The rest of the east coast is of limited interest for tourists because of a rocky coast.

About 6 km south of Phuket City, just north of Chalong junction, is the ostentatious Wat Chalong, best known for its gold-leaf encrusted statues of the previous abbots, Luang Pho Chaem and Luang Pho Chuang. The former was highly respected for his medical skills, which proved to be particularly valuable when Phuket's Chinese miners revolted in 1876. The halving of the international price of tin coupled with Bangkok's attempt to extract excessive taxes from the province inflamed the Chinese. Some 2000 converged on the governor's house and when they failed to take the building, they rampaged through the less well-defended villages. The spree of killing and looting was only brought to an end at Wat Chalong where the two respected monks talked the mob out of their fury. Visible from almost anywhere around the south of Phuket City is Phuket's own Big Buddha statue. Your reward for scaling the enormous and steep Nakkerd Hill is a sweeping view of the island's southern bays and beaches and an up-close glimpse of a 45-m seated Buddha in white Burmese marble. There is also a smaller golden Buddha statue. To get to the Buddha driving from Phuket City, go past Wat Chalong and look for the sign pointing out the right-hand turn to the statue (Soi Jaofa 51).

Cape Panwa

South of Phuket City, down Sakdidej Road which becomes Route 4023, in the grounds of the **Cape Panwa Hotel**, is **Panwa House**, one of Phuket's finest examples of Sino-Portuguese architecture. Panwa House was formerly inhabited by a fishing family from Phuket and, later, by the hotel's official coconut catcher. The catcher's job was to remove coconuts from the trees so the guests would not be concussed. However, he was under orders not to take a coconut from the trees on the beach, and in all his years as official coconut catcher, he never disobeyed. The house is now filled with curious artefacts, like the coconut scraper in the shape of an otter. The first floor has attractive views of guests below at their meals, framed by swaying palms and beach and being serenaded by performers At the tip of Panwa Cape is the popular **Phuket Aquarium** ① *T076-391126, www.phuketaquarium.org, daily 0830-1630 (last admission 1600), ฿100, children ฿50.* The air-conditioned aquarium is well laid out with a moderate collection of salt- and freshwater fish, lobsters, molluscs and turtles and some other weird species. There are regular public songthaews every hour (฿20) from the market on Ranong Road to the aquarium. Watching the sun set along the paved seafront is recommended. There are a few café/restaurants, all open to a view which always seems to include imposing Thai naval boats or cruise ships in the distance. It is possible to charter long-tailed boats from Cape Panwa to **Koh Hii** (฿600), and **Koh Mai Ton** (฿1200), or to go fishing (฿1200). See below.

Koh Tapao Yai, a small island off the cape, is home to a few hotels (see Where to stay, page 61) and around 200 hornbills. Baby brother of Koh Tapao Yai, **Koh Tapao Noi** is another small island, secluded and devoid of almost everything except flora, fauna and hornbills. There is also a lighthouse that was built in 1890. Other than that, enjoy the beach and the sea while you can. To get there, take a boat from Ao Makham Pier (6 km from Phuket City).

Koh Lone, Koh Mai Ton and other southern islands

There are places to stay on several of the islands off the east and southeast coasts of Phuket. All the resorts play on the desert island getaway theme. These places are hard to reach in the monsoon season and often shut for up to three months of the year. Koh Mai Ton, for instance, is a private island 9 km southeast of Phuket with little on it except the Honeymoon Island Phuket Resort (formerly the Maithon Resort).

Koh Maprao (Coconut Island)

Coconut Island, up until recently a tourist-free island off the grid, is now home to the sprawling five-star Village Coconut Island Resort on its northern shoreline, with mains electricity coming soon. A luxury villa development is underway, too, on the opposite side. The traditional island life of its few hundred residents is still intact, however, and the village runs agro-tour and homestay programmes.To get there, make your way to Laem Hin Pier (15 minutes north of Phuket City, on the east coast, about ฿150 in a tuk-tuk), take a long-tailed boat (฿15) over to the island and a short motorcycle ride to the beach.

Koh Rang Yai

This small island off the east coast of Phuket has a focus on day trips, so you might feel like you're being herded in and out like cattle. It's a beautiful island, though, and worth a visit. The island has its own pearl farm and demonstrations are given along with a trip to a pearl shop. Bicycles are available, and there's a putting course. The beach is clean, although the water looks a bit murky and if you just fancy loafing about without many people around, this is a good place to do it.

Boats depart from Sapam Bay, which is about 15 km north of Phuket City, on the east coast. Expect to pay up to ฿300 for a tuk-tuk from Phuket City to Sapam Bay. Bungalows can be rented on the island (see Where to stay, page 61).

Kamala Beach

Kamala Beach, was one of the worst hit by the 2004 tsunami, but it's now fully recovered and changing rapidly from a sleepy Muslim fishing village to a bustling resort town. Some of Phuket's priciest hotels and private villas line the rocky cape, known as the 'Millionaire's Mile, at its south end. The beach is sadly under siege by unabated commercial development, its powder-soft sands nearly completely buried under sun loungers and vendor stands in high season. The northern section is quieter, and there's some decent snorkelling among the rocks just offshore.

Laem Sing

Between Kamala and Surin is a tiny beach by the name of Laem Sing. Though it's getting more crowded with each passing year, the sand is clean and the water is clear. The only problem is the onslaught of jet skis that noisily zip around dangerously close to where people are swimming.

Surin Beach and Pansea Beach → *West coast, north of Patong Beach.*

Surin is developing into something of a 'Tale of Two Beaches'; ritzy beach clubs and cocktail bars visited by the likes of Kate Moss take up ever more beachfront space, while the shrinking public areas, where the locals hang out, appear increasingly neglected and dirty. With numerous private villas and luxury resorts in the surrounding area, Surin's often touted as Phuket's five-star beach, which indeed it is, so long as you avert your eyes from the trash piles. A strong undertow makes swimming at Surin dangerous at times. Pansea Beach has soft sand in a steeply sloping bay just north of Surin, with two exclusive hotels.

Bang Tao Beach → *West coast, north of Patong Beach.*

The **Laguna Phuket** complex at the north of Bang Tao Beach consists of six expensive hotels built around a lagoon. Free tuk-tuks and boats link the hotels, and guests are able to use all the facilities. There is a great range of watersports and good free provision for children. The **Canal Village** offers 40 or so shops and a lagoon-side café serving satay. The adjoining bakery serves good pastries and cakes. To the south of the **Laguna Phuket** are some other places to stay. The southern part of the beach is one of the few areas where you will still see traditional boat builders and the boats themselves in operation, instead of the tourist variety used to take people on island tours.

Nai Thon and Layan

Between Bang Tao and Nai Yang are the isolated beaches of Nai Thon and Layan. These beaches have recently been developed with a luxury resort and spa at Layan occupying the whole bay and similarly expensive developments are moving into Nai Thon, which only has a 400-m-long beach. South of Nai Thon is an exquisite cove, most easily accessible by boat.

Nai Yang and Nai Yang National Park

① *Entrance to beach ฿200 per person.*

Nai Yang is close to the airport and 37 km from Phuket City. To get there, take a bus from the market on Ranong Road in Phuket City. The attractive and often empty forest-lined beach of Nai Yang lies next to the airport and is part of the Nai Yang National Park. It is the ideal place to pass a few hours before an early evening flight. Further south, there is more activity, with a range of luxury hotels and bungalows. The park encompasses Nai Yang and **Mai Khao** beaches, which together form the longest beach on the island (13 km). The area was declared a national park in 1981 to protect the turtles which lay their eggs here from November to March. Eggs are collected by the Fisheries Department and young turtles are released into the sea around the second week of April (check on the date as it changes), on **Turtle Release Festival Day**. The north end of the beach (where there is good snorkelling on the reef) is peaceful and secluded. There is no accommodation in the national park, although camping is possible.

Mai Khao

This is Phuket's northernmost and largest beach, now home to a sprinkling of luxury resorts and a gaudy, underused waterpark in the West Sands resort development, founded by Sir Terry Leahy, former CEO of Tesco's hypermarket. It also encompasses the village of Had Mai Khao and the Sirinath National Park. The village is dominated by shrimp nurseries which sell the grown shrimp on to numerous farms throughout the south of Thailand. These discharge waste to the sea off the Mai Khao beach, but not to the same levels as shrimp farms. Again, sea turtles nest on this beach, including the huge leatherbacks; the Turtle Release Festival is in mid-April. The community effort to conserve the turtles involves collecting the eggs and keeping a hatchery. The beach is steeply shelved, so swimming isn't recommended and it is unsuitable for children. The beach is lined with casuarina trees.

Heroines' Monument and Thalang National Museum

About 12 km north of Phuket City on Route 402, towards the airport, is the village of **Tha Rua**. At the crossroads there is a statue of two female warriors: **Muk** and **Chan**. These are the sisters who repelled an army of Burmese invaders in 1785 by dressing up all the women of the town as men, so fooling the Burmese. Rama I awarded them titles for their deeds and they are celebrated in bronze, swords drawn. The statue was erected in 1966 and Thais rub gold leaf on its base as a sign of respect and to gain merit. The **Thalang National Museum** ① *Wed-Sun 0900-1600 (closed for national holidays), ฿100*, is just east of this crossroads on Route 4027. It has a well-presented collection on Phuket's history and culture.

Khao Phra Thaeo Wildlife Park

① *20 km north of Phuket City, T076-311998, 0600-1800, ฿200, half-price for children.*
To get to this wildlife park turn east off the main road in Thalang and follow signs for Ton Sai Waterfall. The beautiful, peaceful road winds through stands of rubber trees and degraded forest. The park supports wild boar and monkeys and represents the last of the island's natural forest ecosystem. During dry season, a walk around the park is a lot of fun and not particularly gruelling. The primary nature trail has 14 stations where you can stop and learn a bit about the park. There isn't much wildlife to be seen, although you may come across a monitor lizard, gibbon or even wild boar. The main trail is about 2 km long. The park's two waterfalls, Bang Pae Waterfall and Ton Sai Waterfall, are not up to much during the dry season when there isn't any water. When there is water, visitors can paddle in the upper pool. There are bungalows, a lakeside restaurant and a number of hiking routes here.

Bang Pae Waterfall and Gibbon Rehabilitation Project

The road east from Ton Sai Waterfall becomes rough and can only be negotiated on foot or by motorbike; it leads to **Bang Pae Waterfall** ① *0600-1800*. Alternatively, the falls can be approached from the other direction, by turning off Route 4027 and driving 1 km. There is a beautiful lake, refreshment stands, forest trails, and bathing pools. Just south of the waterfall (follow signs off Route 4027) is a **Gibbon Rehabilitation Project** ① *T076-260492, grp@gibbonproject.org, 0900-1600, free, donations welcome as it is run by volunteers*, funded from the US and apparently the only such initiative in Southeast Asia for these endangered animals.

Naka Noi Pearl Farm

① *T076-219870, 0900-1530, ฿500. Long-tailed boats can be chartered at any time, ฿700, and the driver will wait for you.*
Also off Route 4027, at Ao Poh, there is a long wooden jetty where boat tours leave for Naka Noi Island and Pearl Farm – Thailand's largest. At the farm, the owner asks you to wait half an hour while they prepare the oysters for the demonstration, which takes around 1½ hours. Ensure your visit is to Naka Noi, rather than Naka Yai, where the 'Pearl Farm' seems to be a fake.

Phuket Island listings

For hotel and restaurant price codes and other relevant information, see pages 12-16.

🛏 Where to stay

Phuket has hundreds of places to stay, largely at the upper price end. During the low season (Jun-Oct) room rates may be as little as half the high season price. All rates quoted are peak season. Advance booking is recommended during high season (particularly at Christmas and New Year).

Phuket City *p48*

The hotels in town are rather uninspired: most people avoid staying here and head straight for the beaches, however, there are some good guesthouses in the old part of town.

$$$$-$$$ Dara Hotel, 14/18 Moo 4, Chaofa Rd, T076-612846-49, www.daraphuket.com. High-rise hotel with a shocking colour scheme, this is the place to go if you want handy access to the shopping centres. It provides a free tuk-tuk shuttle service to all the nearby malls and, being at the edge of town, it's quicker to get to the beaches from here than from the downtown hotels. A/c rooms and suites, free Wi-Fi, pool.

$$$$-$$$ iPavilion Phuket, 133 Satool Rd, T076-210 445, www.ipavilionhotel. comwww.islandpavilion.com. Almost groovy, circular, high-rise. Nice rooms with an unusual layout. Pool and all facilities.

$$$$-$$$ Novotel Royal Phuket City Hotel, opposite the main bus station in town, T076-233333, www.royalphuketcity. com. Swimming pool, business centre and gym. Expensive but up to 50% discount in the wet season. Hints of Las Vegas with shimmering fountain out front. Rather out of place as it dominates the street.

$$$ Baan Suwantawe, 1/10 Dibuk Rd, T076-212 879, www.baansuwantawe.com. Serviced apartments and hotel opposite Lemongrass restaurant. The rooms are

clean and comfortable and there is a large outdoor swimming pool. Breakfast is not included. Rooms have access to broadband and overlook the pool. The accommodation here really stands out from other choices in Phuket. Cable TV and a/c.

$$$ Bhukitta, 20, 22, 23, 26, 28 Phangnga Rd, T076-215712-3, www.bhukitta.com. Hidden away down a *soi* within walking distance of the bus station. A mid-range hotel with a bar, spa and great restaurant. Rooms have all mod cons and are large and modern. Wi-Fi is offered throughout the hotel. Rooms are spotless and well furnished. There's also a karaoke room, if that's your thing.

$$$ Casa Blanca Boutique Hotel, 26 Phuket Rd, T076-219019, www. casablancaphuket.com. Bright and stylish place with traditional Sino-Portuguese touches in Phuket City centre. Small pool, free Wi-Fi and a cute café tucked away in an indoor garden setting.

$$$ Sino House Phuket, 1 Montree Rd, T076-221 398, www.sinohousephuket.com. A modern hotel with a Chinese twist. The rooms are large and all have Wi-Fi access, a fridge, a/c and cable TV. A decent breakfast is included. Located in a quiet area of town, opposite O'Malley's Irish bar, if you fancy a drink. They also have a spa that comes highly recommended for massages.

$$$-$$ Phuket 346, 15 Soi Rommanee, Talang Rd, T076-258108, www.phuket346. com. Hip little guesthouse with only 3 rooms in a converted Sino-Portugese shophouse. There is lots of art around the place making it quaint and chilled. Rooms have high ceilings, comfortable beds, lovely linen and a/c. You'll feel more like you're in someone's home than a guesthouse. There's also a café and art gallery.

$$ Crystal Inn Hotel, 2/1-10 Soi Surin, Montri Rd, T076-256789, www.phuket crystalinn.com. Comfortable, trendy rooms conveniently close to Surin Circle. There are 54 rooms in total and the hotel also has a lobby bar. Rooms come with twin beds or a large double bed. TV, a/c and artwork come as part of the package. Stylish accommodation at a reasonable price.

$$-$ Phuket Backpacker Hostel, 167 Ranong Rd, T076-256680, www.phuket backpacker.com. By day, Ranong Rd is home to a lively market, but by night, the street has a strange empty charm about it. The hostel may look gloomy from the outside, but inside it's everything you would expect from decent, budget accommodation. There are dorms and rooms with or without air conditioning. The standard rooms are a little pricey for true backpackers (฿900 or ฿1000), but they are clean and the lounge is a cool place to hang out. This place is dubbed a 'boutique hostel', if such a thing is possible.

$ Nana Chart Mansion, 41/34 Montri Rd, T076-230041-2/230050 (extension 3). Spotless, sizeable a/c and fan rooms, although many are slightly airless. It is excellent value and the staff are helpful.

$ On On, 19 Phangnga Rd, T076-211154. Riding on its reputation as Phuket City's first hotel, this establishment, dating from 1929, is in the heart of the Old Town. It has a curious colonial feel with 49 sub-divided a/c and fan rooms with walls that shudder when you sneeze. Cold showers, strip lighting, dark, forbidding wardrobes and the bar downstairs make for an uncomfortable, noisy night. A pity because there are hints, in the lovely worn staircase, that this was once a dignified establishment. Attached a/c coffee shop and good restaurant, plus an excellent tour desk run by the relaxed Woody.

$ Phuket 43, 43 Thalang Rd, T076-258127, www.phuket43guesthouse.com. This tucked-away gem has 4 room types, all with fan and breakfast. The snazziest have private gardens or balconies, as well as outdoor showers. Worth a look.

$ Phuket Old Town Hostel, 42 Krabi Rd, T076-258 272, T08-1569 2519 (mob), www.

phuketoldtownhostel.com. Cheap, cheerful and basic. Not all rooms are en suite, not all have a/c. Prices include breakfast, which is served 0700-1000. The communal bathroom has a hot shower. Run by the same people behind **Thalang Guesthouse**.

$ Thalang Guesthouse, 37 Thalang Rd, T076-214 225, www.thalangguesthouse. com. A pleasant house with old-world charm, large windows, wood floors, double-panelled doors and ceiling fans. It has 13 rooms on 3 floors, with varying prices and standards. Rooms 3 and 21 are best, though a little more expensive; they have balconies overlooking the street, while some rooms look on to a brick wall. This is an excellent base to explore the Old Town. The owner, Mr Tee, has a good reputation with guests, who are encouraged to leave notes and drawings on the landing.

Patong Beach *p51, map p46*

$$$$ Holiday Inn, 52 Thaweewong Rd, T076-370200, www.holiday.phuket.com. This mega-hotel takes up a chunk of Patong. Pool-side rooms need to be reserved. This hotel is suited to couples and families and has all the comforts you would expect from the brand.

$$$$ Patong Merlin Hotel, 44 Moo 4, Thaweewong Rd, T076-340037-41, www. merlinphuket.com/patongmerlin. Large 4-storey hotel, attractively laid out with well-designed rooms. A/c, restaurant, 3 sculptured pools and a children's pool. Recommended.

$$$$ Safari Beach, 136 Thaweewong Rd, T076-341171, www.safaribeachhotel.com. Small hotel set around pool in a leafy compound just north of Soi Bangla. The location is sought after as it is on the beach and the standard rooms are spacious. A/c rooms only, restaurant attached. Recommended.

$$$$ Sunset Beach Resort, 316/2 Phrabarame Rd, T076-342482, www. sunsetphuket.com. What better place to feel safe than a hotel with the tsunami warning tower on the roof? This is another mega-hotel with a double kidney-shaped pool snaking its way between terraced, balconied wings. From the upper floor rooms you can see the sea. There is also a decent spa and good but predictable meals. A 5-min tuk-tuk ride from Bangla Rd. Recommended.

$$$$ Thavorn Beach Village, 6/2 Moo 6, Nakalay Bay (between Kamala and Patong beaches), T076-618217, www.thavornbeach village.com. Giant vulgar concrete Hindu cobras spring from the fountain in front of reception at this otherwise attractively designed resort of Thai-style villas with 4 rooms each, many with verandas, beside the large lagoon-like pool. It's a secluded spot on sparsely populated Nakalay Bay (rocky at low tide). It also offers extras like Thai cooking courses and scuba-diving. The restaurant overlooks the sea.

$$$ Smile Inn, 108/9 Thaweewong Rd, T076-340455. This is a small hotel in the centre of the Patong Beach with rooms painted bright enough to warrant dim light. However, it is only 2 mins from the beach and well maintained for the price.

$$$-$$ Asia Loop Guest House, 2-17/20 Sirirat Rd, T076-364714, www.asialoop.net. Small, nicely designed hotel with 32 a/c rooms and a good range of facilities for the price. Rooftop pool. Close to Bangla Rd so it can get noisy at night.

$$-$ Bodega, 189/3 Rat-U-Thit Rd, T076-602191, www.bodegaphuket.com. Fun and friendly spot with a music cafe and art gallery, some dorm rooms, central location. Its travellers' vibe is unusual for Patong. Excellent value.

Karon and Kata beaches *p51, map p46*
$$$$ Best Western Phuket Ocean Resort, 9/1 Moo 1, T076-396600, www.phuket-ocean.com. On a hillside, this establishment overlooks the Andaman Sea and Karon Lagoon at the quieter, northern end of the bay, away from the beach. It has a/c, restaurant and pool.

$$$$ The Boathouse, southern end of Kata Beach, T076-330015, www.boathouse phuket.com. After changing ownership, one of Phuket's first luxury resorts has emerged from a multi-million-dollar renovation with a fresh look and stylish beach club, RE KÁ TA, plus a boutique and streetside café, pool and spa. Thai cookery classes are offered. The wine cellar is one of the nicest surprises, with over 800 wines – a rarity in the land of whisky and beer. The rooms are relatively small but über-elegant. Recommended.

$$$$ Centara Villa Phuket, 701 Patak Rd, T076-286300-9, www.centarahotelsresorts. com/cvp/cvp_default.asp. This luxury resort and spa is perched almost on the highest point overlooking Karon Bay (between Karon and Patong). The 72 villas are set on a steep hill but there are converted tuk-tuks to transport guests. While all villas are ocean-facing, not all have a good view of the beach, although some have a private pool. The bungalows are nicely decorated and the bathrooms are spacious and airy; some have glass roofs. There's a **Centara Spa** offering a range of services, 2 small swimming pools (that can be crowded), a garden and a walkway to the beach. Friendly staff.

$$$$ Hilton Phuket Arcadia Resort & Spa, 333 Patak Rd, Karon Beach, T076-396433, www.phuket.com/arcadia. Everything you would expect from Hilton. A spa, 5 swimming pools, 24-hr fitness centre, kids' club and free introductory scuba course. Each room has a desk, internet access, balcony and dining table.

$$$$ In on The Beach, 9/23-24 Moo 1, Patak Rd, T076-398220-24, www.karon-inonthebeach.com. Set right on the beach at the quieter northern end, this casual place is one of the few Karon hotels where you can reach the sands without having to cross the busy road. Two-level building with 30 a/c rooms, attractively arranged around a central swimming pool. Restaurant, internet access.

$$$$ Karon Beach Resort, 51 Karon Rd, T076-330006-7, www.katagroup.com/ karonbeach. A/c, restaurant, pool and spa on the beach at the southern end of the bay. Emerged with a snazzy new look after post-tsunami renovations, with much higher prices, too.

$$$$ Kata Beach Resort, 1 Pakbang Rd, T076-330530-4, www.katagroup.com/ kata-beach. 262 rooms in an L-shaped block are set around a free-form beachfront pool. This is a smoothly operated hotel at the southern end of the beach, paired with **Karon Beach Resort**, see above.

$$$$ Katathani Phuket Beach Resort, 14 Kata Noi Rd, T076-330124-26, www. katathani.com. Stunning location in this quiet cove. All rooms have a seafront balcony and there are even louvered panels in the bathroom that can be opened if you want to gaze at the sea from your bath. Recommended.

$$$$ Marina Phuket (formerly **Marina Cottage**), 47 Karon Rd, southern end of beach, T076-330625, www.marinaphuket. com. A/c, 2 good restaurants, beautiful secluded pool, individual cottages in lush grounds set on a hilltop. **Marina Divers** runs tours and boat trips from here. Recommended.

$$$ Kata Minta Resort, 6/56-58 Moo 2, Patak Rd, T076-333283, www.kataminta. com. A/c rooms, close to Kata Yai and Noi beaches. Typical Thai luxury look with pointed roof and stone Buddhas in the **Elephant** restaurant. Predictable but pleasant enough.

$$$ Kata Noi Pavilion 3/71 Patak Rd, near **Kata Thani Hotel**, T076-284346, www.katanoi-pavilion.com. Small rooms crowded into a tall building with TV, fridge, hot water and cheap furniture.

$ P&T Kata House 104/1 Koktanod Rd, T076-284203. One of several guesthouses at the southern end of Kata Beach set back from the shore, past a 7-11, offering some of the island's cheapest rooms outside Phuket City. The rooms are clean and many

overlook a garden. There is no hot water but a/c rooms are available. Recommended.

Nai Harn and Promthep Cape *p52, map p46*
$$$$-$$$ Baan Krating Jungle Beach, 11/3 Moo 1, Witset Rd, T076-288264, www.baankrating.com/phuket. Accessible through the **Royal Phuket Yacht Club**, this is in a remote, attractive position on Ao Sane Beach, which is nicknamed Jungle Beach for the foliage around it. There are 30 villas, all with sea views from the balconies and a pool overlooking Nai Harn Bay. The rooms have a slightly rustic Western feel, picked up again by the presence of a pool table and big screens in the relaxation area. If you like to explore, your own transport is a good idea here as it is an isolated spot.

$$ Ao Sane Bungalow, 11/12 Ao Sane Moo 1, Witset Rd, T076-288306. Also accessible through the yacht club's car park. Bungalows on a small rocky bay with coral. But this is a refreshingly secluded part of Phuket.

Laem Ka and Chalong beaches *p53, map p46*
$$$$ Evason Phuket & Bon Island, 100 Vised Rd, Moo 2, Rawai, T076-381010, www.sixsenses.com/evason-phuket. Large 260-room resort on the tip of Laem Ka with stunning views across to its own private island, Koh Bon, and over Chalong Bay. While the buildings are quiet large, the rooms are exquisite with a cool, airy feel. There are tennis courts and a refined spa.

$$$-$$ Shanti Lodge, 1/2 Soi Bangrae, Chaofa Nok Rd, T076-280233, www.shanti lodge.com/page/shanti-phuket. Just metres from the busy 4-lane thoroughfare, this Thai-South African family-run place is surprisingly serene, with landscaped gardens and a lagoon-style pool adding a real jungle feel. Fan and a/c rooms come in various sizes, some with shared bathrooms. It has a quirky boho atmosphere and service can be pretty laissez-faire, but the restaurant is excellent, with many vegetarian choices using ingredients from the owner's own farm.

___

Cape Panwa *p53, map p46*
$$$$ Cape Panwa, 27 Moo 8, Sakdidej Rd, T076-391123, www.capepanwa.com. Beautifully secluded, with a variety of accommodation, including bungalows. There are Italian and Thai fusion restaurants, an excellent cocktail bar and a good breakfast buffet. While you may never wish to leave the hotel, there is also a shuttle service into Phuket Old Town. Recommended.
$$$$ Sri Panwa, 88 Moo 8, Sakdidej Rd, T076-371000, www.sripanwa.com. This resort sets the pace for up-and-coming designer luxury. Each of the enormous pool villas are brilliantly put together and clustered in a small community on a hillside with gorgeous views over the Cape. All the cutting-edge facilities you'd expect, with iPods and players in each room, giant plasma screens, day beds, giant bathtubs and even kitchens in the bigger villas. No beach though. Highly recommended.
$$$$-$$$ The Kantary Bay Hotel, 31/11 Moo 8, Sakdidej Rd, T07-6391514, www.thebay-phuket.com. A seafront hotel 15 mins' drive from Phuket. Rooms have sofa and dining table, stereo and large balcony. There is a gym, 2 pools and a garden. Selection of studios and suites make this place excellent value.

___

Koh Lone, Koh Mai Ton and other southern islands *p54, map p46*
$$$$ Baan Mai Cottages, 35/1 Moo 3, Koh Lone, T02-6730966, www.baanmai.com. Bungalow/houses decorated with faux 19th-century Burmese furniture and Balinese-style bathrooms. Thai and French cuisine. Pool.
$$$$ Honeymoon Island (formerly Maiton Island Resort), Koh Mai Ton, T076-214954-8, www.honeymoonislandphuket.com. The only resort on the island has 37 a/c rooms and 6 pool villas, plus good

sports facilities, not to mention beautiful white beaches with a decent coral reef.
$$$$-$$$ Coral Island Resort, Koh Hii, T076-281060, www.coralislandresort.com. The 70 a/c bungalows – poolside and beachfront – are nice, but starting to look tired in places. The location, however, is near perfect: white beaches with coral reefs fit for snorkelling. On the other side of the island, you can also visit pleasant secluded bays.

___

Koh Rang Yai *p54*
$$ Richy Island Phuket Co, T076-239893-4/238565, www.rangyaiisland-phuket.com. Rang Yai is privately owned and, as such, everything on the island is run by one company. Bungalows can be rented for ฿1000 a night for overnight stays. The bungalows are basic, with bedding on the floor and mosquito nets above. There's no a/c, but electricity is provided 24 hrs. There is also the option of camping out. Hotel pickups can be arranged, and boats depart from Sapam Bay. The food on the island is excellent. There is the option of taking your vows on Rang Yai, if you fancy getting married on a tropical island. Full-day tours cost up to ฿2500 for adults, ฿1250 for children, without an overnight stay.

___

Koh Naka Yai
$$$$ The Naka Island, 32 Moo 5 Paklok, T076-371400. This 5-star resort has been rebranded a few times since opening and is now operated by Starwood Hotels. It has 67 rustic-chic villas, with private plunge pools and outdoor bathrooms, a spa, restaurants and loads of activities. Too soon to tell if Starwood has found the winning formula for this prime piece of property, but early reviews are looking good.
$$$ Tenta Nakara, www.tentanakara.com. Just a 10-min boat ride from Phuket but a world away, this 'luxury tent' eco-friendly resort offers a real island escape. Tents are set on semi-permanent structures with wooden floors and en suite bathrooms, all with views across Phangnga Bay. Electricity

available only in the common areas and restaurant for a few hrs a day. Under the same management as the long-running **Joy Bungalow** on Koh Jum.

Kamala Beach *p54, map p46*

$$$ Papa Crab Guesthouse, 93/5 Moo 3, Kamala Beach, T076-385315, www.phuket papacrab.com. 10 air-conditioned rooms and 3 bungalows at this unusually named guesthouse. Basic accommodation next to the beach. Has tour information and can arrange a taxi to the airport. The rooms are simple, clean and with comfortable beds. Everything is very white, so it all looks a bit post-modern. Big discounts in low season.

$$ Popeye's Place, 99/25 Moo 3, Soi 10, T076-385815, www.popeyes-place.com. Run by a Danish-Thai couple combo, there are 11 rooms and 5 bungalows. Also features a minimart, restaurant and internet access. Well priced, although a little sparse. Rooms are large, with a/c, TV, fridge and double bed. The bungalows have hot showers. Located 400 m from the beach.

Surin Beach and Pansea Beach *p54, map p46*

$$$$ Amanpuri Resort, 118/1 Pansea Beach, T076-324333, www.amanresorts. com. This is undoubtedly one of the best resorts on Phuket. The more expensive rooms are beautifully designed Thai pavilions with attention to every detail. Super facilities include private yacht, watersports, tennis and squash courts, fitness centre, private beach and library. Guests include political figures.

$$$$ The Surin Phuket (formerly The Chedi Resort), 118 Moo 3, T076-621580, www.thesurinphuket.com. South of Amanpuri, this chic, exclusive resort is set into the hillside above a perfectly secluded sandy white beach. There's a choice of 1- or 2-bedroom thatched-roof cottages in a contemporary design with private verandas. Superb facilities include watersports, tennis court, library, games

room, restaurants, spa and pool. Known for its exceptional service, especially for dining and events. Extensively renovated with the brand name change.

$$$$-$$$ Pen Villa Hotel, 9/1 Moo 3 Surin Beach, Srisootorn Rd, T076-621652, www.penvilla-phuket.com. Bland red-roofed complex with decent pool and big clean rooms. Suitable for families. Free transfers to 2 local beaches – Surin and Laem Sing. The hotel also arranges daytrips, fishing and golf.

Bang Tao Beach *p55, map p46*

$$$$ Angsana Laguna (formerly the Sheraton Grande), T076-324101, www. lagunaphuket.com/hotels/angsana/index. php. Good choice of rooms, stilted lofts and pool villas. Facilities include a yoga/ pilates studio, fitness centre, spa, kids' club, 7 restaurants (with a good choice of cuisine), and a large pool with interlinked sections, including a sandy 'beach' and a sunken bar.

$$$$ Banyan Tree, 33, 33/27 Moo 4, Srisoonthorn Rd, T076-324374, www. banyantree.com. Spa pool villas with private pool, jacuzzi, sunken baths, outdoor showers and beds sheathed in silk that 'float' over lily ponds. The spa itself is similarly spectacular.

$$$$ Dusit Thani Laguna, T076-362999, www.lagunaphuket.com/hotels/dusitthani/ index.php. The quietest and most refined of the **Laguna Phuket** complex, this beautifully laid out, unimposing hotel has a/c, restaurants, attractive pool, tennis courts, water-sports and excellent service. Its new 2-bedroom pool villas are rather swanky.

Nai Thon and Layan *p55, map p46*

$$$$ The Pavilions, T076-317600, www. thepavilionsresorts.com. A hilltop all-villa resort overlooking Layan Bay, aimed at the honeymoon market, so children under 16 are not permitted. Each villa has a private pool and there's a rooftop restaurant and bar with fantastic sunset views. It's a bit of a distance to the beach, but free shuttle bus service is provided.

Nai Yang and Nai Yang National Park *p55, map p46*

Camping in the national park costs ฿60.

$$$$ Indigo Pearl, T076-327006, www.indigo-pearl.com. Built in 2006 in a stark, chic fashion with stand-alone bathtubs, marble and grey stone walls. The sprawling resort dominates the underdeveloped southern end of the bay.

$$$$ Nai Yang Beach Resort, 65/23-24 Nai Yang Beach Rd, T076-328300, www.naiyangbeachresort.com. Well-built bungalows with good facilities and simple decor. Some a/c. Set in large grounds with plenty of trees for shade. Friendly staff. A bit pricey at the upper end but excellent value at the lower end.

$$$-$$ Garden Cottage, 53/1 Moo 1, T076-327293, www.garden-cottage.org. Charming cottage-style bungalows 2 mins from the airport and walking distance from beach. The friendly Swiss-Thai owners are willing to show you the island. Excellent value, with a masseur, restaurant and communal areas.

Mai Khao *p55, map p46*

$$$$ Marriott's Phuket Beach Club T076-338000, www.marriott.com. Take the turn-off at the sign on the main road (402) travelling north from the airport. The rooms are elegant and spacious, and the 2-bedroom villas with full kitchens are ideal for groups. Service is impeccable and guests have access to the facilities of the nearby JW Marriott Resort, with a total of 3 pools and 10 restaurants to choose from. Brightly painted traditional boats (*korlae*) are dotted throughout the resort. Sea turtle-nesting grounds are close by, and the hotel has donated a large sum to the Thai World Wildlife Fund to start up a turtle conservation project. Watersports are banned, and guests are asked to use the pools rather than the sea to avoid disturbing the turtles.

$$$-$ Seaside Cottages, 129/1 Moo 3, T08-0522 8392 (mob), www.mai-khao-beach.com. This is quite a find for Phuket, tucked away in a grassy clearing, shaded by large casuarina trees and shrubs, right on the beach. There are smaller bamboo and palm-roof huts with shared bathrooms and larger en suite concrete and wood rooms. The owners set up a regular campfire for guests at night. Contact the owners in advance to arrange transport. Recommended.

Phuket City *p48*

There are quite a few reasonably priced Thai restaurants in the old town. The food in Phuket is highly rated throughout Thailand, for the range of dishes and the invigorating and sophisticated spices and herbs used in Southern Thai cuisine.

$$$ Ka Jok See, 26 Takua Pa Rd, T076-217903. Excellent Thai restaurant. The success of the restaurant is leading to some pretty sharp pricing but the atmosphere, character, style and first-rate cuisine make it worth paying extra. Gets pretty wild late into the night, when the tables get pushed aside to make way for dancing. Booking is essential.

$$$ La Gaetana, Phuket Rd, T076-250253, T08-1397 1227 (mob). The best Italian food in Phuket. Owners Gianni Ferrara and Chonticha Buasukhon offer impeccable service. There is also a decent wine list. Booking is recommended, as the restaurant is rather small and fills up early.

$$$ Raya Thai Cuisine, 48 New Deebuk Rd, T076-218155. This restaurant is in a well-preserved 70-year-old Macao-style house with original fittings and garden. It serves Thai dishes and local specialities; try the spicy *nam bu bai cha plu* (crab curry with local herbs served with Chinese rice noodles).

$$ Dibuk Restaurant, Dibuk Rd, T076-258148. Daily 1100-2300. French and

Thai cuisine in a restored shophouse that has just the right balance of chic and dusty old mystery. Great spot for a French fix at good value.

$$ Farang Restaurant, off Chaloem Kiat Rd, next to **Index**, T076-249512. Amazing little restaurant that serves cheap, quality fusion dishes. Sausages, steaks, pasta, pizza, it's all here. There is also a second branch at 120/6 Cherngtalay, Thalang, T08-1620 7429 (mob).

$$$ Kanda Bakery, 31-33 Rasada Rd. This spotlessly clean a/c restaurant with art deco undertones, serves breakfast, Thai and international dishes and good cakes like cinnamon rolls, croissant and chocolate brownies.

$$ Khanasutra, 18-20 Takuapa Rd, T076-256192. If you're in Phuket City and feel like eating Indian, this is the place to go. The portions are generous, although the atmosphere is a little gloomy. The management and staff are a friendly bunch.

$$ Natural Restaurant, Soi Phutorn, T076-224287, T076-214037. A long-time favorite in Phuket City, with fish swimming in televisions and all manner of plants everywhere. The oysters are perhaps the best in Phuket. The sushi is average, but the Thai food is exceptional. Check out the range of curries for some spicy excitement.

$$ Roak Ros, opposite **Fresh Mart** on Phuket Rd and Soi Thalang Chan. Popular with locals. Spartan interior with stainless steel table-tops, and cutlery and plates in a plastic tray screwed into the wall above your table. The favourite here is clams in chilli paste. Shellfish can be small, though.

$$ Salvatore's, Rassada Rd, T076-225958, T08-9871 1184 (mob). A jolly little restaurant that looks and feels like a cliché but has some decent pasta dishes to choose from. A little expensive for what it is. Aimed at tourists.

$$$ Santana Coffee, 54/8-9 Montri Rd. A nicely decorated European-style café that serves Thai food, steaks and European food as well as an excellent selection of coffees. Brews range from Jamaica Pea to Kilamanjaro.

$$ Siam Indigo, Phangnga Rd, T076-256697, T08-1892 4885 (mob). Reasonable restaurant with Thai dishes and a few international splashes here and there. Does a decent rack of lamb.

$$ Suay Restaurant, 50/2 Takuapa Rd, T08-1747 2424 (mob). Cheerful place in a garden setting with white picket fences. Creative Thai and fusion food and healthy herbal juices. The Chiang Mai style crispy noodles with salmon is fantastic. Excellent value. Brings in a big local crowd in evenings.

$ Baan Talang Restaurant, 65 Thalang Rd. Tasty Thai and Islamic food (the lamb curry is excellent but hot). As with most places in this part of town, the walls are lined with photographs of old Phuket and there is an old-world feel.

$ Fine Day, Chumphon Rd, finedayphuket. multiply.com. Fine Day is an institution in Phuket. It's a hip hotspot where people hang out, eat and drink. Stays open until about midnight and is always busy. The staff are friendly and although there isn't a menu in English, there is always someone on hand to help out.

$ Food Court, 4th floor, around the corner from the cinema, **Central Festival Phuket**. An excellent food court serving cheap Thai nosh. You can get everything from *kao man gai* (boiled chicken meat on a bed of rice and a side of spicy, ginger sauce) to noodles. Much better than most of the restaurants at Central Festival.

$ Kow-Tom-Hua-Pla (**Boiled Fish Rice**) opposite **Caramba Bar** on Phuket Rd past Thalang Rd. Daily 1700-2400. Popular with locals, this simple café serves an eclectic mix of noodle dishes. Recommended.

$ Lemon Grass, Dibuk Rd. Decent Thai food at a large, outdoor restaurant. A bit out of the way but worth the journey.

$ Mee Ton Pho, at the clock circle opposite the Metropole Hotel. For decades this has been the go-to lunch spot for cheap and tasty Hokkien yellow noodles with seafood, served hot and fresh. Pork satay with a rich peanut sauce is also sold here.

$ NC Bakery and Food, 183/6 Phang Nga Rd (near the bus station). Serves up fairly standard cakes and coffee but it excels at Thai dishes. The massaman curry's a favourite.

$ Nong Jote Café, 16 Yaowarat Rd. This 100-plus-year-old building looks like a café in Lisbon with high ceilings and, along one side, ceiling-to-floor antique glassed cabinets in teak. Excellent southern Thai food. Try the spicy *yum tour plu*. Recommended.

$ Vegetarian restaurants, Ranong Rd, just beyond the bus stop area. A handful of simple shops serve curries and stir-fried tofu and vegetable dishes, accompanied by brown rice or glass noodles. No English menu but you can simply point to the ready-made choices in the display containers. Tasty and very cheap.

Foodstalls

There is a late-night *khanom jeen* vendor on Surin Rd (towards Damrong Rd, just up the road from the Shell garage). While usually a breakfast dish, there is no better meal to have late at night when you get a case of the munchies then *khanom jeen*. Choose your curry, throw in a few condiments and enjoy some of the best Thai food on offer. Look for the large brown pots at the side of the road.

The best place to browse on the street is around the market on **Ranong Rd**. A good and cheap restaurant close by is **Koh Lao Luat Mu** (name only in Thai), on the round-about linking Ranong and Rasada roads, which serves tasty noodle and rice dishes. Alternatively, **Khai Muk**, Rasada Rd (opposite the **Thavorn Hotel**) serves superb *kwaytio* (noodle soup). Just round the corner from Robinson on Ong Sim Phai Rd, is a lively collection of night-time street food vendors serving cheap Thai dishes to locals. There is a wide choice of food, much better than the nearby burgers and pizza.

Patong Beach *p51, map p46*
Many of the sois off Patong Beach Rd sell a good range of international food.

$$$ Da Maurizio, Kalim Beach, north of Patong, opposite **Diamond Cliff Hotel**, T076-344079. Italian food in an attractive setting.

$$$ White Box, 247/5 Prabaramee Rd, Patong, Kathu, T076-346271, www.white boxrestaurant.com. A simple concept: it's white and it looks like a large box. The setting is ideal, far enough away from the madness of Patong, but with decent views over Patong Bay. Good Mediterranean and Thai food.

$$$-$$ Lim's, Soi 7, Kalim Bay. This opened in a small house in 1999 and now has a vast dining room with high ceilings and outdoor courtyard. Also features bold abstract paintings by one of the owners, 'Gop'. Has a *Sex in the City* feel. The food concentrates more on the quality of the ingredients rather than overwhelming with spices. Suits an exhausted palate. Choices of dishes range from grilled pork ribs to Vietnamese spring rolls with, among other things, capsicum.

$$ Joe's Downstairs, 223/3 Prabaramee Rd, Kalim Beach, near Patong, T076-618245. A cool place to watch the sun set while sipping on a cocktail and enjoying the view of Kalim Bay. They have some great tapas here.

$$ Nicky's Handlebar, 41 Rat-U-Thit 200 Year Rd. Friendly open-air bar and restaurant lined floor-to-ceiling with big-bike memorabilia. The cheerful but eccentric Thai owner speaks fluent English and German. Thai and western dishes are just OK but it's a fun spot to dine, drink and soak in the biker atmosphere. At the back is a Harley rental and tour shop and cool industrial-style rooms for rent. A must for motorheads.

$$ Pan Yaah, Kalim Bay. Clinging to a rocky cliffside with wide views across Patong Bay, this sea-breezy Thai restaurant is a good choice for reasonably priced seafood and curries. Has a more authentic taste than most of the resort fare you'll find in Patong. Gets busy at sunset.

$$ Rock Hard Café, 82/51 Bangla Rd.
Garden, steaks, pizzas, served in a perfect
spot to view the bewildering Bangla
scene in full bloom. There's an a-go-go
bar upstairs. Not to be confused with
the Hard Rock Café around the corner.
$$ Sea Hag, 78/5 Permpong Soi 3, Soi
Wattana Clinic Rd, T076-341111. Fresh,
authentic Thai fare in a low-key, intimate
setting. A/c or outdoor seating. Owner
Khun Kenya is a colourful character, even
by Patong standards.
$ Woody's Sandwich Shoppe, Aroonsom
Plaza, T076-290468, www.khunwoody.com.
Woody's Shoppe, run by local computer
guru Woody Leonhard, is something of an
institution in Phuket. For about ฿100 to
฿150, you can get a sandwich that puts
Subway to shame. Woody also offers free
Wi-Fi access, and has another 3 branches
scattered around the island.

Karon and Kata beaches *p51, map p46*
$$$ Royale Namtok, Soi Nam Tok Rd,
T08-7263 7327, www.royalenamtok.com.
The classic Gallic fare at this secluded
private house is served fine-dining style at
white linen tables set with silverware and
candelabras. Good for romantic dates.
$$ JaoJong Seafood, 4/2 Patak Rd,
KataNoi, T076-330136. Unpretentious sea-
shanty feel to this spacious open-fronted
seafood restaurant. Good selection of
freshly caught seafood and well executed.
Recommended.
$ Hua Soi, Koktanod Rd. Its location is
nothing to cheer about but the food at
this simple family-run eatery is delicious
and well-priced. Big portions and a real
Thai taste. Try the chicken and cashew
nut stir fry. Recently moved to Kata-Karon
after running for a decade in Chalong.
$ Swiss Bakery, Bougainvillea Terrace
House, 117/1 Patak Rd, Kata beach,
T076-330139. Swiss delicacies here
include Bouguionne and Tartaren Hut.
Also burgers and sandwiches from
฿120. There's an open-air terrace,

Rawai *p52, map p46*
There are several Thai seafood restaurants
lining the beachfront. Try any; they're
all pretty good and cheap compared to
Phuket's busier resort areas.
$$ The Green Man, 82/15 Moo 4, Patak Rd,
T076-281445, www.the-green-man.net.
Claims to be the only Tudor-style pub
in Asia. In terms of pub grub, it's all very
British and it's all very tasty. They even have
pickled eggs. Busy on Thu quiz nights and
when they switch on the gigantic screen for
English and international football matches.
$$ Nikita's, 44 Viset Rd, T076-288338.
Waterfront restaurant and bar that's a
favourite haunt for expats. Big menu
with the standard Thai fare and pizza
made in the wood-fired oven. Staff
unsmiling but efficient.

Laem Ka and Chalong beaches *p53,
map p46*
Ao Chalong
$$$-$$ Kan Eang @ Pier, 44/1 Viset Rd
Moo 5, T076-381212, www.kaneang-pier.
com. Venerable seafood joint with a long
terrace stretching along the bay and an
enviable word-of-mouth reputation for
snagging the best catches.

Cape Panwa *p53, map p46*
$$$-$$ Panwa House, Cape Panwa (see
Where to stay), on the beach. Everything
is here for the perfect meal: a stately
Sino-Portugese mansion with indoor and
outdoor dining, excellent service and
deliciously executed dishes. Try their lobster
with shavings of caramelized shallot, palm
sugar and tamarind. Recommended.
$$ Live India, Sakdidej Rd (down a small soi
off the espalande near the aquarium), T076-
391480. Bit of a hidden treasure, with fresh,
flavourful Indian fare in a simple setting.
$ Sawasdee Restaurant, 31/4 Sakdidej Rd.
The food here is average and caters to a
perceived Western taste which is bland,
slightly sugary and somewhat slippery
with oil. However, the set-up is fun. You sit

at old Singer sewing tables in a brick rustic Thai-style bungalow with an open front and a great view of the ocean. The 80-year-old bricks were taken from the owner's home on the Malaysian border. A good place to snack.

Surin Beach and Pansea Beach *p54, map p46*
$$$ Amanpuri, see Where to stay, above, T076-324394. Considered one of the best Thai restaurants on the island and the setting is sensational. At least 48 hrs advanced booking needed during peak season.
$$$-$$ Catch Beach Club, catchbeach club.com. Its wild success since opening 4 years ago has sparked a rush to add fine dining and 5-star partying to Phuket's beaches. Serves a mix of Thai and Western fare, plus rather indulgent daily lunch and dinner buffets. There are beachfront lounging sofas, an a/c covered area and a reception area to book yacht cruises and 'Champagne' sun beds. Pricey, but the 'wow' factor can't be denied.

Bang Tao Beach *p55, map p46*
$$$ Lotus Restaurant, 31/13 Banyan Tree Beachfront, T076-362625, T08-1797 3110 (mob), www.lotusphuket.com. Quite expensive, but the seafood is good and the vibe next to the sea unbeatable.

Nai Yang and Nai Yang National Park *p55, map p46*
$$ Nai Yang Seafood, Nai Yang beach. One of several charming spots next to the empty beach, all of which serve excellent seafood.

Mai Khao *p55, map p46*
There is a full range of restaurants in the **Marriott** and a simple in-house restaurant at the **Mai Khao Beach Bungalows**.
$$$ Rivet Grill, Indigo Pearl Resort, Mai Khao, www.indigo-pearl.com/dining/ rivet-grill-rebar. Serves the best steaks in Phuket and probably the whole of Southern Thailand. Countless touches reflect the resort's tin mining theme.

⚬ Bars and clubs

Phuket's club scene has experienced something of a resurgence and is now attracting the attention of DJs and promoters who have previously favoured Koh Phangan and Koh Samui. International DJs such as Louie Vega, Judge Jules and Brandon Block have passed through. Whether you want house, electro, hip-hop, rock, pop or reggae, you'll find somewhere to go in Phuket.

Phuket City *p48*
9Richter, Rassada Rd. Despite the strange name, this is a great place to hang out, as very few foreigners make it inside. Stays open until about 0100 with the usual Thai songs sung by live bands and a DJ who isn't afraid to rupture eardrums with bizarre techno music.
Balé, 445/2 Phuket Rd. While karaoke may not be top on your list of things to do, if you fancy screaming your lungs out in a small booth while drinking copious amounts of whisky, this is the place to do it. If you didn't bring your singing voice, there's a cool open-air beer garden that stays open reasonably late.
Barzah FunClub, Phun Pol Rd. Although Barzah is supposedly located in the 'bad' area of town, this extremely loud hip-hop club is a fun place to drink and dance, often after other clubs have closed their doors. The locals are friendly and there is almost never any trouble.
Blue Marina, Phuket Merlin Hotel, 158/1 Yaowarat Rd, T076-212866-70. A long-standing favorite with the locals. Offers up standard Thai hits and other random treats from bands and DJs. Fri and Sat are always very busy.
Kor Tor Mor, Chana Charoen Rd, near Nimit Circle, T076-232285. Large Thai pub that gets ludicrously busy on Fri and Sat. Get there early or else you may be turned away. Buy a bottle of whisky, drink, kick back and dance.

Oasis, Mae Luan Rd. Oasis is quintessentially Thai and a lot of fun. It's a small venue that doesn't attract too big a crowd so you've always got a bit of space to drink and dance in. As usual, expect bands singing Thai favorites and the occasional Green Day number. The in-house DJ usually closes the night with blistering dance music. The Thais will be surprised to see you, but you'll be welcomed as long as you join in the fun.

O'Malleys, 2/20-21 Montri Rd, T076-220170, www.omalleys-phuket.com. An Irish-style pub that serves pints as well as a knock-out all-day breakfast. Upstairs there is free pool, darts and table football.

Timber Hut, 118/1 Yaowarat Rd, T076-211839. Something of an institution, Timber Hut has been around for about 20 years. The crowd is a mix of Thai and foreigners. Arrive early on Fri and Sat because once midnight hits, you won't be able to move. A standard selection of Thai songs and the odd Western classic is the order of the night.

Patong Beach *p51, map p46*

Bars in Patong are concentrated along Rat Uthit Rd and Bangla Rd. Similar to Pattaya's Walking St, Patong's Bangla Road is a brash neon rash of go-go bars, beer bars and nightclubs that throb until the police bribes run dry. It's couple-friendlier, though, and the sex-for-sale element is less in-your-face.

Banana Disco, on the beach road, T076-340306. A firm favourite with the locals. It's always very busy with a large number of tourists finding their way there. The club doesn't stay open very late and the drinks are reasonably priced. Expect to hear a range of rock music, hip hop and pop. As Phuket's longest-running night-club, you can count on a decent night out. The scruffy shophouses beside it have now been torn down, and this prime section of the beach road is soon set to open as a more upscale entertainment and shopping complex with the giggle-inducing name, Banana Walk.

BYD Lofts, 5/28 Haad Patong Rd, T076-343024-7, www.bydlofts.com. In Patong,

but sufficiently away from the madness of Soi Bangla, this restaurant doubles as a bar. The food is average but for pre-club drinks, it's a chilled affair.

Famous, Jungceylon shopping centre, Rat-U-Thit Rd, www.famousphuket.com. Big, well-designed rooftop bar with plush lounging areas. Being inside a mall, the vibe at Famous feels a bit disconnected from Patong's lively nightlife scene, but the glass-bottom pool with bikini-clad babes paddling about gives an ambience of a different sort. Fire shows and DJ music nightly.

Hollywood, 7 Bangla Road, T076-294 216, www.hollywoodpatong.com. Patong's busiest late-night disco/meat market.

Paradise Complex, Rat-U-Thit Rd. Paradise Complex is like the gay community's version of Soi Bangla. The complex is huge, comprising numerous gay bars, hotels, cafés and restaurants. The fun is hedonistic and there are endless cabaret shows to be watched. This is a popular, friendly area where all walks of life are accepted and celebrated. It can get pretty raunchy, but you won't come across any trouble. Visit www.gaypatong.com for info about the gay scene.

Rock City, 169 Rat-U-Thit 200 Pee Rd. Get your rocks off at Rock City. Cover bands steam through Bon Jovi, Metallica, Megadeath and even Bryan Adams. The place is usually packed on Fri and Sat. The bands are pretty good and, for a kind of nostalgic, 80s-themed night out, you can't go far wrong. Recent reports of thuggish behaviour by its staff is something to watch out for, however.

Safari, located on the hill between Patong and Karon. Where most people go after the other clubs have closed. There's a climbing wall that drunk tourists try to scale, not recommended if you've had a few. There are also opportunities to drench ladyboys by dunking them in large pools of water. You have to see it to believe it. The music is pumping and the people range from tired tourists through to drunk locals and every hanger-on in between.

Seduction Beach Club & Disco, 39/1
Bangla Rd, www.seductiondisco.com.
This place has been around for a while
and provides reasonably priced drinks
and 2 floors of hip-hop and dance beats.
It has a younger crowd than many Patong
clubs and tries to give an exclusive feel with
VIP and 'members-only' rooms upstairs.
Tai Pan, at the far end of Soi Bangla on the
opposite side to the beach, www.taipan.st.
A rowdy nightspot with live bands,
cheap drinks, lots of shouting and
dancers. Open late.

Karon and Kata beaches p51, map p46

Ratri Jazztaurant, Kata Hill, T076-333 538,
www.ratrijazztaurant.com. The perfect
spot for a romantic dinner for 2 or just
for kicking back for a few drinks while
enjoying the splendid view. As the name
suggests, this place is all about jazz, though
not always live. It isn't the cheapest or
friendliest spot, but it can't be beaten for
setting and ambience.
Rick n Roll Music Café, 100/51 Kata Rd,
www.ricknrollmusiccafe.com. Cheesy but
cheerful Vegas-inspired lounge hosting live
music and jam sessions. Have a go at the
karaoke and release your inner Tom Jones.

Nai Harn and Promthep Cape p52, map p46

Reggae Bar, Nai Harn Lake. Definitely
worth a visit. This is about as real a reggae
bar as you'll find in Thailand, complete with
Rastafarians. It's chilled and peaceful next
to the lake. Usually stays open later than
regular closing times.

Cape Panwa p53, map p46

Baba Dining Lounge, Sri Panwa, T076-
371006, www.sripanwa.com. Hip, happening
and with killer views of the sea at sunrise
and sunset. The food and drinks are priced
at the upper end of the Phuket scale, but
you expect quality when you're at a place
like Baba. When they have special events the

venue becomes a hive of nocturnal activity
with lots of dancing. Requires a trip to the
southernmost point of Phuket.
The Top of the Reef Bar, Cape Panwa
Hotel, see Where to stay, above. Excellent
house cocktails and a view of the sea on a
wicker-chaired veranda. Even if you are not
staying here, it is worth dropping in for the
feeling of tropical indulgence and glamour.
There's a jazz singer taking your requests.
Dress for the occasion.

☻ Entertainment

Phuket City p48

Siam Niramit, 55/81 Chalermprakiat
(bypass) Rd, T076-335000, www.siam
niramit.com. The popular Bangkok stage
show has now opened a Phuket branch
with a huge 1740-seat theatre on the
outskirts of the city. It's a grand spectacle,
with more than 100 performers and
dazzling special effects depicting Thai
legends and myths. The buffet dinner is
extra, but probably not worth it.

Patong Beach p51, map p46

Danze Fantasy Theatre, Bangla Rd (next
to the Tiger Entertainment complex), T08
3504 1028 (mob), www.danzefantasy.com.
Big baht was spent creating this 580-seat
theatre hosting an elaborately staged
performance, with illusionists, acrobatics,
song and dance, put on by a production
team that runs several shows around
the world. Quite well done and a classier
alternative to the usual chrome-pole
twirling acts that Patong's best known for.

Kamala Beach p54, map p46

Phuket Fantasea, 99 Moo 3, T076-385111,
www.phuket-fantasea.com. For a long
time, this has been a firm favourite with
visitors. It's billed as the ultimate in nightlife
entertainment. The entire complex is huge
and includes a carnival village, a restaurant
and Las Vegas-style shows involving lots of
animals, lighting effects and acrobatics.

✹ Festivals

Phuket Island *p48*

Jan-Feb Chinese New Year.

Jan-Feb Old Phuket Town Festival. In the days following Chinese New Year, the locals close off Thalang Rd, Krabi Rd and Soi Rommanee to celebrate Old Phuket Town with foodstalls, music, plays and exhibitions.

Feb Phuket Blues Festival, www.phuket bluesfestival.com. One of the few music festivals held in Phuket. Great bands, a good crowd and lots of booze.

March Phuket Food Festival. Held every year in Saphan Hin over a period of about 10 days. Enjoy Thai food accompanied by the world's most out-of-tune brass band, some karaoke singing and carnival games where you can win fish.

13 Mar Thao Thep Kasattri and Thao Srisunthon Fair. Celebrates the 2 heroines who saved Phuket from Burmese invaders.

Apr Turtle Releasing Festival timed to coincide with Songkran or Thai New Year. Baby turtles are released at several of Phuket's beaches.

Apr Phuket Bike Week at Patong Beach – held just before Songkran. Get your kicks with Harley and Co.

End May Rugby Tournament, held at Karon Beach and Karon Municipal Stadium.

Between the 6th and 11th lunar month Chao Le Boat Floating Festival, involving the Rawai, Sapan, Koh Sire and Laem Ka Chaolay or 'sea gypsy' communities. This festival is held at night as small boats are set adrift to ward off evil.

Jun Laguna Phuket International Marathon (2nd week).

Aug Por Tor Festival, in Phuket City. This means 'hungry ghosts' and is a time when ancestors are honoured. Ghosts are supposedly released into the world for the whole month. To keep them quiet and reasonable, they are given food, flowers and candles at family altars. Bribes include cakes in the shape of turtles – the Chinese symbol of longevity.

Sep-Oct (movable) Chinese Vegetarian Festival, *Tetsakan Kin Jeh*, lasts 9 days and marks the beginning of Taoist lent. No meat is eaten, alcohol consumed nor sex indulged in (in order to cleanse the soul). Men pierce their cheeks or tongues with long spears and other sharp objects and walk over hot coals and (supposedly) feel no pain. The festival is celebrated elsewhere, but most enthusiastically in Phuket, especially at Wat Jui Tui on Ranong Rd in Phuket City. It's one of Phuket's star attractions; visitors are welcomed and pictures make the international newspapers.

25 Nov Laguna Phuket Triathlon, 1.8-km swim, 55-km bike ride and 12-km run. For international athletes.

Dec Patong Carnival welcomes in the tourist season.

5 Dec King's Cup Regatta is a yachting competition in the Andaman Sea, timed to coincide with the king's birthday (he is a yachtsman of international repute). The event attracts competitors from across the globe.

○ Shopping

Phuket City *p48*

Most souvenirs found here can be bought more cheaply elsewhere in Thailand, and if travelling back to Bangkok, it is best to wait. Best buys are pearls and gold jewellery.

Weekend Market, located on the outskirts of Phuket City, just off Chao Fa West Rd, opposite Wat Naka. A sprawling mass of cheap T-shirts, shoes and knick-knacks. Definitely worth a visit. Sat-Sun from 1600.

Antiques

Ban Boran Antiques, 51 Yaowarat Rd (near the circle), recently moved from Rasada Rd. This is arguably the best antique shop on Phuket; interesting pieces from Thailand and Burma especially; well priced.

Chan's Antiques, Thepkrasatri Rd, just south of the Heroines' Monument. Not many 'antiques', but a selection of Thai artefacts.

The Dream Gallery, 96 Krabi Rd. Antiques, porcelain, wood furniture, mostly sourced from China, set within the dazzling interior of the Blue Elephant Governor Mansion (see Restaurants), in one of Phuket's biggest and most beautifully restored old homes.

Food
Methee Cashew Nut Factory, 9/1-2 Tilok Uthit Rd, T076-219622/3. The factory offers tours so you learn just why cashew nuts are so damned expensive. The Methee experts have been around for over 40 years. Stock up on a weird and wonderful range of cashews, including garlic, chilli and palm sugar flavour.

Handicrafts
Radsada Handmade, 29 Rasada Rd, textiles wood carvings and home decor items from around Southeast Asia; **Prachanukhao Road**, numerous stalls leading to Karon which sell hand-painted copies of great artists, including Gauguin, Van Gogh and Da Vinci.

⦿ What to do

Phuket Island *p48*
While cultural activites may be thin on the ground in Phuket, there's plenty for outdoor and water sports lovers to enjoy. A growing arts and culinary scene provide some good alternatives to check out beyond the beaches.

Art galleries
Lat Design and Art Garden, 95/33 Sai Yuan Rd, Rawai, T08-6294 3971 (mob). Mon-Sat 0900-2100. Original paintings and sculptures by an artist from Thailand's deep south.
Sarasil Art Gallery, 121 Phangnga Rd, Phuket City, T076-224532. Daily 0800-2200. Original work by 5 local artists.
Wua Art Gallery, 95 Phang Nga Rd, Phuket City, www.wua-artgallery.com. Daily 1000-2200. Quirky, modern, cartoonish paintings by Mr Zen.

Boating
Several operators offer crewed or bareboat yacht rentals and speedboat trips. No-frills (no equipment or insurance) long-tail boat trips can be arranged at most beaches directly with the boatman.
Coral Seekers, 16 Soi Tueson, Phuket City, T076-354074, www.coralseekers.com. Pricier than other speedboat tour operators but its trips are designed to avoid the crowds. More safety-conscious, too.
Seal Superyachts, 96/68, Praphuketkhew Rd, Kathu, T076-612654, www.superyacht-charters.com. This well-established outfit goes to the Similan and Surin islands and offers PADI courses. Professional crews, fishing and snorkelling equipment.

Bungee jumping
Phuket Jungle Bungy Jump, 61/3 Vichitsongkram Rd, Kathu, T076-321351, www.phuketbungy.com. Daily 0900-1800. Get your kicks with a bungee jump over a lagoon or try catapult bungeeing or trampoline bungeeing. There is also a bar in case you need to steady your nerves. Jumps are said to be to New Zealand standards.
World Bungy Jump, 2/59 Sai Nam Yen Rd (next to Patong Boxing Stadium), Patong, T076-345185. Daily 0930-1830. Leap from a 60-m crane over a swamp and water spring.

Canopying
Phuket Cable Jungle Adventure, 232/17 Bansuanneramit, Moo 8, Srisoonthorn, Thalang, T076-527054, www.phuketcanopy.com. Some people get their kicks bungee jumping, others choose to zip through the jungle on cables. There are 15 stations about 20 m above the ground. The adventure costs ฿2150. They can pick you up from the pretty much anywhere on the island. Call for details.

Cookery courses
Many luxury spa resorts and 4-star hotels are now offering Thai cookery courses. Check out what dishes you want to learn

and find out if they can teach them; these courses can often be tailored to your needs.
Boathouse Cookery School, Kata Beach, T076-3300157, see Where to stay, page 59.
 Phuket Thai Cookery School, 39/4 Thepatan Rd, Rassada, T076-252354, www.phuketthaicookery.com. Hands-on 1-5 day courses; ฿2500 per day, free hotel roundtrips.

Diving
The greatest concentration of dive companies is to be found along Patong Beach Rd, on Kata and Karon beaches, at Ao Chalong and in Phuket City. Dive centres – over 25 of them – offer a range of courses (introductory to advanced), day trips and liveaboard – leading to one of the internationally recognized certificates such as PADI and NAUI. For an open-water course the cost is about ฿14500. The course stretches over 4 days, beginning in a hotel pool and ending on a reef. An advance open-water diver course costs around ฿13500. A simple introductory dive, fully supervised, will cost about ฿4500-5500 (2 dives). For those with experience, there are a range of tours from single day, 2-dive outings to dive spots like Koh Racha Yai and Koh Racha Noi (south of Phuket), and Shark Point (east of Phuket) which cost ฿3500-5500 depending on the location, to 1-week expeditions to offshore islands such as the Similan and Surin islands. 5 days and 4 nights to the Similans costs around ฿25,000. Other liveaboards, depending on location and length of trip, vary from ฿18,000-30,000. Snorkelling is good on the outer islands; the waters around Phuket itself are mediocre. For the best snorkelling and diving it is necessary to go to the Similan Islands, see page 35.
All 4 Diving, 5/4 Sawatdirak Rd, Patong Beach, T076-344611, www.all4diving.com. Offers a diving service with other dive operators and sells equipment.
Andaman Divers, 62 Prabaramee Rd, Patong Beach,T076-346932, www.

andamandivers.com. 17 years in the business, this operation does liveaboards to the Similan Islands and PADI courses. Japanese-, English- and French-speaking instructors. Claims to offer the best rates.
Dive Asia, Boomerang Village Resort, 9/11-13 Patak Rd, Kata Beach, T076-330598/284117. Established 18 years ago.
Marina Divers, 45 Karon Rd, Karon Beach, T076-330272. PADI-certified courses, professional set-up. Recommended.
Phuket Scuba Club, 241 Koktanod Rd, Kata Beach, T076-284026, www.phuket-scuba-club.com. South African-owned. Good reports of a Similans liveaboard with this outfit, which offers instructors of varying nationalities. Thai and English spoken. Half-day dive trips from ฿1000.
Santana, 49 Thaweewong Rd, Patong Beach, T076-294220, www.santanaphuket. com. A prestigious 5-star PADI instructor training centre. This operation has 30 years' experience. As well as day trips, it offers liveaboards to the Similan Islands, Surin and Hin Daeng. Courses in English, German and Thai.
Scuba Cat Diving, 94 Thaweewong Rd, Patong Beach, T076-293120, www. scubacat.com. 5-star PADI dive centre offering liveaboards to the Similan Islands, Koh Bon, Koh Tachai and Richelieu Rock as well as fun dives. Phuket's first **National Geographic Dive Centre**, it is also a Go-Eco operator and is involved in marine clean-up.
Sea Bees Diving, Chalong Beach, T076-381765, www.sea-bees.com.
Seafarer Divers, 1/10-11 Moo 5, Soi Ao Chalong Pier, T076-280644, www.seafarer-divers.com.
Sunrise Divers, 269/24 Patak Rd, Karon Beach, T076-398040, www.sunrise-divers. com. Small operation known for its personalized service. Day trips, 5-star PADI instruction, discovery dives and liveaboards.

Elephant trekking
Camp Chang Kalim, Phrabarami Soi 9, Phrabarami Rd, Kalim (north of Patong),

T08-7898 2260 (mob), www.campchang.com. Among the many Phuket elephant riding operations, this one is said to take better care of its animals.

Fitness
Le Fitness, Le Méridien Phuket Beach Resort, Karon Noi Beach (between Karon and Patong), T076-370100. Big gym, 4 tennis courts and 2 a/c squash courts. Aerobics, yoga and pilates classes on offer. Lessons and membership available for outside guests.

Game fishing
Dorado Big Game Fishing, 46/17-18 1 Moo 9, Ao Chalong Pier Rd, T076-202679, www.phuket-fishing.com. Offers Phuket's largest deep-sea fishing boat – a 65-ft hardwood timber cruiser with shaded deck, sundeck and lounge that is big enough for 21 passengers. Does day trips and sleeps 6 passengers for liveaboard safaris. The English owner is an ex-oilman. The company specializes in long-range liveaboard safaris to the Similan Islands.
Wahoo Big Game Fishing, Sea Center, 48/20 Moo 9, Soi Ao Chalong, T076-281510, www.wahoo.ws. Has been in business for over 20 years and knows the area inside-out.

Go-karting
Patong Go-Kart Speedway, 118/5 Moo 6, Pra Baramee Rd, Kathu, T076-321949, www.gokartthailand.com. Open daily. Go-karting is a popular activity for visitors to Phuket. Just turn up and drive. If you have 5 or more people you can race in a mini-grand prix. There are kids' karts and 2-seater karts available. There's also an off-road track if you're feeling a little more adventurous.

Golf
Blue Canyon Country Club, 165 Moo 1, Thepkrasatri Rd, Thalang, T076-328088, www.bluecanyonclub.com. The Canyon Course and the Lakes Course are here Top pros from around the world have walked the fairways at both. Blue Canyon has received numerous awards over the years.
Laguna Phuket Golf Club (formerly Banyan Tree Golf Club), 34 Moo 4, Srisoonthorn Rd, Cherng Talay, T076-270991/2, www.laguna phuket.com/leisure-and-tours/golf/index.php. Located in the Laguna compound, this golf club offers some fine greens with a range of challenging hazards. Rated as one of the best courses in Thailand, golf pros like Nick Faldo have had good things to say about it.
Loch Palm Golf Club, 38 Moo 5 Wichit Songkram Rd, Kathu, T076-321929-34, www.lochpalm.com. The serene setting of this established course makes it a firm favourite on the island.
Mission Hills Phuket Golf Club Resort and Spa, 195 Moo 4 Pakhlok, Thalang, T076-310888, www.missionhillsphuket.com. Seaside course with plenty of water hazards to keep things interesting.
Phuket Country Club, 80/1 Moo 7, Wichit Songkram Rd, Kathu, T076-319200, www.phuketcountryclub.com. Has been around for 20 years on a former tin-mining site. As with all of Phuket's golf courses, the scenery is stunning and the course is challenging.
Red Mountain Golf Course, Kathu, T076-321929-34, www.lochpalm.com. This is the sister course of **Loch Palm**. It's billed as the most challenging course in Phuket.

Horse riding
Phuket International Horse Club, 47 Lagoon Rd, Bang Tao Beach, T076-324199. Trails lead through grassland, past the golf course and along the beach.
Phuket Riding Club, 95 Viset Rd, south of Chalong traffic circle, T076-288213. ฿1000 per hr.

Kiteboarding
This challenging water sport has recently become popular in Phuket, and it gained a bit of prestige by being part of the King's Cup sailing regatta in 2011.

Kite Thailand Phuket Kitesurfing School, 2 bases in Chalong and Koh Lone, T08-1090 3730/9970 1797, www.kitethailand.com. Offers lessons for all levels, rental and can arrange other water sports, activities and tours.
Kite Zone Phuket, Friendship Beach Resort, Rawai, T08-3395 2005 (mob), www.kitesurfingphuket.com. Lessons and equipment rental.

Lawn bowls
Kamala Lawn Bowling Club, 71/26 Moo 5, Kamala, T076-385912, www.lawnbowlphuket.com. Believe it or not, Phuket has its own dedicated lawn bowls club. Evening games can be fun with a group of friends and a few cold beers. Afternoon games usually kick off about 1500 and you can be picked up from your hotel for a small fee. Tuition is available and there is an on-site bar.

Motorbike and jeep tours
Hiring a motorbike, car or jeep for the day is a great way to see the island, if you can brave the traffic. A suggested route might run north from Phuket City or east from Patong to Tha Rua, the Heroines' Monument and the National Museum at Thalang. Take a side trip to Ton Sai Waterfall and the national park, then continue north on Route 402, before turning left for Nai Yang Beach and the national park. Crossing Route 402, drive east through rubber plantations, taking in Bang Pae Waterfall, before returning to the main road at the Heroines' Monument.

Muay Thai (Thai boxing)
Bangla Boxing Stadium, 198/4 Rat-u-thit 200 Pee Rd, Patong. A decent place to watch a fight. Near enough to Patong's nightlife so that you can sneak out when you want and you're not in the middle of nowhere. They have some high-calibre fights here.

Patong Boxing Stadium, 2/59 Sai Nam Yen Rd, Patong, T076-345578. Boxing stadium where fights are held every Mon and Thu. Ring-side seats will set you back ฿1500.
Phuket Thai Boxing Gym, 82/5 Moo 4, Patak Rd, Kata, T076-281090, Open Tue-Sun.
Rawai Muay Thai, Rawai Beach, T08-1537 6038 (mob), www.rawaimuaythai.com. Thai boxing and fitness training gym. Train 6 hrs a day with knowledgeable coaches. Beginners are welcome. They also have accommodation available.
Saphan Hin Stadium, South Phuket Rd, T076-258393. Charge ฿350. Every Fri at 2000 (tickets available from 1600). A place to join the locals in watching a Muay Thai match.
Suwit Muay Thai Camp, 15 Moo 1, Chao Fa Rd, Chalong, T076-374313, www.bestmuaythai.com. This camp has been around for more than 15 years. Pick up a few tricks from boxing pros.
Tiger Muay Thai and MMA Training Camp, 7/6 Moo 5 Soi Tad-ied, Chalong, T076-367 071, T076-383107, www.tiger muaythai.com. Mon-Sat 0700-1900. One of the most famous camps in Phuket. Anyone, from beginners to advanced fighters, is invited to attend for some serious training. Walk-ins welcome.

Nature tours
Siam Safari, 45 Chao Fah Rd, Chalong, T076-280116, www.siamsafari.com. Offers tours to forests, rice fields, villages, plantations, secluded beaches and elephant camps.

Sea kayaking
Andaman Sea Kayak, T076-235353, www.andamanseakayak.com. Hires out 2-man canoes to explore the grottoes, capes and bays that line Phuket's coast, but which are often not accessible by road. Day trips cost about ฿2800-3300; 4-day expeditions, all-inclusive, ฿22,000.
John Gray's Sea Canoe Thailand, 124 Soi 1 Yaowarat Rd, T076-254505, www.johngray-seacanoe.com. John Gray has had over 20

years' experience and is the man for day trips and overnights with the advantage being the limited number of expedition guests. Many people swear by the John Gray experience.

Paddle Asia, 18/58 Thanon, Rasdanusorn, Ban Kuku, T076-241519, www.paddleasia. com. Traditional kayaks take tours around the marine parks. Specializes in multi-day, customised trips.

Sea Canoe Thailand, 125/461 Moo 5, Baan Tung Ka-Baan Sapam Rd, Rassada, T076-528839, www.seacanoe.net. Established watersports company offering day trips and longer tours from Phuket.

Shooting

Expect to pay up to ฿1200 to fire off 10 real bullets.

Kathu International Shooting Club, 86/3 Soi Kathu Waterfall, Wichit Songkram Rd, Kathu, T076-323996. Learn various tricks and techniques for firing rifles and handguns. Tuition is provided along with all safety equipment. Several choices from classic Smith & Wessons to Glocks. Archery, too. Fewer people find their way here than **Phuket Shooting Range** so you may well have the place to yourself, but the staff are terminally bored.

Phuket Shooting Range, 82/2 Moo 4 Patak Rd, Rawai, T076-381667. Standard shooting range where all manner of guns can be fired for a hefty price. There are revolvers and shotguns, but thankfully no machine guns. The staff are more into the whole experience than at the **Kathu Range**. Archery, Airsoft BB Gun war games, paintball, ATV riding and snake shows also on offer in this large compound.

Surfing

There is a small but tight community of surfers in Phuket. Every year there are small-scale international surfing competitions held at Kalim or Kata beaches. While Phuket is not the most renowned surfing destination, it is possible to catch a

wave, especially during the wetter months. Boards in varying conditions can be rented from most of the beaches.

Patong Beach is generally considered the worst place to surf, though Kalim just north of it gets some decent wave action. Kamala and Nai Yang are reasonable, while Kata is the most popular spot on the island. Nai Harn is quieter and often gets the best waves in Phuket.

Phuket Surf, south end of Kata Beach, T08-7889 7308 (mob), www.phuketsurf.com. Surf lessons for ages 5 and up and board rental. Also runs a surfer-friendly bar, **The Tube**, just up the street.

Saltwater Dreaming Surf Shop, 108/3 Moo 3, Cherng Thalay, Thalang, T076-271050, www.saltwater-dreaming.com. Keeps tabs on the surf in Phuket and also has information about renting boards and where to go.Stand Up Paddle Thai, Layan Beach, T076-20095, www.standuppaddle thai.com. Phuket's first stand-up paddle operator, offers lessons and board rental for this Hawaiian-born water sport.

Therapies

Traditional Thai massage is available from countless (usually untrained) women and men on the beaches and in shops around the island. Check for a certificate from Wat Po.

Mai Khao Sand Spa, follow Thepkrastri Rd past the airport, turn left at Wat Mai Khao and then turn left at Mai Khao Village until you come to the 'spa', T08-1895 4833 (mob). This isn't a spa as such because it's out on the beach. There are some people in Phuket who are convinced that being buried in sand with all of your clothes on is good for you.

Tour operators

Full-day tours to the **Similan Islands** (see page 35), **Phangnga Bay** and **Coral Island** (Koh Hii) usually cost ฿1500-4000, including swimming, snorkelling and fishing. It's best not to go with the cheapest tours unless you enjoy snorkelling with more people than fish.

Buffalo Tours, 60/6 Raj-u-thit 200 years road, www.buffalotours.com. Arranges tours throughout the region. Also offices in Bangkok and Chiang Mai.

Waterskiing

Phuket Cable Ski, 86/3 Moo 6, Soi Nam Tok Kathu, near Kathu Waterfall, T076-202525/7, www.phuketcableski.com. Inland waterskiing course on a man-made lake. Skiers are pulled around an oval track at up to 30 kph by giant overhead cables.

⊖ Transport

Phuket Island *p48, map p46*
Air

The airport is to the north of the island, 30 km from Phuket City, T076-3272307, www.phuketairportonline.com. There are regular **Air Asia**, **Bangkok Airways**, **Nok Air** and **THAI** connections to **Bangkok** and **Chiang Mai**. Bangkok Airways runs daily connections to **Koh Samui**. For a list of other airlines that fly between Bangkok and Phuket, see www.tourismthailand.org. There are also flights to **Beijing**, **Hong Kong**, **Penang** and **Kuala Lumpur** (Malaysia), **Singapore**, **Taipei**, **Tokyo**, **Munich**, **Dusseldorf**, Copenhagen and Helsinki.

Airline offices Air Asia, airport 3rd floor, T076-328601, and on Thaweewong Rd in Patong (opposite La Flora resort), T076-341792. **Bangkok Airways**, 158/2-3 Yaowarat Rd, T076-225033. **THAI**, 78 Ranong Rd, T076-360444. Dragonair, 156/14 Phangnga Rd, T076-215734 (from Hong Kong); Malaysia Airlines, 1/8-9 Tungka Rd (opposite Merlin Hotel), T076-216675; SilkAir, 183/103 Phangnga Rd, T076-213891; Firefly, airport 3rd floor, T076-351477.

Boat

Ferries run year round to and from **Koh Phi Phi**, leaving from Rassada Pier on Phuket's east coast. Tickets for ฿300-350 single can be bought at tourist offices on the dock or around the island, as well as from many guesthouses and hotels. In high season (Nov-May), Tigerline (www.tigerlinetravel.com) runs a ferry boat from Chalong Pier, departing daily at 0800, 1 hr. The return trip from Phi Phi departs at 1700. It costs more than double that of the other services but the boat is much less crowded, doesn't allow the annoying hotel touts aboard and arrives a good 2 hrs before the other ferries.

There are many boats to **Koh Yao Yai**, with vessels leaving from Laem Hin Pier, Tien Sin Pier and Rassada Port. 5 boats a day leave Bang Rong Pier to **Koh Yao Noi**.

There's a direct ferry and speedboat service to Koh Lanta (฿850, 3 hrs) or on Tigerline ferry (see above) with brief a stop at Phi Phi on the way, only available from Nov-Apr. In low season, it is best to catch one of the regular buses to Krabi and go from there via the car ferry.

Long-tailed boats can be hired to visit reefs and more isolated coves, ฿500 per hr or up to ฿2000 a day, negotiable.

Bus

The station (*bor ko sor* – BKS) is on Phangnga Rd in Phuket City, T076-211480. It's cheaper to buy tickets here than through travel agents. The information desk usually has a timetable and fare list produced by the TAT detailing all departures as well as local transport. A new station is being built on Thepkrassatri Rd, but it's been beset with delays. At the time of writing, it had not yet opened.

Regular a/c and non-a/c connections with **Bangkok**'s Southern bus terminal (14 hrs). Regular morning connections with **Hat Yai** (8 hrs), **Trang** (6 hrs), **Surat Thani** (6 hrs) and **Satun** (7 hrs). Regular connections with **Phangnga** (2 hrs), **Takua Pa** (3 hrs), **Ranong** (6 hrs) and **Krabi** (4 hrs). Journey times for these buses will vary between 30 mins and 1 hr.

Car

Small outfits along most beaches, expect to pay ฿900-1200 per day, depending on the age of car, etc. It is worth picking up an updated map of the island from the TAT office in Phuket City as the roads in the north can be confusing. **Avis** has an office in the Phuket airport arrival hall, T08-9969 8674, from ฿1100 per day. **Hertz**, at the airport, T076-328545; prices are similar to **Avis**. The tour desks at a number of the bigger resorts can arrange bookings with these international brands, too. There are other rental companies down Rasada Rd in Phuket City and in all the towns and beaches across the island.

Motorbike

As for car hire above, ฿200-350 per day. There are easy-to-find rental shops in all the towns and beach areas. Some places insist on taking your passport as a deposit/collateral but it is best not to let it out of your hands if you can help it.

Motorbike taxi and tuk-tuk

Men (and women) with red vests will whisk passengers almost anywhere for a minimum of about ฿40. The motorbike taxis congregate at intersections.

Avoid tuk-tuks if possible – they are overpriced and uncomfortable. From Patong to Phuket City, or vice versa, will cost you about ฿450. Travel within Phuket City shouldn't be more than about ฿100.

Taxi

There are minibus and car taxi services to Surat Thani, Khao Lak, Krabi and other mainland destinations, which may be booked at hotel tour desks or with agents near the bus terminal on Phangnga Rd. Prices range from about ฿2000 for a 3-passenger car to Khao Lak to ฿6000 for a 9-seater minibus to Surat Thani. Plenty of freelance 'black' taxi drivers are willing to drive you there more cheaply, but are uninsured.

Phuket City *p48*
Songthaew and minibus

For Patong, Kamala, Surin, Makham Bay, Nai Yang, Kata, Karon, Nai Harn, Rawai, Thalang and Chalong buses leave every 30 mins, 0600-1800 from the market on Ranong Rd in Phuket City. Fares range from ฿20-25 to whatever the collector thinks he can get away with.

Phangnga Bay

Phangnga Bay is best known as the location for the 1974 James Bond movie *The Man with the Golden Gun*. Limestone rocks tower out of the sea (some as high as 100 m); boats can be hired to tour the area from Tha Don, the Phangnga customs pier.

Travelling from Phuket to Phangnga the road passes through limestone scenery. Much of the land looks scrubby and dry, punctuated by shrimp farms and scrappy farms. But en route, it is possible to watch rubber being processed by smallholders. Not long ago, over-mature rubber trees (those more than 25 years old) were cut down and processed into charcoal. Today, due to the efforts of an enterprising Taiwanese businessman, a rubber-wood furniture industry has developed.

Arriving in Phangnga

Getting there and around
Phangnga has no train station or airport – the only way here is by bus (or private transport). Buses leave through the day from Bangkok's Southern bus terminal, including overnight VIP coaches (15 hours). Phangnga bus station is on Petkasem Road, near the centre of town. There are regular bus connections with Phuket, Krabi and towns south to the Malaysian border and north to Bangkok. Motorcycle taxis will wait at the bus station to take passengers further afield. Cramped but rather extraordinary teak wood *songthaews* with unpadded seats constantly ply the main road, ฿30. They are the main form of transport around town (which is easy to cover on foot) and to surrounding villages.
▸▸ *See Transport, page 85, for further information.*

Phangnga town and around → *For listings, see pages 82-85.*

The poor relation to its neighbouring tourist hotspots of Phuket and Krabi, Phangnga is often overlooked by visitors. Its relaxed, authentic Thai feel, dramatic setting and interesting daytrips make it an excellent place to pass a few days. There is one main road that goes through the centre of town which nestles narrowly between striking limestone crags. If you want urban sophistication and multiple culinary options, then Phangnga may disappoint. It is a non-tourist Thai experience, and Phangnga folk come across as almost grumpy with tourists – a relief after the feigned jollity of so many Thailand's tourist-drenched resorts.

In the centre of town, behind the **Rattanapong Hotel** is the fresh produce and early morning market while along the main street near the Thaweesuk Hotel are some remaining examples of the **Chinese shophouses** that used to line the street.

Around Phangnga town

Due to the limestone geology, there are a number of caves in the vicinity. The most memorable, and by far the most disgusting, are at **Wat Thomtharpan Amphoe Muang**, the so-called 'Heaven and Hell Caves', around 2 km to the south of town on the road to Phuket. It's hard to see where Heaven is in this Buddhist depiction of Hell, designed to teach youngsters about the consequences of sinning. Cheap plaster models of human are burned on spits, chopped in half, sent through a mangle, torn apart by birds and gutted by dogs. Hideously distorted demons with metre-long tongues and outsized genitalia glare down on the visitor. Eat before you arrive at this eerily deserted compound. Just on the outskirts of town on Route 4 towards Phuket, on the left-hand side, is the **Somdet Phra Sinakharin Park**, surrounded by limestone mountains; it is visible from the road and opposite the former city hall. Within this park are **Tham Luk Sua** and **Tham Ruesi Sawan**, two adjoining caves with streams, stalactites and stalagmites. These watery, sun-filled caves have rather unsympathic concrete paths. At the entrance to the cave sits Luu Sii, the cave guardian, under an umbrella. **Tham Phung Chang** is a little closer into town on the other side of the road, within the precincts of **Wat Phraphat Phrachim Khet**. To get to the arched entrance to the wat, take a *songthaew* about 300 m past the traffic lights

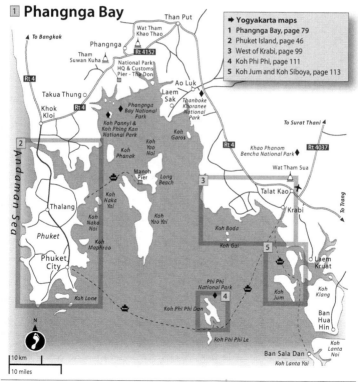

1 Phangnga Bay

10 km
10 miles

(themselves past the **New Lak Muang Hotel**). The cave is actually inside the symbol of Phangnga – a huge mountain that apparently looks like a crouched elephant called Khao Chang. It can be found behind Phangnga's former city hall. In this long dark cave, again dripping with stalactites and stalagmites, there is a spring, Buddha images and a small pool where boys swim. The wat is more visually interesting though not as quirky. It enjoys a fine position against the limestone cliff and set within a large compound.

Tham Suwan Kuha ① ฿10, is 12 km from Phangnga on Route 4 to Phuket, take a southwest-bound bus. A turning to the right leads to this cave temple. It is popular with Thais and is full of Buddhas. Stairs lead up to a series of tunnels, containing some natural rock formations. King Chulalongkorn visited the cave in 1890 and his initials are carved into the rock.

Several kilometres out of town, and a right turn off the Krabi road, the **Sra Nang Manora Forest Park** (probably best reached on a scooter) offers a delightful break from the midday heat. The forest is free to enter and offers an easy, shaded 90-minute walk past several caves and sheer limestone cliffs. Thai visitors congregate at the park entrance to picnic next to the gushing stream, but anyone prepared to walk for a few minutes will have the forest to themselves.

Wat Tham Khao Thao is 12 km from Phangnga on Route 4152 to Krabi, on the left-hand side of the road, under a cliff wall (buses travel the route). Views of the surrounding plain can be seen from a stairway up the cliff face. The road here passes through nipa palm which then becomes an area of mangrove. Aquaculture is an important sideline industry, and tiger prawns are raised in the brackish waters of the mangroves and in purpose-built ponds.

Phangnga Bay National Park → *For listings, see pages 82-85.*

① *Park entrance fee, ฿200 (check to make sure it is included in the tour price). To get there take a songthaew to the pier, ฿30, from Phangnga town. 7 km along Route 4 there is a turning to the left (Route 4144 – signposted Phangnga Bay and the Ao Phangnga National Park Headquarters) and the pier is another 3 km down this road.*

Relaxed, excellent-value boat tours of Phangnga Bay can be booked from one of the travel agents in the town's bus station. They cost about ฿1100, and include the park entrance fee, accomodation, meals and a guided canoe tour, where someone does the paddling for you. The trips are just sightseeing tours as the boat drivers speak little English.

The standard tour winds through mangrove swamps, which act as a buffer between land and sea and nipa palm, and past striking limestone cliffs before arriving at **Tham Lod Cave**. This is not really a cave at all, but a tunnel cut into the limestone and dripping with stalagmites that look like petrified chickens hanging upside down. From Tham Lod, the route skirts past **Koh Panyi** – a Muslim fishing village built on stilts which extends out into the bay; its most striking feature being a golden mosque and the sheer peak rearing up behind it. Through the narrow lanes, the main transport is bicycle. There are also overpriced seafood restaurants in this village.

Other sights include **Khao Mah Ju**, a small mountain between Tha Dan and Koh Pnay which resembles a dog. There is also **Khao Khian** or 'Mountain of Writings' with ancient depictions of animals and sea life dating back more than 3000 years. These drawings include a cartoon-like dolphin which looks suspiciously contemporary. It is believed that seamen who used the place to escape from the monsoon, painted these vivid images. While all of these sights may seem highlights in themselves, it is the 'James Bond' island that is touted as the raison d'être for these tours. **James Bond Island** or **Koh Tapu** lies in the little bay of Koh Phing Kan or 'Leaning Mountain' which is a huge rock split into two parts with the smaller part having slid down so that the taller section appears to be leaning. The limestone karst stack that sticks up out from the sea just off this island is called **Koh Tapu** (Nail Island). The 'famous' rock, like a chisel, seems much smaller than it should be, and the tiny beach and cave are littered with trinket-stalls (refreshments available) and other tourists. Endless tour groups are spewed onto the small beach throughout the day to barge into each other as they wander past tatty souvenirs. There are few tackier sights in Asia. For details on the two large islands in the bay, Koh Yao Yai and Koh Yao Noi, see below.

Koh Yao Noi and Koh Yao Yai

Koh Yao Noi and Koh Yao Yai, equidistant from Krabi mainland and Phuket, are the two most important islands in the 44-strong cluster of islands known as Koh Yao, to the east of Phuket. They are so close to each other that it only takes around eight minutes by long-tailed boat to cross over from Koh Yao Yai to Koh Yao Noi.

There's a strong Muslim and Sea Gypsy community here, and most locals are keen to preserve and promote their traditional way of life. They prefer outsiders to dress modestly and not to drink alcohol outside resorts or restaurants. Traditional handicrafts still persist, such as the inventive 'fish-scale flowers' created by the housewives of Koh Yao. The unusual rural heritage is seen in other ways too, and eco-activities include rubber collecting and fishing demonstrations, kayaking, hiking and snorkelling.

Getting there From Phuket's Bang Rong Pier, eight long-tail and six speedboat ferry trips depart for Koh Yao Noi daily 0730 to 1745, with returns daily 0715 to 1700. A less frequent service is available from Laem Hin Pier and Rassada Port, both on Phuket's east coast. From Krabi's Thalen Pier there are seven trips daily 0900 to 1700, and eight daily return trips 0730 to 1700. From Phang Nga there's one boat a day departing 1300 and returning from Yao Noi at 0730. The boats make a brief stop at Koh Yao Yai first, less than 10 minutes away from Yao Noi. Fares are ฿120-200 and the journey takes up to one hour 30 minutes. Private long-tail or speedboat transfers may also be arranged.

Koh Yao Yai, the larger of the two islands, has better beaches for swimming but fewer places to stay, most of which tend to be overpriced. Although expensive resorts are appearing, there are still wooden houses, rubber plantations and wandering buffalos. There's a spectacular view where the road ends on the west side of the island, overlooking Klong Son Bay. The main attraction is the peace and quiet.

Koh Yao Noi is considerably more advanced than its bigger sister, with better facilities, including a hospital and internet shops but very few restaurants and shops. There is an award-winning homestay programme, the Koh Yao Noi Homestay Club, run by local fishermen and their families, and a few sensitively designed resorts, while most other operations are basic bungalows. A partially paved road encircles Koh Yao Noi, with its village in the middle and huts scattered throughout the island. On the northern tip of this island and best reached by boat, is an enormous tree, the trunk of which takes 23 men to span. Hire a bike for a delightful few hours taking in the beauty of the island while negotiating the (sometimes difficult) roads. Koh Yao Noi has become a bit of a hotspot for alternative traveller groups, who have bagged the place as good for retreats ranging from yoga to healing crystal workshops. For little trips there are beautiful beaches, especially on Koh Nok, and a dreamy lagoon on Koh Hong. Mobile phones operate throughout both the islands.

Phangnga to Krabi

From Phangnga to Krabi, the road passes mangrove swamps and nipa palm, more dramatic karst formations and impressive stands of tropical forest. For those travelling independently by car or motorbike, there is a lovely detour worth taking for about an hour. Look out for signs to **Tham Raird** or **Ban Bang Toei** and turn left down towards the towering karst formations. The road leads through a pass into a valley in the heart of the karst. It is a little like stepping back in time, and several Thai television commercials idealizing rural life have been filmed here. The backdrop of lush forest on towering karst, with a foreground of rice fields and small villages, is wonderful. Rainy season visitors will be well rewarded with mist and cloud on the peaks and a golden light on the wet paddy. Sadly, behind these wonderful, almost circular limestone crags there are several large limestone concessions blasting the mountains away. To the front there are similar scenes of rice farming against a backdrop of towering mountains, interspersed with the occasional village or temple.

Phangnga Bay listings

For hotel and restaurant price codes and other relevant information, see pages 12-16.

⊜ Where to stay

Phangnga town *p78*
$$-$ Phangnga Inn, 2/2 Soi Lohakit, Pet-kasem Rd, T076-411963. A beautiful family house converted into a cosy hotel with a range of contrasting, immaculately clean en suite rooms. It is off the main road, and clearly marked by a purple sign. Recommended.
$ Rattanapong, 111 Petkasem Rd, T076-411247. In the town centre, this 5-storey building is a converted hospital. It is a friendly establishment with large, cleanish a/c and fan rooms. A few with balconies overlooking the market.
$ Thawesuk, 79 Petkasem Rd, T076-412100. Clean rooms, thin walls, basic, run by an eccentric family. Mr Thawesuk is an amiable character with a sharp eye for anyone who's not a guest, so the security is excellent, despite having to walk through what feels like an open garage to get to the rooms. A narrow stone staircase leads to a roof terrace at the back of the building where you can view the surrounding limestone

mountains. Rooms have been recently renovated. Recommended.

Koh Yao Noi and Koh Yao Yai *p81*
Koh Yao Noi
$$$$ Koyao Island Resort, 24/2 Moo 5, T076-597474, www.koyao.com. 15 villas incorporating traditional thatched Thai architecture mixed with the latest in French style are set around a garden in a coconut plantation. They look out onto an island-spotted stretch of the Andaman Sea and the only non-rocky beach on the island. Villas have small private gardens, satellite TV, phone and fax, minibar, etc. A largely outdoor spa offers sauna, jacuzzi and traditional Thai massage in a relaxed and airy setting.
$$$$ The Paradise Koh Yao Boutique Beach Resort and Spa, 24 Moo 4, T076-584450, www.theparadise.biz. 48 superior studios, 16 deluxe studios and 6 pool villas on the beach in the north of Koh Yao Noi. Has its own passenger transfer boats.
$$$$ Six Senses Yao Noi Beyond Phuket, 56 Moo 5, T076-418500, www.sixsenses.com. Set amid trees – you hardly notice they're there at all – are 56 luxurious wooden villas, all complete with private pool, sunken tubs and sala. Everything is done in natural

fabrics and materials, with only a hint of concrete. Six Senses donate a percentage of revenue to carefully selected local projects. Eating here is unforgettable; they have an in-house deli stocking the best cheeses and charcuterie you'll find anywhere in Thailand. Prices are high but you get a lot for your money. Highly recommended.

$$$$-$$$ Lom Lae Beach Resort, T076-597486, www.lomlae.com. Thatched roof fan bungalows in a peaceful garden setting. Cookery courses, local nature trips and a dive shop on site.

$$$-$$ Ban Tha Khao Bungalows, T076-597564, www.kohyaobungalow.com. Several decently sized bamboo and wooden structures with chairs, table, wardrobes, Western toilets and mini balconies. No a/c. This is a picturesque choice near a deserted cove up a rough road in the centre of the island, so it's a bit of a hike, but the Mut family who runs it can arrange for a pick-up by motorcycle taxi. The owners also manage the **Sea Canoe** company.

$$$-$$ Sabai Corner Bungalows, T076-597497, T08-1892 1827 (mob), www.sabai cornerbungalows.com. 10 romantic bungalows are set among cashew and coconut trees with magnificent views over Pasai Beach. Attached toilets. A popular option, often full, ring ahead.

$$-$ Koh Yao Noi Homestay Club, Koh Yao District, Pang Nga Province, 82160, Coordinating Office T076-597244, T08-1968-0877/6942 7999. You'll be housed in any one of several family homes run by this award-winning homestay programme. All monies go directly to the local community with a percentage of income being used to protect the fishing stocks of crab and prawn available locally. Expect reasonably basic accommodation but an unforgettably freindly welcome and some of the best seafood you're ever likely eat. The basic price covers food and accommodation but they can organize an entire programme for you at extra cost that takes in fishing trips, visits to secret islands complete with stunning beaches and cooking courses. One of the most highly recommended places to stay in Thailand. Some details are also available on www.cbt-i.org, a website dedicated to Community Based Tourism.

Koh Yao Yai

The choice on Koh Yao Yai isn't as great as on its smaller neighbour, and much of it is overpriced, although the lack of visitors does make a degree of bargaining possible.

$$$$ The Elixir Resort, 99 Moo 3, T08-7808 3838, www.elixirresort.com. Beachfront resort with 44 a/c bungalow villas, some with private pools. Well crafted with a good design that blends rustic and contemporary style. Shared pool, spa, gym, restaurants, dive centre and other water sport activities. Popular with honeymooners.

$$$-$$ Thiwson Bungalows, 58/2 Moo 4, T08-1956 7582 (mob), www.thiwsonbeach. com. Sweet, clean rooms in the usual bamboo-and-wood style, with bedside lights and Western toilets. Restaurant, deck chairs on the verandas and a pleasant garden overlooking one of the nicest beaches on the island. Recommended.

$$$-$$ Yao Yai Resort, Moo 7, Ban Lopareh, T08-1968 4641, www.yaoyairesort. com. Located on a beach that's decent even at low tide, this west-facing resort allows you to enjoy the setting sun. Good bungalows come complete with eccentric wood furnishings, everything is en suite though there is the choice of fan and a/c. If you can help it, don't get suckered into taking the resort's overpriced transfer boat.

❼ Restaurants

Phangnga town *p78*

Cafés on Petkasem Rd, near the market, sell the usual array of Thai dishes, including excellent *khaaw man kai* (chicken and rice) and *khaaw mu daeng* (red pork and rice). There is also a good shop selling all manner of rice crackers, nuts and Thai biscuits on Petakasem Rd past **Thaweesuk Hotel**. Try the popular **Kha Muu Restaurant** opposite the **Thaweesuk Hotel**.

There is an early morning market behind **Rattanapong Hotel**, which begins as early as 0500. There are a couple very good cafés here that do traditional morning rice soup (khaaw thom) to perfection until around about 0900. This soup is a rice porridge with coriander, basil, ginger, spices, onion, lemongrass, pepper and minced pork. You can also get a fix of sweet tea. The market itself, though small, sells an astonishing array of foodstuffs, fish, meat, flowers for making garlands and lots of sarongs. Recommended.

$$ Duang Seafood, 122 Petkasem Rd (opposite **Bank of Ayudhya**). Mediocre seafood restaurant if you go for the *farang* menu and Chinese specialities. But the Thai menu is completely different so the best move is to be emphatic and point to what the locals are eating.

$$-$ Khru Thai (Thai Teacher), Petkasem Rd (opposite the post office). Clean and cheap place, where the dishes are openly displayed making selection easy.

$ Open-air cinema eaterie, Petkasem Rd and around Soi Bamrungrat. This no-name eatery (the sign in Thai script simply describes what it sells) is not to be missed. There is a 100-year-old-plus tree that grows through part of it and a gigantic screen that can be heard along Petkasem Rd as it blares Southeast Asian martial arts flicks and straight-to-video Western horror movies. Outside this open-air restaurant and cinema, nocturnal stalls also sell sweet pastries. The food is of good quality. Popular with the locals, this Cinema Paradiso is a magical treat. Recommended.

Koh Yao Noi and Koh Yao Yai *p81*
Most people eat at the restaurant attached to their bungalows, although there is **Tha Khao Seafood** right next to the pier. Otherwise a good option is to pick your choice of fish from the fishermen's huts on Tha Tondo Pier to the northwest of the island, and take it to the local restaurant just by the pier for cooking while watching arguably the best sunset the island can offer.

For a local delicacy on Koh Yao Yai, it is worth trying/buying the *pla ching chang* dried anchovy paste which is used with rices and noodles to liven things up.

🎵 Bars and clubs

Koh Yao Noi and Koh Yao Yai *p81*
Koh Yao Noi
Pyramid Bar, a nice beachfront bar offering beer and cocktails.
Reggae Bar, on the non-beach side of the road between **Sabai Corner** and **Holiday Resort**. Offers beer and cocktails and consists of a few tables set outside.

⏱ What to do

Phangnga town *p78*
Tour operators
Sayan, next to the bus terminal on Phetkasem Rd, T076-430348. Experienced operator offering half-day, full-day and overnight island tours. The tours are worthwhile and good value. **Mr Hassim**, who operates **MT Tours** is an affable and endearing man who grew up in Koh Panyi and comes from a long line of fishermen. For an extra ฿250 he will put you up in his stilted Muslim village for the night and provide a seafood dinner. He is a very accommodating host who speaks relatively good English and who has quite a loyal following.

Phangnga Bay National Park *p80*, map *p79*
Tour operators
Long-tailed boats can be chartered from the National Park pier for a trip around the sights of Phangnga Bay for about ฿500 per person although it is cheaper for 1 person to take a tour with **Sayan**, **Kean** or Mr Hassim at **MT Tours** (see Phangnga town, above).

There are other ways of getting down to the bay and taking tours: as the widened and rather fast road nears Phangnga, there are a number of roads down to the coast, from where tours to Phangnga Bay depart. Look out for signs. The first of these leads down a long winding road through rubber plantations and over hills to **Khlong Khian pier**. Although there are several tour operators here, they are small-scale efforts; most of the boatmen speak little English, but can take you to caves and islands you will never see on larger tours. They are also more flexible in terms of timing, and take no more than 8 people per boat.

Further down the road, another route to the Phangnga Bay tours is along a well-marked narrow *soi* leading to a pier in **Takua Thung** town, which has been partially bypassed by the main road to Krabi. At the pier, there are several restaurants, souvenir shops and parking for tour buses. Independent travellers will find plenty of tour operators willing to book them on a boat. The boats here are large, taking up to 20 passengers, and more reminiscent of Bangkok long-tailed boats than local fishing boats. A similar scene is to be found on the last main turn-off to Phangnga Bay, near the national park offices. The national park offices themselves contain some interesting information on the bay and feature a mangrove interpretive walk and some accommodation. This last bay attracts smaller independent tour operators so it is possible to get away from the crowds in this location too.

Koh Yao Noi and Koh Yao Yai *p81*
Koh Yao Noi
Reggae Tour, next to Reggae Bar, see Bars and clubs, above. Rents a long-tailed boat (฿800 for ½-day, or ฿1200 for a full day), and kayaks (฿250 for ½-day, ฿500, full day).

🚍 Transport

Phangnga town *p78*
Bus
The bus station is on Petkasem Rd, a short walk from the **Thaweesuk** and **Lak Muang 1** hotels. Call T076-412300 or T076-412014. Buses to **Bangkok**'s Southern bus terminal, 15 hrs. 3 VIP buses leave in the evenings for Bangkok. Regular connections with **Phuket**'s bus terminal on Phangnga Rd, 2 hrs, and with **Krabi**, 2 hrs. Also buses to **Ranong**, **Takua Pa**, **Hat Yai** and **Trang**. You can wave down these buses if you catch them coming out of the station and pay on board.

Motorbike
Hire from the **Thaweesuk Hotel** and **MT Hotel** for ฿200 daily.

Krabi and around

Krabi is a small provincial capital on the banks of the Krabi river. It is fairly touristy and a jumping-off point for Koh Phi Phi (see page 110), Koh Lanta (see page 120), Ao Nang and Rai Leh and smaller islands like Koh Jum, Koh Bubu and Koh Siboya (see pages 113 and 114). Krabi town itself is a shambling and amiable waterfront port with excellent, easily accessible tourist sites like the Tham Lod cave and Tiger Temple.

In the past, the town acquired the unfortunate reputation of being a haven for junkies and a place where you really shouldn't leave anything in your hotel room. But in recent years Krabi has attempted to cash in on its heritage in an idiosyncratic way. Hence, the kitsch iron statues on Muharat Road of four bearded prehistoric men carrying the traffic signals. This vision, best viewed at twilight with the jungle foliage behind, is meant to remind visitors that big human skulls were found in Tham Phi Hua To Cave, which means Big-Headed Ghost Cave. Aside from anthropological joys, Krabi town is a perfect place to either prepare for, or recuperate from, island-hopping, especially for those who have been on islands with limited electricity and luxuries. Here, you can stock up on bread – Krabi has excellent bakeries – fetch your newspapers and get a decent café latte before heading back to the nature reserve for some more hammock swinging.

Rock climbing, river trips, birdwatching, hiking at national parks and reserves, motorcycle treks and sea canoeing are all available and most tour companies also operate daily and overnight tours around Phangnga Bay (see page 78) often incorporating a visit to Wat Tham Suwan Kuha and other sights.

Arriving in Krabi

Getting there and around

Krabi is well connected with scheduled and charter flights. Krabi International Airport, 17 km from town, offers seven daily flights from Bangkok. The taxi to town from the airport is around ฿400 and to Ao Nang ฿500. *Songthaews* offer a cheaper option. There are also boats to Koh Phi Phi – still worth a day-trip – and Koh Lanta, from the new pier on the outskirts of Krabi town. Free courtesy tuk-tuks from the old pier at Chao Fah to the new one may still be offered, so don't be too keen to flag down a taxi. Meanwhile, Chao Fah Pier continues to operate services to Rai Leh beach and there is a white minibus for ฿50 to Ao Nang from there as well.

There is no train station in Krabi but Phun Phin (the stop for Surat Thani) is a three-hour bus ride away. The overnight sleeper is met by buses for those going on to Krabi. Buses drop travellers at the tourist office in Krabi, where bookings for the islands can be made. Alternatively, travel to Trang or Nakhon Si Thammarat and take buses from there. Combination tickets from Bangkok via Surat Thani are available and can be booked through travel agencies. From the bus station, around 5 km from the centre in Talat Kao (Old Market), close to the intersection of Uttarakit Road and Route 4, there are regular connections with Bangkok's Southern bus terminal (16 hours) as well as with all major towns in the south. The VIP bus from Bangkok is a 12-hour overnight journey. However, do your homework and don't economize – Krabi hoteliers are now warning tourists of a rogue bus service with contraband 'passengers'. For Koh Samui, companies offer combination bus/boat tickets. Motorcycle taxis also wait to ferry bus passengers into town. *Songthaews* are the main form of local transport, they drive through town stopping at various places such as Phattana Road, in front of **Travel & Tour**, for Ao Phra Nang and in front of the foodstalls on Uttarakit Rpad for Noppharat Thara Beach. Red *songthaews* regularly run between the bus station and town, ฿20. Motorbikes are widely available for hire.
▶▶ *See Transport, page 96, for further information.*

Tourist information

Small **TAT office** ① *Uttarakit Rd, across from Kasikorn Bank, 0830-1630.* For more information on Krabi, Ao Nang, Phra Nang, Rai Leh, Koh Phi Phi and Koh Lanta and some good articles, pick up the free *Krabi Magazine* or Krabi Miniguide, available at various bars and guesthouses. Many other places offer 'tourist information', usually to sell tours, tickets and rooms, which can be either offensive or convenient.

Background

Krabi's economy used to be based on agriculture and fishing but since the mid- to late 1980s, tourism has grown although rubber and palm-oil plantations are still a mainstay. The tourism takeover in Krabi is all down to the growth in the late 1970s and 1980s of surfaced roads at Ao Nang, Ao Luk, Klong Tom and Panom Bencha. Indeed, in the early 1970s communists bandits operated the roadblocks at night, along the only surfaced road in Krabi – Highway 4 – which linked the town with Phangnga. Only those motorists who knew an ever-changing password would be allowed to travel while locals learned not to venture out after dusk. What scant tourists there were clung to their guesthouses, not that maps were even available for the more adventurous among them. Ever mindful of the possible spread of Communism, a watchful Royal Thai Survey Department along with the US Defence Mapping Agency in Washington, published a secret map of the area that no civilian was permitted to see. Then, as the communist threat receded, Ao Nang, which persisted with a dirt track to Krabi until the mid-1970s, got in on a budding asphalted network. This resulted in a bungalow and bar boom that transformed what was once an isolated beachside village into a Costa Del Sol with a twist of Patong. Meanwhile, Krabi

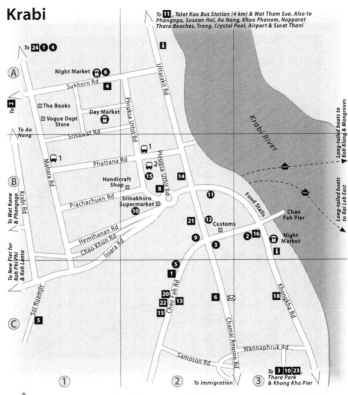

Krabi

To **11**, Talat Kao Bus Station (4 km) & Wat Tham Sua. Also to Phangnga, Susaan Hoi, Ao Nang, Khao Phanom, Nopparat Thara Beaches, Trang, Crystal Pool, Airport & Surat Thani

Boon Siam **2** A1
Chan Chalay **6** C2
City **4** A1
Europa Café &
  Guesthouse **5** C1
K Guest House **13** C2
Krabi City Sea View **10** C3
Krabi River **3** C3
Maritime Park &
  Spa Resort **11** A2
P Guesthouse **15** C2
Star Guest House **18** C3

Thai **21** B2
Thara Guesthouse **23** C3
Theparat Travel Lodge
  & Restaurant **24** A1
Up To You **14** B2

Restaurants
89 Café **5** C2
Bolero **12** B2
Chao Sua **4** A1
Chok Dee **3** B2
I-Oon **9** B2W

May & Mark's **10** B2
Pizzeria Firenze **11** B2
Relax Coffee **2** B3
Ruen Mai **1** A1
Seafood Restaurant **6** A1
Viva **15** B2

Transport
White Songthaews to
  Ao Nang & Nopparat
  Thara **1** B1, B2
Minibus to Talat Kao **2** B2

50 metres
50 yards

Where to stay
A Mansion **1** C2
Andaman Legacy **20** C2
B&B House & Hostel **8** B2
Bai Fern Guesthouse **22** C2
Blue Juice **16** B3

town, on the beach route, steadily grew as a tourist layby and is, today, exceptionally well served with well-priced cafés and restaurants, catering for both tourists and locals and good quirky bars. There is even talk of an annual Thai reggae and Moken 'sea gypsy' summer music festival as more musicians are attracted to the area's laid-back nightlife. Over the past five years the demographics of Krabi have also shifted and the present burgeoning Muslim population – well over half – has clearly influenced the food. Along with hot Thai salads, halal meat, roti and Malaysian-Thai fusion cuisine are commonplace.

Krabi town → *For listings, see pages 92-97.*

There is a **general market** on Srisawat and Sukhon roads, and a **night market** close to the Chao Fah Pier. Chao Fah Pier at night is flooded with foodstalls frequented mainly by locals. The food is highly varied and cheap, although the cooking is quick-fire so you need to make sure everything is properly cooked. However, for a nocturnal nibble alfresco and a promenade walk, the pier is ideal, especially as the streets are thronged with people around twilight. Depending on how you feel about young elephants performing tricks for a cucumber, visitors can pay to feed the gentle beasts. There are also a handful of guesthouses, some shabby but intriguing, along the river and opposite the market if you want to be close to the action.

Around Krabi → *For listings, see pages 92-97.*

Wat Tham Sua (Tiger Cave Temple)

ⓘ *Wat Tham Sua is east along Route 4. Take a red songthaew from Phattana Rd in town for ฿20 to Route 4 (the songthaew is marked 'Airport/Fossil Beach'). From here either walk along Route 4 to the Cave Temple or take a motorcycle taxi (about ฿25). Walk to the cave from the main road.*
Wat Tham Sua is 8 km northeast of town just past Talat Kao down a track on the left and has dozens of *kutis* (monastic cells) set into the limestone cliff. Here, the monks still meditate in the forest. Tiger Cave is so called because once a large tiger apparently lived there and left his pawprints behind as proof, although some visitors have found this a dubious claim and grumble that the pawprints are not at all paw-like. Real wild creatures can be found in the surrounding rocky hillsides and mangrove forest. Here, trees that are hundreds of years old ensconce garrulous macaque monkeys. Walk behind the ridge where the bot is situated to find a network of limestone caves, which eventually lead back to the entrance. There is also a staircase on the left; 1237 steps leading to the top of a 600-m-high karst peak with fantastic views and meditation areas for the monks which are often occupied. This is a demanding climb as it is steep; it is best reserved for cool weather and early morning. Take water and a sunhat.

Tham Phi Hua To and Tham Lod

ⓘ *The caves of Tham Phi Hua To and Tham Lod can be reached by boat from a pier just down the road from Hat Nopparat Thara (take the first left as you exit towards Khlong Muang), or you can take one of many tours by boat or canoe to the same caves. It is also possible to visit these areas with companies offering sea canoeing. While generally more expensive than the trips via long-tailed boat (bear in mind that sea canoes cost upwards of US$350 each in Thailand), a more private trip is worth it, particularly when passing through the lush and mysterious limestone canyons. Then you can be assured that the main sounds will be eerie watery echos and the dipping of oars rather than tourist chatter.*
Phi Hua To Cave (Big-Headed Ghost Cave) is famous for the discovery there of ancient and unusually large human skulls as well as 70 paintings in red and black of people and

animals, all of which upholds Krabi Province's claim to having hosted the oldest human settlements in Thailand. A large pile of shells was also discovered in the cave. There are two paths in the cave. Take the left for a cathedral-like cavern illuminated by a shaft of light and the right for a hall reputed to have been a shelter for prehistoric people.

Tham Lod Tai is a cavern in the limestone karst through which you can travel by boat along narrow passages filled with stalactites and stalagmites. Tham Lod Nua is a longer and larger cavern with more meandering passages. Both are passable only at low-tide. The boat ride to the caves passes mangroves and limestone karst outcrops.

Mangrove trips
① *Long-tailed boats can be hired for a trip into the mangroves at the Chao Fah Pier (rates are negotiable and depend on the time of year, length of time and number of passengers). For this trip it may also be possible to get a rua jaew – the traditional boat used in the Krabi area (including Koh Lanta). Paddles are used instead of a motor (though most now use both).*
Mangroves line the river opposite Krabi. This is a protected area although heavy logging has left most of the forest quite immature. It is worth visiting for the birds and other wildlife including several families of macaques, but ask the boatman to go slowly when in the mangroves so as not to startle the wildlife.

Thanboke Khoranee National Park
① *Entry is ฿400 (the same as for Phanom Bencha National Park and Khao Nor Chu Chi). Take Route 4 towards Phangnga; turn left down Route 4039 for Ao Luk after 45 km. About 2 km down this road there is a sign for the gardens, to the left. By public transport, take a songthaew from Krabi to Ao Luk, and then walk or catch a songthaew.*
Thanboke Khoranee National Park is a beautiful, cool and peaceful forest grove with emerald rock pools, streams and walkways. In the park, swimming is permitted in the upper pool which is near a small nature trail leading up into the limestone cliffs (sturdy shoes are advised).

Laem Sak
① *Turn left as you exit Thanboke Khoranee National Park and continue on Route 4039 into the town of Ao Luk and beyond down a small road to the end of the peninsula.*
Laem Sak juts out from the mainland just north of Ao Luk and makes a good trip before or after a visit to the Thanboke Khoranee National Park. Views back towards the mainland are impressive with a wall of limestone karst in the distance fringed by mangroves. Out to sea and to the west are a group of rocky islands. The fishing pier is working with plenty of activity and there are restaurants serving fresh seafood. This is a good place to watch the fishing boats pass by and eat reasonably priced fish.

Garos Island
① *A tour leaves from a pier down a rough dirt track which can be reached from Ban Thung. (Turn left at Ban Thung, drive about 500 m and take a right turn down the dirt track. There are signs to the pier after about 5 km, and the pier is about 12 km from the main road). Pre-arrange a tour by calling T076-649149. Mr Mos speaks reasonably good English. His partner (Mr Mudura), can also take the tour but speaks much less English, although he knows more about the area having lived there for most of his 60 years.*
Garos Island lies off the coast of mainland Krabi near Ban Thung (before Ao Luk). A day trip in a small long-tailed fishing boat will take you past mangroves and limestone karst islands to Garos, where you can see somewhat sinister prehistoric wall paintings and several caves

used as traditional burial grounds for 'sea gypsies' (Chao Le). It's good for birdwatching and for seeing the traditional lifestyles of fishing communities. The tour, which provides a fantastic lunch cooked on a small island beach where you can also enjoy a swim, is operated by members of the community. Recommended.

Khao Phanom Bencha National Park

ⓘ *Take a motorcycle or other transport out on the main road going towards Trang (past Talat Kao). The turn-off comes before the exit for Wat Tham Sua. Motorcycle theft from the car park at Kho Panom Bencha happens regularly.*

Khao Phanom Bencha National Park provides a magnificent backdrop to the town with a peak rising more than 600 m above the surrounding land. Near the park entrance is the lovely **Huai To Waterfall** best seen between September and December after the monsoon. The drive to the waterfall is pleasant with a distinctly rural feel and the area around the park entrance has some charming trees and open grassland, good for picnics. Park rangers lead treks up to the peak and to a waterfall on the other side. The level of English spoken by rangers can vary – check that you feel comfortable with any potential guide before setting out. The trek takes more than a day as the climb is quite steep.

Khao Nor Chu Chi forest, Crystal Pool and hot springs

ⓘ *Tours can be arranged from most tour offices in town. For self-drive, the turn-off to Khao Nor Chu Chi is just after the major intersection in Khlong Thom town, it's marked. Once you get on to the road to the Crystal Pool and hot springs, you will find clear signposting.*

These sights are all in Khlong Thom district to the south of Krabi province. Khao Nor Chu Chi, which is in the middle of nowhere, is a mere parcel of rainforest surrounded by plantations. It has a forest trail and bungalow-style accommodation (**Morakot Resort**) that was initiated as part of an ecotourism project aimed at conserving the seriously endangered **gurney's pitta**, a bird believed to be extinct; it was re-discovered by the ornithologists Philip Round and Uthai Treesucon. Prince Charles, a keen ornithologist, has also endorsed the fight to save the comically named bird with its flashes of turquoise, red and brown. Gurney's pitta, which favours heavy forest, can be almost impossible to find and visitors have spent two days looking for a glimpse of this jewel-winged bird, which is listed as one of the top 50 endangered birds in the world. The ongoing fear now is that gurney's pitta will become extinct in the next 10 years as deforestation due to rubber and palm-oil plantations continues to dominate over ecological concerns. Tourism could save the day as the Tourism Authority of Thailand gets increasingly involved in the plight of gurney's pitta.

The **Crystal Pool** ⓘ *entrance ₿200*, is visited by the Queen and other royals annually and is so-called because of the exceptional clarity of the water and its emerald colour. The colour derives from mineral deposits that are visible through the water. The pool is shallow and the water buoyant. However, while the pool may look attractive enough, the deposits feel rather crunchy and not particularly pleasant under foot and the slopes are slippery.

A visit to hot springs (₿100) on a hot day may seem rather odd, but the temperature of the water is comfortable and it's a relaxing place to spend some time. The springs have been developed into Thai-style mineral baths with changing rooms, walkway to the original springs and landscaped gardens for the walk through to the river. There are eight of these springs, all with enticing names. They are **Nam Lod** (Water Passing Through), **Cheng Kao** (Valley), **Jorakeh Kao** (White Crocodile), **Nam Tip** (Heavenly Waters) **Nam Krahm** (Indigo Water), **Morakot** (Emerald Water), **Hun Kaeo** (Barking Deer) and **Noi** (Small).

Krabi and around listings

For hotel and restaurant price codes and other relevant information, see pages 12-16.

🛏 Where to stay

Krabi *p86, map p88*

With the rising cost of accommodation at nearby beach resorts and the spectre of burgeoning 4-star complexes on Koh Lanta, Krabi has found a niche in providing low-cost but often friendly and imaginative accommodation for the lower-budget crowd. This has also meant a lot more guesthouses are cropping up, which has forced some of the original dross out.

Generally, the older guesthouses on Ruen-Ruedee Rd are cramped and stuffy; those up the hill and elsewhere in the town are more spacious, better maintained and often cheaper. Note that prices during the high season can double. Another good reason to give the nearby beaches a miss for overnight stays is the food. Krabi town boasts 2 night markets, a morning market, excellent restaurants offering an eclectic range of cuisines and fine cafés with good coffee, tea and pastries.

$$$$ Maritime Park & Spa Resort, 1 Tungfah Rd, T075-620028-35, www.maritimeparkandspa.com. Krabi town's first luxury hotel, about 2 km from town, is off the road towards the bus station. Rooms are large and clean with balconies overlooking huge twin limestone outcrops. Big pool, cycling paths and a pond for canoeing.

$$$ Theparat Travel Lodge and Restaurant, 151-155 Maharat Rd, T075-622048, www.thepparatlodge.com. This white 4-storey offers a/c and fan rooms with satellite TV and mini-bar. It does an extensive range of tours, including one to a King Cobra Show, and has a bakery. Not bad service and clean rooms. Worth checking out but you may find it lacking in atmosphere.

$$$-$$ City Hotel, 15/2-3 Sukhon Rd, T075-621280, www.citykrabi.com. Some a/c, 3-storey hotel for which we have received mixed reports, rooms are clean with attached bathrooms, faces onto one of the quieter streets in town. Rooms can be hot and airless and staff unfriendly. Nothing special, but great location by the night market.

$$ Boon Siam Hotel, 27 Chao Khul Rd, T075-632511-5, www.boonsiamhotel.com. This 5-storey hotel block has a concrete exterior. Rooms are all a/c with hot water, spacious and comfortable, with satellite TV. A bit far out of the town, but still within walking distance of the centre. Does a brisk trade around Chinese New Year. Good value.

$$ Krabi City Sea View Hotel, 77/1 Khongkha Rd, T075-622885-8, www.krabicityseaview.com. Hotel block on the promenade, down the road from the Immigration Department. Great views from the top storey. The lower floor rooms have no view, but all are fitted out with TVs and fridges. The restaurant at the top is a fine place for breakfast if you do not mind the sound of long-tailed boats that are initially part of the charm but soon become piercing.

$$ Krabi River Hotel, 73/1 Khongkha Rd, T075-612321, www.krabiriverhotel.com. A 5-storey hotel with a splendid view of the river, the mangroves and the hustle and bustle of the boats. Rooms are bright, if uninspiring. Recommended.

$$-$ A Mansion, 12/6 Chao Fah Rd, T075-630511-3, www.a-mansionkrabi.com. Hotel-style facilities and prices. The rooms are all a/c and should have hot water. Rooms, though box-like, are clean and smell fresh. This is centrally located. It is possible to ask for a discount on the top-end price and staff can be swayed.

$$-$ Bai Fern Guesthouse, 24/2 Chao Fah Rd, T075-630530, www.baifern-mansion.com. Clean rooms in this well-run guesthouse Some attempt has been

92 • Andaman Coast Krabi & around listings

made to personalize the entrance with an aquarium by the stairs but overall the establishment craves a more intimate touch. However, it is safe, secure and clean with trustworthy family staff who try to help and, if you choose your room carefully, it is decent value. Excellent advice on tours and travel.

$$-$ B&B House and Hostel, 98 Pleugsa Uthit Rd, T075-632315. Rooms are a little sterile and bleak but various options are available, from dorm rooms with shared bathroom, to private a/c rooms. The real bonus here is that there's free Wi-Fi access for all guests.

$$-$ Blue Juice, 1/1 Chaofa Rd, T075-630679. Just before the pier, where the boats leave for Railay, this concrete building houses 16 fan and 2 a/c rooms. The cheaper ones have a shared clean bathroom. The teak floors and whitewashed walls makes this place bright and airy. There's a PADI dive shop and restaurant on the ground floor.

$$-$ Chan Chalay, 55 Uttarakit Rd, T075-620952, www.chanchalay.com. Pleasant white-and-blue building on Uttarakit Rd near the post office. Reasonably priced, clean and airy rooms are set back a little from the road. Serves breakfasts and provides a reliable tour operator service. Recommended.

$$-$ K Guest House, 15-25 Chao Fah Rd, T075-623166. Mainly fan rooms with mosquito nets. 2-storey building with a long wooden veranda balcony along the first floor. Views over town. Wonderful potted foliage along the front intensifies the feeling of being in a hideaway. Wooden floor and ambient lighting. Get a room in the wooden part and not the airless ones with shared bathroom at the back. Restaurant, laundry service and internet. Good bargain. Recommended.

$$-$ Thara Guesthouse, 79/3 Kongkha Rd, T075-630499. Next to the **Krabi City Sea View Hotel**. The rooms are bright and airy, they have fridges and TVs with some overlooking the river. The staff are considerate and everything is well maintained. In this price range – recommended.

$ Andaman Legacy (formerly the Ban Chaofa), 20/1 Chao Fah Rd, T075-630359. This 2-storey hotel is edging towards 2-star standards. It has a Japanese/Ikea feel, with clean, chic and minimalist rooms, some with fan, others with a/c. Rooms overlooking street have small balconies. The owner speaks fairly good English and has put care into his venture. Internet and laundry. Restaurant on ground floor. Recommended.

$ Baan Sabaidee Guest House, 65 Maharat Rd, T075-611981, www.krabi-baansabaidee.com. A/c rooms with TV, Wi-Fi, hot water and private bathrooms. Some rooms lack windows. Friendly, central location. Good value.

$ Europa Café and Guesthouse, 1/9 Soi Ruamjit Rd, T075-620407, www.cafe europa-krabi.com. Under Thai and Danish management, the **Europa Café** has 5 rooms above the restaurant. All rooms are nicely decorated and clean but the smallest lack windows. Shared spotless bathroom with hot water. The restaurant is cosy and inviting, rather like a Danish café, and serves good-quality northern European food (imported meats and cheeses). The owners are enter-taining sources of information – all speak excellent English, German and Danish. The guesthouse closes at 2300 and security is excellent. Recommended, although some may prefer a more laissez-faire approach.

$ Hello KR Mansion, 52/1 Chao Fah Rd, T075-612761, www.krmansionkrabi.com. Some a/c, clean, bright and airy rooms, rooftop balcony for an evening beer and good views. At the quieter top end of town, a 10-min walk from most of the bars and restaurants.

$ P Guesthouse, 34-36 Chaofa Rd, T075-630382. The rather garish colour scheme of lilac and lime green in the hallways, thankfully doesn't continue into the rooms, which are well appointed with TV and hot water showers. Good level of comfort for this price range. Internet and tours on the ground floor.

$ Star Guest House, Khongkha Rd, T075-630234. A charming wooden guesthouse over the top of a small convenience store and tour office, the 7 rooms are tiny, leaving little space for more than a bed, but there is a pleasant balcony with tables and chairs overlooking the night market and the river. Separate bathrooms are downstairs near a small bar in a garden at the back. Recommended.

Restaurants

Krabi *p86, map p88*

$$ Bolero, Oottahanahkit Rd. Italian restaurant run by 2 Thais. Good pizza and pasta. There's also a live band in the evening.

$$ Chao Sua, on Maharat Rd, along the road from the **Ruen Mai** (the sign, with a leopard on it, is in Thai). Considered by many locals to be one of the best restaurants in Krabi. The restaurant itself has a rambling feel and service is sometimes a little haphazard. Excellent Thai food. Barbecued seafood, crispy duck salad and virtually anything that is fried is especially good; the *pad pak pung* is delicious. An original menu with lots of house specialities, for example, the *chao sua* eggs are well worth trying – like a Thai scotch egg although the appearance may put one off.

$$ Pizzeria Firenze, Khongkha Rd. No-nonsense decor, though not much atmosphere. Usual mix of Thai and Italian dishes. Perfectly acceptable when the taste buds have reached overload with one too many papaya salads. Unobtrusive staff.

$$ Ruen Mai, on Maharat Rd well beyond the **Vogue Department Store** up the hill on the left-hand side as you leave the town. Excellent Thai food in a quiet garden. Popular with locals, with good English-language menu and helpful staff. Has a number of southern specialities. Fish dishes are particularly good, as are the salads.

$$-$ Europa Café, 1/9 Soi Ruamjit Rd, T075-620407, www.cafeeuropa-krabi.com.

A favourite with locals and expats. Serves tasty Scandinavian food as well as possibly the best Western breakfast in town.

$$-$ The Seafood Restaurant, Sukhorn Rd, in front of the night market. Offers excellent cheap food but do get there early for the best selection.

$$-$ Viva, 29 Phruksa-Uthit Rd, between Phattana and Issara roads. Serves a range of Italian and Thai food and good fresh coffee (Lavazza). This is a hang-out for travellers having a break from the rigours of no-frills bungalow huts but unfortunately also for the British lager lout and his Thai bargirl travelling companion. The music is often loud. However, reassuring Italian favourites like bruschetta and pizza are good and the place has proper olive oil and grappa and other Italian liquors. Reasonable prices and portions.

$ 89 Café, Chaofa Rd. Very popular place that also serves reasonable Thai and Western food. Nightly movies. Fresh coffees and herbal teas. Free Wi-Fi.

$ Chok Dee, Chao Fah Rd. Reasonable prices, some dishes are delicious and good value for the quality and quantity. TVs with cable and a good selection of movies. Friendly management and staff.

$ I-Oon, 73 Chao Fah Rd, near the **Grand Tower Hotel**. Excellent little café, with good breakfasts and special deals for dinners.

$ Kanchanee Bakery, 12-14 Maharat Soi 6, T075-630501. Spacious, bright and airy café, maybe a little too bright if you have a hangover but the pastries are good and the coffee is superb. Also has newspapers.

$ May and Mark's Restaurant, Ruen-Ruedee Rd, T075-612562. Good information, friendly atmosphere and it attracts expats so the conversation goes beyond predictable backpacker chat. However, this tiny and well-loved hang-out seems to be resting on its laurels. It's not as clean as it could be and the much-touted bread needs to appear more often. Thai, Italian, Mexican and German food, along with the traveller usuals and vegetarian options.

$ Relax Coffee and Restaurant, 7/4 Chaofa Rd, T075-611570. Said to serve some of the best breakfasts and coffee in town. Family run and friendly.

Foodstalls

A **night market** sets up in the early evening on Khlong Kha Rd, along the Krabi river, and serves good seafood dishes. Halal and Chinese dishes can be found here. Instead of opting for *banana roti* it's worth trying the *mataba* as a savoury dish. This is made in the area near the town – slightly spicy, sweet and with a pleasant taste of curry and vegetables. Tasty ice cream and good Thai desserts further up the hill. There should also be a stall selling *khao man kai* (Hainanese chicken with rice), red pork and soups with real ginger and soy sauce to go with the chicken.

A second **night market** is based in the parking lot near the Provincial Electricity Authority office on the road running between Uttarakit and Maharat roads. This market sells fruit at night, at much cheaper prices than the market by the pier. Keep your eyes peeled for mango and sticky rice. It also has an excellent selection of halal stalls, *phat thai*, noodle soups, *khanom jeen* (noodles with sauces and vegetables) and desserts. There is a beer garden in the grounds plus clothes and cheap goods stalls. The hum begins in the early evening, continuing until 2200.

Stall food is also available from the **fresh market** between Srisawat and Sukhon roads, and from scattered places along Uttarakit Rd, facing onto the Krabi river. For a real treat, try the **morning market** on Soi 7 off Maharat Rd. In the middle aisles, are stalls selling extraordinarily complex salads that can be found for around ฿25. Order noodle soup and the stall-owner will set before you a series of tiny dishes that are variously pickled, shredded and dry, prawn-festooned plus baby aubergine salads. There will also be a plate of fresh herbs including mint, coriander, basil and lemon grass. The salads are eaten separately and the herbs added to your noodle soup. All the produce is fresh daily and there is constant dicing, chopping, washing and peeling. The market is packed with other vendors and the only place to eat is at long tables where elbows jostle for space so it is well worth getting up early. The fresh fish stalls are also impressive – if you are going back to a smaller island, you can purchase things like shellfish here and have it cooked back at your bungalow.

The **Vogue Department Store** on Maharat Rd also has an a/c food court on the 3rd floor.

🕯 Bars and clubs

Krabi *p86, map p88*
Bar Chaofa Rd. A laid-back vibe with lots of comfy places to sit and chill. There are also numerous other bars along this road worth checking out.

Kwan Fang Live Music, Sudmongkol Rd, next to **Mixer Pub**. For a sense of weirdness and longing, there is always Kwan Fang with its staple of country and western bands. This out-of-place haunt looks a little like a western saloon with some of the space out in the wide open air. An older crowd than **Mixer**.

Mixer Pub, 100 Sudmongkol Rd. Pulls in a solid local crowd. At **Mixer** they prepare your poison all night with your choice of mixer. Mischievous staff will also videotape you through the stages of drunkenness, table-top dancing and singing. Doubling the fun (or horror), this is later played on a screen, so not a place for shrinking violets. Suits a younger crowd. Great for anthropological viewing and for the brave – unparalleled for shameless exhibitionism.

Nyhavn, across from **Europa**, Soi Ruamjit. They only play jazz and sometimes have live performances. You also get sandwiches and baguettes with roast beef, imported cheese, salami, etc. It has a small garden too.

❄ Festivals

Krabi *p86, map p88*
Boat races on the river can be thrilling,
particularly when the Samsong rum
is flowing.
Nov Andaman Sea Festival in the gardens
beyond the pier (coinciding with *Loi
Krathong*) – a showcase for traditional
dancing and singing from around Thailand.
Also features Andaman handicrafts.

🛍 Shopping

Krabi *p86, map p88*
Books
Many of the guesthouses and tour
companies also run book exchanges.
The Books, 78-80 Maharat Rd, next to
Vogue Department Store.

Clothes and tailoring
There is a tailor on the corner of Issara and
Khongkha roads. Lots of clothes stores on
Phattana, Prachachuen and Uttarakit roads,
mostly selling beachwear.

Department stores and
supermarkets
Sri Nakhorn, opposite the Thai Hotel;
Vogue Department Store, Maharat Rd.
Near the airport are 2 busy a/c
hypermarkets, Tesco-Lotus and Big C.

Souvenirs
Khun B Souvenir, and other souvenir
shops on Khongkha and Uttarakit Rd, sell
a range of souvenirs from all over Thailand
and Southeast Asia.
Thai Silver, opposite Thai Hotel. Sells silver-
ware mostly from Nakhon Sri Thammarat.

🎯 What to do

Krabi *p86, map p88*
Canoeing tours
Europa Café, see Restaurants, above. Offers
a mangrove/canoeing tour but with an

English-speaking guide, which is necessary
if you wish to learn a little en route about
local history and why mangroves are so
important. The tour, which goes near Bor
Thor village close to Ao Luk, takes in caves
and allows for swimming.

Golf
Krabi Golf, 12 Kongka Rd, T08-1538 8608
(mob), www.krabigolftours.com. Booking
agency for golf courses in the region,
including Krabi's Pakasai Country Club, a
scenic and challenging 18-hole course with
tricky water hazards and bunkers, 40 km
south of Krabi Town. Rates include transfers
and club rental.

Tour operators
Tour operators are concentrated on Uttarakit
and Ruen-Ruedee roads and close to the
Chao Fah Pier. There are so many tour and
travel agents, and information is so freely
and widely available, that it is not necessary
to list numerous outfits here. Prices and
schedules are all openly posted and a
30-min walk around town will reveal all.
Krabi Full Moon Tours, 66/17 Moo 5 Sai
Thai, T08-1606 1916, www.krabifullmoon
tours.com. Diving, snorkelling, cultural or
adventure tours. Free hotel transfers.
Krabi Somporn Travel and Service, 72
Khongkha Rd, opposite the old pier, T08-
1895 7873 (mob). This is run by Mrs Tree.
She is friendly and doesn't overcharge.

🚌 Transport

Krabi *p86, map p88*
Air
Krabi Airport is 17 km south of the town.
Air Asia (www.airasia.com) flies to
Bangkok and Kuala Lumpur, THAI
(www.thaiair.com) flies to Bangkok, and
Bangkok Airways (www.bangkokair.com)
flies to Samui. Krabi is also served by
several charter airlines.

Boat

Note that the southwest monsoon months of May-Oct affect all boat timetables. Klong Jirad Pier on Tharua Rd, about 4 km outside town, is now the main ferry departure point, though it's still possible to catch boats at Chao Fah Pier (see Krabi map). During high season (Nov-Apr), there are 4 or 5 boats a day to **Phi Phi** (1½ hrs, ฿350-400; service is halved in low season), and 1 daily to and from **Koh Jum** (1½ hrs, ฿350-400), **Koh Lanta** (2 hrs, ฿350-400) and **Phuket** (2 hrs, ฿850-950); for further details, see www.phuketferryboats.com or ask at any tour desk. In the wet season (May-Oct), a minibus runs from Klong Jirad Pier via 2 short car ferries across Lanta Noi to Ban Sala Dan on Koh Lanta, 2 hrs; contact a tour operator and see Arriving in Koh Lanta, page 121, for details. Tigerline high-speed ferry (www.tigerlinetravel.com) runs a service Nov-Apr between Ao Nang and Langkawi in Malaysia, stopping at Krabi, **Koh Jum**, **Koh Lanta**, **Koh Ngai**, **Koh Kradan**, **Koh Mook**, Had Yao Pier in **Trang** and **Koh Lipe**; you can book any leg of this trip separately to do some island-hopping. Ferries to **Koh Yao Noi** depart from Thalen Pier, near Ao Nang (see West of Krabi map), 8 times daily 0730-1700, with 7 return trips daily 0900-1700. Boats to **Rai Leh** (฿150) depart from Khlong Kha Pier (see Krabi map). The boatman will wait till the boat fills before departing, or you can charter it for ฿1500.

Bus

Numerous evening a/c, VIP and non-a/c connections with **Bangkok**'s Southern bus terminal, 16 hrs. There is also a service that departs for Bangkok's Khaosan Rd at 1600. Regular a/c and non-a/c connections with **Phuket**, 3 hrs via **Phangnga**, 1½ hrs. Minivan to Phuket, daily 0900, 1130, 1430, pick-up from guesthouse, ฿350. Regular connections with **Surat Thani**, 3 hrs and **Trang**, a/c minibuses to **Hat Yai**. Tickets and information about bus connection (both public buses and private tour buses) available from travel agents.

To **Koh Samui** (฿500) and **Koh Phangnan** (฿550), bus and boat, 1100 and 1600. One connection daily with Koh Tao at 1600, ฿850.

International connections with Malaysia and Singapore By a/c mini-bus to **Singapore**, 0700, ฿1000; **Kuala Lumpur**, 0700, ฿1000 (there's also a VIP bus at 1200), **Penang**, 0700 and 1100, 7-11 hrs, ฿750) and Langawi, 0700 (฿850). Buses stop in **Hat Yai**, for passport checks. Some travel agents charge ฿10 'border service', avoid paying if possible.

Motorbike and jeep

Scooters cost ฿150-200 per day. Jeeps and cars, ฿900-1500 per day.

Songthaew

Songthaews drive through town, stopping at various places such as Phattana Rd. They also run to the bus station at Talaat Kao, 5 km from town. They charge ฿40-60 0600-1830, and ฿50-70 after dark.

West of Krabi

The road to the coast from Krabi winds for 15 km past limestone cliffs, a large reclining Buddha, rubber stands and verdant forest. Arriving at the coast in the evening, with the setting sun turning the limestone cliffs of Ao Nang a rich orange and the sea interspersed with precipitous limestone crags, is a beautiful first impression.

The coast west of Krabi consists of the beach areas of Ao Nang and Hat Nopparat Thara (which lie 18 km and 22 km respectively to the west of Krabi town), and also Ao Phra Nang, Ao Rai Leh East, Ao Rai Leh West and Ao Ton Sai.

More than half the native population are now Muslim Thais, discreetly signalled by the absence of pork on restaurant menus, even though you will not hear the call of the muzzein at prayer times. Buying alcohol in public at a beach bar should be disallowed, but in typical Thai-style, bar staff are Buddhist in Muslim-run and owned operations, which nicely gets around that dilemma. It should be remembered that topless sunbathing is very definitely frowned upon. It is rare to see Thai women even in bikinis at the beach – due to modesty and also an abhorrence of tanning. But, while most sun-starved Westerners come to Thailand to sunbathe and indeed are encouraged, with ever-present deckchairs, cold towels and beach masseurs, it is still a good idea to cover up when you leave the beach for restaurants. These establishments will often be staffed by Thai-Muslims even if the bars aren't. If you get too hot and bothered by this option, there's always takeaway.

Ao Nang, Nopparat Thara and Khlong Muang → For listings, see pages 102-109.

Ao Nang is neither sweeping nor glorious and has coarse dirty yellow sand intermingled with millions of broken shells that are unpleasant to walk on. One end of the beach is filled with kayaks and long-tailed boats for transporting tourists to nearby islands and it is these motorized long-tailed boats that punctuate the quiet with ferocious regularity. The concrete wall behind the beachfront, the construction of which initially excited much antagonism, saved Ao Nang from the greater force of the tsunami and has since been rebuilt. Behind this is the commercial outcrop of Ao Nang itself which has taken up the whole of the beach road and swarmed inland. The town itself is a generic collection of souvenir shops, small resorts and bad restaurants – it is mind-boggling to think that just 20 years ago, Ao Nang was a sleepy fishing hamlet. On the whole, there is little to do in today's Ao Nang, including eating. The food is dreadful; if you don't count the gas-oven pizzerias of which there are far too many, even something simple like a fruit salad or toast is substandard and often served grudgingly. The whole set-up utterly lacks the shameless

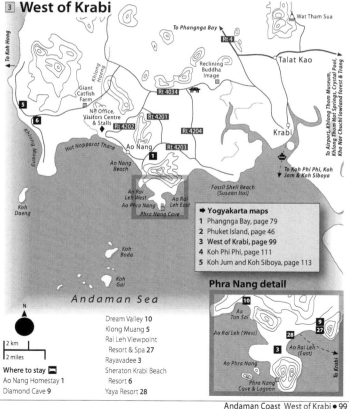

West of Krabi

→ **Yogyakarta maps**
1 Phangnga Bay, page 79
2 Phuket Island, page 46
3 West of Krabi, page 99
4 Koh Phi Phi, page 111
5 Koh Jum and Koh Siboya, page 113

Phra Nang detail

Where to stay
Ao Nang Homestay 1
Diamond Cave 9
Dream Valley 10
Klong Muang 5
Rai Leh Viewpoint
  Resort & Spa 27
Rayavadee 3
Sheraton Krabi Beach
  Resort 6
Yaya Resort 28

exuberance of Patong or the charm of Kata Noi and the tourists reflect this. However, there are pleasant features in spite of all this, which makes the current development even more regrettable. The beachfront is lined with coconut palms and mango trees with limestone walls at one end and lovely views of the islands on the horizon. Ao Nang also has good facilities for diving, windsurfing, fishing and tours to the surrounding islands. It is still relatively quiet and the beach water is fine for swimming, out of the monsoon season, with calm waters and beautiful limestone scenery. But it is really the surrounding beaches, coves, caves and grottoes that make the place bearable.

At **Hat Nopparat Thara**, about 3 km northwest of Ao Nang, is a deliciously long stretch of soft, pale beige sand covered in tiny seashells and lined with tall casuarinas at the beachside. To the back are paperbark forests. Locals used to call this place 'Hat Khlong Haeng' or dried canal beach because at low tide the canal dries up, leaving a long beach. Khlong Haeng is also the name of the village closest to the beach – around 900 m away. This 5-km-long beach is divided by a river with the side closest to Ao Nang being the most developed as it is bordered by a main road. The other side, which is lousy with sandflies, can only be accessed by boat or by a dirt track from the road to Khlong Muang.

Khlong Muang, a more remote stretch of average beach, is attracting ever-greater interest from upmarket developers who tout the hotels on the shore as having 'private beaches' (despite these being shallow and rocky) because there is only indirect public access to them once the hotels are up. Many of the bungalows here are closed during the monsoon season and there is little in the way of dining or nightlife outside the resorts.

There are a couple of interesting places on the road in from Ao Nang. The main one, about 8 km before Khlong Muang, is the **Giant Catfish Farm** ① *daily 0800-1800, ฿50*. Set up by Nina, an American expat and her Thai husband, Paichit, a visit here is a genuinely eccentric and fascinating experience. More like an adventure zoo than anything else – there are crocodiles, tarantulas, monitor lizards and ponds of huge catfish – the entire place is set up amid the jungle with gorgeous waterfalls and refreshing pools on hand should you require a dip. They also run a very popular restaurant.

Nopparat Thara has three distinct sections. The first is closest to Ao Nang and is where most of the bungalow and hotel developments have taken place and where most Western tourists wander. This area has limited shade. Further down the beach near the **Hat Nopparat Thara-Mu Ko Phi Phi National Park office** ① *0830-1630*, is the area where most Thai tourists congregate – this area is well shaded with picnic grounds under the casuarina trees. The final section is across the canal, adjacent to the national parks office and by the harbour used by local fishermen. This stretch of beach is home to affordable bungalow resorts, and has a completely different character to Ao Nang and the other parts of Nopparat Thara. These bungalows are accessible by boat across the canal and by road. Although it is a pleasant place to rest with great views and more peace and quiet than in Ao Nang, the water is very shallow, making swimming during anything except high tide next to impossible. Well inhabited with crustaceans and other sea creatures you never know what you might step on, so wear sandals if you decide to paddle in the shallowest waters. Some guests even wear shoes. But there are some sweet sights to be had here – monkeys, kingfishers and sea eagles at the west end of the beach – as well as caves to explore. At low tide it is also possible to walk out to some of the islands in the bay. In these ways, it is an ideal place for children. ▸▸ *See What to do, page 107, for details on snorkelling, canoeing and kayaking.*

In the opposite direction, beyond the limestone crags, is drop-dead gorgeous Phra Nang, see page 101, and the beaches (and accommodation) of boho-chic Rai Leh, which has been visited by the likes of Mick Jagger, Colin Farrel, and Fatboy Slim who gave an impromptu set.

Susaan Hoi (Fossil Shell Beach)

① *Take the white songthaews from the corner of Phattana and Maharat Rd in Krabi. ฿50. Coincide your visit with low tide when more pavement is exposed.*

Susaan Hoi, literally 'shell cemetery', lies 20 km southwest of Krabi near the village of Laem Pho (not far from Ao Nang Beach) and 5 km east of Ao Nang. Great slabs of what looks like concrete are littered along the shoreline but on closer inspection turn out to be countless fossilized freshwater shells, laid down 40 million years ago. It is one of only three such cemeteries in the world; the others are in the US and Japan. It is an impressive and curious sight.

Koh Boda and Koh Gai

Koh Boda is 30 minutes by boat from Ao Nang. It is hugely popular with snorkellers for its wonderfully clear water. Round-trip excursions last five hours. The nearby Koh Gai is also a 30-minute boat trip from Ao Nang. Ao Thalen combines the curious and wonderful shapes of the mangrove, with extraordinary limestone crags, cave paintings, monkey troupes, and an overall sense of mystery in the gorges that is quite magical. ▸▸ *See Where to stay, page 105, and What to do, page 108.*

Phra Nang and Rai Leh → *For listings, see pages 102-109.*

Phra Nang is the peninsula to the south of Ao Nang. There are no roads on Phra Nang, which lends it a secret-hideaway ambience – albeit an exclusive one as all the land behind the beach is occupied by the **Rayavadee Resort**. The point consists of **Rai Leh West** and **Ao Phra Nang** on the west side and **Rai Leh East** on the east. Further west from Rai Leh West is **Ao Ton Sai**. Rai Leh has become something of a mecca for rock climbers, partly because limestone is porous so that the water cuts into it and makes natural grips ideal for climbers. But, equally alluring, say climbers, is the combination of landscape, climate and rock, which rarely come together in such harmonious splendour.

The best beach is on the west side – a truly picture-postcard affair. However, the east coast beach is still amazing at low tide in a sci-fi end-of-the-world way as the landscape transforms into a 300-m stretch of sinister shining mud. When Rai Leh East is not a mudbath, there are still the mangroves lining the beach so that it is fairly impossible to get any swimming in here. Rai Leh East also acts as a pier for taxi boats to and from Krabi and you will often spy tourists slogging across the mud with luggage over their heads. Pretty Rai Leh West, also knows as 'Sunset Beach', is about 10 minutes' walk away from the other beach – this means there is no escaping the daytime noises of the long-tailed boats although the evenings are delightful. There is also good snorkelling and swimming in archetypal crystal-clear water. The limestone rock formations are spectacular, and there are interesting caves with stalagmites and stalactites to explore though they require patience and fortitude as the paths are not always straightforward nor easygoing. At the southern extremity of the bay is a mountain cave (**Outer Princess Cave**) on Phra Nang Beach that is dedicated to the goddess of the area and considered 'her summer palace'. Here, you may be delighted to find an abundance of wooden and stone penises, many in wonderful colours of candy pink, lime green and pillar box red. It is believed local fishermen put the penises there to bribe the goddess into granting them plenty of fish on the sea. Be that as it may, many non-sailors also like to drop by a penis or two and the cave is suitably endowed. Near the penis cave are lots of monkeys that are rather friendly and several beachside stalls selling trinkets, clothes, beer and snacks like barbecued corn on the cob. There is also one outrageously priced bar that looks totally out of place. If you feel you must make an effort, there is Sa Phra Nang (Princess Pool) to explore. This is a pond inside the cliff that can be accessed along a cave trail at the side of the mountain. You can get to the top of the mountain if you keep climbing. There's a walkway to Rai Leh east from Ao Phra Nang if you care to visit the Inner Princess Cave, better known as the Diamond Cave, which is three caverns, one of which has a waterfall of quartz-like frozen amber. Entry is ฿40 or ฿20 for kids.

There are several climbing schools (see What to do, page 109), as the tower karst formations offer some truly outstanding climbing opportunities along with spectacular views.

Rai Leh is suffering from being too popular. The area available for development is small, sandwiched between limestone cliffs and crags, and already the bungalows are cheek-by-jowl in places. It is also going upscale with the recent appearances of superstars, so prices are starting to soar. On the whole, the entertainment here remains coffee houses/bars/bookshops during the day and low-key parties on the east side at night – still more reggae than rave. Electricity, ATMs and high-speed internet have now arrived on Rai Leh but foodies will be seriously disappointed as the closest and most patronized outpost for food is Ao Nang.

Ao Ton Sai, north of Ao Rai Leh West, largely appeals to climbers who can manage far more than five-minute walks. Climbing is the main activity here, followed by frisbee, volleyball and assorted refreshments à la *Big Lebowski*.

West of Krabi listings

For hotel and restaurant price codes and other relevant information, see pages 12-16.

◉ Where to stay

Ao Nang, Nopparat Thara and Khlong Muang *p99, map p99*
High-season (Nov-May) room rates may be as much as double (or more) the low-season (Jun-Oct) rates.

Accommodation in Ao Nang seems to have settled down into 2 broad groups – fairly faceless 4- to 5-star hotels with a pool or 2- to 3-star hotels without a pool. Since the difference is negligible and no one is there for the museums, the pool question does need to be considered – we've tried to list the best in each category. Most of the places here are populated with package tourists. Rates are slashed May-Oct.

Ao Nang
$$$$ Emerald Garden Beach Resort, 90 Moo 3, T075-637692, www.krabiemerald.

net. Italian-owned timeshare property that rents out 20 villa cottages. Up on the hill away from the beach in a quiet location with 2 pools, a gym and bar plus good facilities (excellent bathrooms with bidets). Variable decorations. A bit far from everything, but represents pretty good value for the facilities.
$$$$ Golden Beach Resort, 254 Moo 2, T075-637870-4, www.goldenbeach-resort. com. This has one of the best locations on the beach with good views across to the islands. Rooms are in cute green-roofed, white bungalows and low-rise hotel blocks. Pool and well-tended gardens. The Thai restaurant (Thai Thai) is probably the best in Ao Nang.
$$$$ Pavilion Queen's Bay, 56/3 Moo 3, T075-637611-18, www.pavilionhotels. com/queensbay. This huge hotel of more than 100 rooms is certainly luxurious and has very friendly staff, but is hampered with some silly design flaws, and lack of attention to detail. International, Thai

and Japanese restaurants (the last highly exclusive with top-class sushi on offer), very large spacious rooms but somewhat cramped bathrooms. Luxurious spa – one of the best features of the hotel and open to non-residents too. All the other facilities expected from a hotel like this, including a 3-layered swimming pool. Good views. Big discounts online.

$$$$ Princeville Resort, 164 Moo 2, T075-637971, www.aonangprinceville.com. The rooms are spacious and decorated in warm, rustic tones, all overlooking the swimming pool. De luxe rooms have a bathtub. Restaurant and massage areas are hidden in thick foliage.

$$$$-$$$ Beach Terrace Hotel, 154 Moo 2, T075-637180, www.krabibeachterrace. com. All rooms have a/c, fridge and TV. The rooms without balconies have small windows and are a little dark. Try to get a sea-view room. Offers better value than before, now that it's been refurbished. Swimming pool and massage area.

$$$$-$$$ Pakasai Resort, 88 Moo 3, T075-637777, www.pakasai.com. Has all the facilities that you would expect at this price range. Nice design features such as a bathtub on the balcony in the Andora rooms.

$$$$-$$$ Royal Nakara, 155/4-7 Moo 3, T075-661441, www.royalnakara.com. Built on the edge of a steep drop, the rooms are reached by descending several flights of stairs. All are very light and spacious, with modern furniture, TV and DVD player. Premium rooms have pantry kitchen and dining area. Infinity pool. Recommended.

$$$$-$$$ Thai Village Resort, 260 Moo 2, T075-637710-9, www.krabithaivillage.com. This huge red-winged traditional Thai-roofed hotel shoots out of the forest in a rather predatory way. 3 large swimming pools, pool bar and children's pool. Large dull buffets and unadventurous food. At night you can hear the crickets.

$$$$-$$$ Vogue Resort and Spa, 244 Moo 2, T075-637635, www.oamhotels.com/ vogue-resort-spa. One of the more appealing of the luxury hotels. Nestled into mountain foliage, this complex sprawls beautifully through landscaped gardens and has a very nicepool. It is especially good for honeymooners who like to go from the bath to the poolside.

$$$ Ao Nang Beach Home, 132 Moo 2, T075-695260, www.aonangbeachhome krabi.com. Offers large, well appointed a/c rooms, with spacious bathrooms and nice touches such as beach mats in the rooms. Laminate teak furniture, modern and comfortable. Restaurant overlooking the beach. Recommended for price (includes breakfast) and location.

$$$ Ao Nang Village, 49/3 Moo 2, T075-637544, www.aonangvillage.com. Quite a walk from the beach. Concrete a/c bungalows and rooms in a 2-storey building. Basic but very clean. Quiet garden setting. **Me Me** offers a similar, slightly cheaper set-up next door.

$$$ Ben's House, next to **Royal Nakara**, T075-661595, www.aonang-benshouse. com. Various styles of rooms located over 6 floors, the rooms on the top floors have a sea cottage feel and are the best designed. For a modern hotel with swimming pool and a good range of facilities, it's not bad for the price.

$$$ Harvest House, 420/18-19 Moo 2, T075-695256, www.harvesthousekrabi.com. Rooms are comfortably furnished with balcony, a/c, cable TV, bath. It is quite a walk to the beach from here but these rooms are very good value.

$$$-$$ Baan Pimphaka Bungalows, 115/2 Moo 3, T075-637562, www.baan pimphaka.com. Comfortable chalet-style rooms with hot water showers and large comfy beds. Homely restaurant and friendly staff. Discounts available for longer stays. Recommended.

$$$-$$ Blue Village, 105 Moo 3, T075-637887, www.bluevillagekrabi.com. Fantastic layout, with huts and palm trees growing through the roofs, futon-style beds and sunken bathrooms. Good, cheap food. Recommended.

$$$-$ Ao Nang Home Stay, 262/2 Leela Valley, T08-1732 1273 (mob), www.aonang homestay.com. Fan and a/c rooms, all with balconies and mini-fridges. Quite a distance from the sea but cheap.

$$$-$ Green View Village Resort, 279 Moo 2, T075-637481 www.greenview aonang.com. Attractive wood and brick and a/c bungalows in a garden setting with swimming pool. Some family villas. Wi-Fi, restaurant. Free shuttle service to the beach, about a 15-min walk away. Excellent value.

$$ Dream Garden House, 86/2 Moo 2, T075-637338, www.krabidir.com/dream gardenhostel. Some of the 16 rooms here have balconies which look onto walls so don't believe the advertorials. Quite noisy at night with a bar nearby but the service is good.

$$ Scandinavian Residence, 278 Moo 2, T075-695622. www.scandinavianresidence. net. Well-run small guesthouse just outside the main centre of Ao Nang. There's a petite pool, some nice shaded garden areas, plus each room is a/c and comes with TV and en suite. The guesthouse serves food and has a bar as well. A good deal, though you might need your own transport.

Nopparat Thara

$$$$-$$$ Emerald Bungalow, catch a boat from Nopparat Thara pier across the estuary, westwards, T08-1892 1072 (mob). This place is very peaceful with around 40 large, fan bungalows and some a/c rooms. Restaurant. Location is the high point; it is south facing so you get a good sunset and there is also a river to swim in at the end of the beach. Can arrange transfers for you. Friendly staff.

$$$ Jinnie's Place, 101 Moo 3, T075-661 398, www.jinniesplace.com. Red brick a/c bungalows have bags of character and charm. The bathrooms are possibly the largest in Krabi and have baths and even a garden. There's a children's pool and a main pool. Recommended.

$$$ Na-Thai Resort, near Nopparat Thara and Phi Phi Island National Park Headquarters and the Montessori School, T075-637752. It's 5-10 mins by motorbike or car from Hat Phra Ao Nang and Hat Nopparat Thara. Free pick up. Surrounded by oil palms and rubber trees, this is a husband and wife set-up – Gerard and Walee who have more of an eco-friendly approach to running things. There are bungalows and apartments set around a small pool that you can swim in at night and a restaurant where they can trot out Western favourites or excellent Thai food. Not the most imaginative place, but great attitude and good for a more isolated getaway. Prices depend on the month. Recommended.

$$$-$$ Lakeside Bungalow, 119 Moo 3, T075-637751, www.aonanglakeside.com. Typically designed bamboo huts in a very quiet area. Facilities include TV. A/c rooms are also available. Restaurant and lounge area where football matches are often shown.

$$$-$ Cashew Nut Bungalows, 96 Moo 3, T075-637560. Concrete bungalows set amongst cashew trees (hence the name). Family run. Rooms range from fan and cold water, to a/c with hot water. Basic but clean. Very quiet. 5 mins from the beach.

$$-$ Nopparat Thara and Phi Phi Islands National Park Headquarters, PO Box 23, Muang District, Krabi 8100, T075-637436 or make reservations at the Royal Forestry Department in Bangkok, T02-5790529. Has some bungalows and camping facilities but you have to make reservations ahead of time.

Khlong Muang

New accommodation is springing up along this stretch of beach with some big players moving in.

$$$$ Phulay Bay, 111 Moo 3 Nongthalay, Tubkaak Beach, just north of Khlong Muang, T075-628111, reserve.ritzcarlton. com/phulay_bay. Dubbed a '6-star' hotel,

Phulay Bay is a Ritz-Carlton Reserve and one of Krabi's priciest resorts, with 54 huge, almost imposing villas with private plunge pools, 24-hr butler service and a ridiculously lavish spa. Caters to weddings and honeymooners. This is about the best you can find in the area, if you can afford it, but the beach here is not the most appealing.

$$$$ Sheraton Krabi Beach Resort, 155 Moo 2, Nong Thale, T075-628000, www.sheraton.com/krabi. A large and luxurious resort. It's very well planned with nice gardens and good beach access. You can opt for either hotel rooms or bungalows – both are of a very high standard and include all the usual top-end trimmings. 2 large pools, kids play area, elephants and an excellent wood-fired pizza restaurant. Lots of other facilities, including a spa, gym, etc.

$$$-$$ Klong Muang Inn, 36/13 Moo 3, Nong Thale, T08-9971 9938 (mob), www.klong-muang-inn.com. All rooms are clean with a/c and en suite in this small guesthouse – go for the rooms on the upper floors. Set about 200 m from the sea and run by German expat, Freddy.

Ban Nanteen

$$ Home Stay Ban Nateen, Bannateen 4/2 Moo 4, T075-637390, www.homestay inthailand.com. Excellent programme, run and managed entirely by the friendly local Muslim villagers. You can choose to stay either in a small compound of bungalows or in other dwellings scattered throughout the village. Accommodation is basic but the rates include all meals plus one daily activity such as cooking, fishing, tuk-tuk tours. Awesome value and highly recommended.

Koh Boda *p101*

$$$-$$ Poda Island Resort, 232 Moo 2, T075-637030-5, www.podaislandresort. com. Concrete and bamboo fan bungalows. Restaurant, Western toilets and not particularly friendly staff. No electricity overnight. Camping is possible on the

island. Quiet after the day trippers leave, but sadly the beach is left full of trash.

Phra Nang and Rai Leh *p101*

There is not much to distinguish between the various lower-end bungalow operations at Rai Leh. The cheapest rooms are found at Ao Ton Sai and Rai Leh East, which has no beach and faces out on mangroves and mudflats. The area has been turned into an unpleasant building site as some of the more quaint establishments are replaced by concrete chicken sheds. Rai Leh East is a short walk from the beaches at Phra Nang and Rai Leh West. Many of the owners have crammed too many structures onto too small an area, and others have grown too large (with 40 or more cottages) and service has consequently suffered. All have their own restaurants, bars and often minimarts, tour desks and telephones. Many also have exchange services often offering poor rates.

Rai Leh West

A beautiful beach but huts have been built too closely together, making for overcrowded conditions and basic (but not cheap) accommodation.

$$$$ Railay Bay Resort, West/East Rai Leh, T08-1915 2700, www.railaybayresort.com. Occupies a long thin slice of land stretching from Rai Leh east to west. Most of the recently renovated a/c rooms and cottages sit in distinctively styled zones amid the central gardens. Includes 2 pools and one of West Rai Leh's most popular terrace restaurants. A good option but very pricey at its top end.

$$$$-$$$ Railei Beach Club, Rai Leh West, T08-6685 9359 (mob), www.railei beachclub.com. Hugging the cliffs at the northern corner of Rai Leh West, these traditional Thai-style teak houses are private holiday homes that the owners let out. Each unique, they range from cute open-plan affairs that sleep 2 up to rambling multi-wing ones that can sleep 8 or more. Kitchens and bathrooms, Wi-Fi, but no a/c. Public amenities are slim – no pool or restaurant – but the quiet natural setting humming with critters is blissful. Bring cooking supplies. Recommended

Phra Nang headland
$$$$ Rayavadee, T075-620740-3, www.rayavadee.com. 98 2-storey pavilions and 5 villas set amid luscious grounds studded with coconut palms in this luxurious, isolated getaway. Every service imaginable is provided in the beautifully furnished pavilions, including lovely, exclusive bathrooms and bedtime chocolates. Some rooms have private pools. The strikingly large main pool faces Rai Leh beach. Restaurants include the **Krua Phranang**, on the renowned Phra Nang beach, where the Mieng Kana, small parcels of kale leaves filled with lime, chilli, shallots, ginger, cashew and shrimp, are to be savoured. Indulge in the magnificent spa and the **Rayavadee** signature massage, including a hot herb compress. Excursions are offered. Due to its location, bordering 3 beaches and caves, it feels more like an adventure than just a hotel. Price includes airport transfer. Recommended.

Rai Leh East
$$$$-$$$ Rai Leh Viewpoint Resort and Spa, T075-819 428, T08-5629 7070 (mob), www.viewpointresort66.com. Large upgraded resort. Friendly, well run and clean. Good restaurant, mini-mart, internet and pool. Some of the best bungalows.
$$$ Diamond Cave, 36 Moo 1, T075-622 589, www.diamondcave-railay.com. Next to a huge limestone outcrop. Almost monstrous number (for the space) of solidly built and clean concrete a/c bungalows set on a hill on the sunrise side of Rai Leh peninsula. Pool, massage and minimart. Clean and secure.
$$$-$$ Ya Ya Resort, T075-622998-9, yaya-resort.com. Formerly the long-running and somewhat infamous Ya Ya bungalows, it was taken over by Railay Princess Resort

in late 2011 and revamped into a 'budget wing' of the larger resort. The 2-3 storey wooden block structures, with small fan and a/c rooms, remain but have been spruced up and given a spring clean. Though it looks to have improved from its notoriously filthy rat-infested days', it remains far from certain if Ya Ya's upgrade justifies its higher prices.

Ao Ton Sai
Ao Ton Sai has transformed from a hippy hang-out to a building site, with a resort set for development across a large central section of the beachfront. The restaurants here are generally poor, even for the area, and most of the accommodation is a 5-min walk uphill behind the sand.
    Cheaper rooms can be found further up the hill at **Andaman Nature**, **Krabi Mountain View** and **Phoenix Bungalow** resorts.
$$$-$$ Dream Valley, T075-621772. Revolutionized in recent years, with a field full of concrete, characterless a/c bungalows that have hot water and patios where there used to be a few bamboo huts.

🍴 Restaurants

Ao Nang, Nopparat Thara and Khlong Muang *p99, map p99*
Food in Ao Nang and Rai Leh remains dominated by sloppy Western and tourist Thai restaurants with a silly number of pizzerias. As one would expect, the best food available at Ao Nang is fresh seafood. Almost all the restaurants along the beach-front road, and then lining the path north-west towards the **Krabi Resort**, serve BBQ fish, chilli crab, steamed crab, prawns and so on. There is little to choose between these restaurants – they tend to serve the same dishes, prepared in the same way, in rather lacklustre sauces; food does not come close to the standards set by the better restaurants in Krabi. Most lay their catches out on icefor customers to peruse – snapper, shark, pomfret, tiger prawns and

glistening crabs. Those concerned about conserving the marine environment should avoid the shark and coral fish which usually come at a much higher price than the tag you see on the fish. Evening is certainly the best time to eat, drink and relax, with the sun illuminating the cliffs and a breeze taking the heat off the day.

$$$-$$ Freddy and Jurgen, next to the Klong Muang, see Where to stay, above. Thai and German food, along with pizza and a massive array of beer should keep most people happy.

$$$-$$ Giant Catfish Farm, 8 km before Khlong Muang. Great little restaurant nestling beside the eccentric adventure zoo set up by American expat, Nina. Combine a visit there with a meal here. Excellent, affordable Thai food. Recommended.

$$$-$$ Lavinia restaurant, on the Beach Front Rd, next to Encore Café and Kodak Shop, Ao Nang. Great view of beach, good selection of bread but London prices for a sandwich. Service slow and scatty.

$$$-$$ Sushi Hut and Grill, Ao Nang Beach Rd, Ao Nang. See if you can get uni (sea urchin) or toro (tuna belly). It also does tempura, miso soups, tofu steak in mirin, edamame and all the standards. Steak and Thai food also available.

$$ Azzurra, Beach Front Rd, ao Nang. Can become rather dusty during the drier months of Jan-Mar. Good unpredictable Italian fare with decent ingredients.

There's a cluster of open-air thatched-roof shacks all selling fresh seafood and Thai dishes on the Airport Rd, near the Ao Nang Paradise Resort. Prices (**$$-$**) are only marginally cheaper than more tourist-orientated places but they have a more local ambience.

🕙 Bars and clubs

Ao Nang, Nopparat Thara and Khlong Muang *p99, map p99*

Plenty to choose from but they tend to open and close with great frequency.

A 'bar-beer' scene has opened up off the beachfront in Hat Nopparat Thara behind the front row of dive and souvenir shops and is complete with massage services, pink lights, cocktails, etc.

Fisherman Bar, Ao Nang. for a drink on the beach. Flexible closing hours.

Full Moon Bar, formerly the Full Moon House. Tried and trusted and right in the centre of Ao Nang.

Irish Rover and Grill, 247/8 Moo 2, Ao Nang. Theme pub but still, sometimes, Guinness is good for you. Good selection of draughts and cider, too. Well run, with a fairly high standard of bar food, including chilli con carne, toasties, pies and chops. Does roast dinner but this can be heavy for a tropical climate. Live sports. Recommended.

Luna Beach Bar, Hat Nopparat Thara, Ao Nang. Has fantastic cocktail prices (for Ao Nang anyway), and a very loose interpretation of closing hours. Can get raucous with Happy Hour becoming unhappy hours.

🛍 Shopping

Ao Nang, Nopparat Thara and Khlong Muang *p99, map p99*

Shops open on the beachfront at Ao Nang during the evening selling garments, leather goods, jewellery and other products made specifically for the tourist market. There isn't much that's unusual, except for batik 'paintings', usually illustrating marine scenes, which are made in small workshops here.

🎯 What to do

Ao Nang, Nopparat Thara and Khlong Muang *p99, map p99*
Canoeing

Sea Canoe, T076-528839, www.seacanoe. net, hen@seacanoe.net. Offers small-scale sea canoeing trips (self-paddle), exploring the overhanging cliffs and caves and the rocky coastline of Phra Nang, Rai Leh and nearby islands.

Sea Canoe boasts about its strong environmental policies, including restrictions on the number of people per trip, and no foam or plastic-packaged lunches. Some of the other operators have adopted these policies too, particularly in the Ao Thalen area where there is a small group of companies operating in amicable fashion. The best thing is probably to spend some time chatting to your prospective guide to see if you like the way they operate and whether you are happy with the level of English they speak. You should also try to get some guarantees on the number of people on the tour. Sea Kayak Krabi, on the front, T075-630270/T08-9724 8579 (mob), www.sea kayak-krabi.com, has been known to promise no more than 10 participants but then take up to 30. Remember too that sea canoes in Thailand are open, so you should either wear a strong waterproof sun block or go for long trousers/sleeves and a hat.

Diving
Ao Nang Divers, 208/2-3 Moo 2, T075-637246, www.aonang-divers.com. Easily the best in town. A 5-star PADI dive centre on the main street.
Poseidon, 23/27 Moo 2, Ban Ao Nang, T075-637 263, www.poseidon-krabi.com.

Muay Thai (Thai boxing)
There is a well-supported stadium for Thai boxing in the Ao Nang area. The old one was next to **Ao Nang Paradise**. This much larger stadium which attracts national standard boxers is set back from Hat Nopparat Thara beach by about 300 m.

Rock climbing
King Climbers has an office down towards Phra Nang Inn.

Golf
Phookeethra Golf, 200 Moo 3, Khlong Muang, T075-627800, www.phokeethragolf. com. A 9-hole course operated by the neighbouring Sofitel Krabi resort.

Shooting
Ao Nang Shooting Range, 99/9 Moo 2, Ao Nang Rd, Ao Nang, T075-695555. You can fire shotguns, Berettas, semi-automatics and Magnums at this well-run shooting range. Prices start at around ฿890 for a full clip.

Therapies
Most luxury hotels are now offering spa facilities.
Pavilion Queen's Bay, see Where to stay, above. Offers the best in-hotel spa. Others offer the services one might expect, but don't have that aura of peace and tranquillity that leads to a truly pampering experience.
Tropical Herbal Spa, 20/1 Moo 2, Ao Nang, www.tropicalherbalspa.com. A glorious day spa, a little away from the beach but set in beautiful gardens and mostly open to the air.

Tour operators
Ao Nang Ban Lae Travel, close to Krabi Resort. Runs boat tours to various islands and beaches, including Rai Leh and Phi Phi.
Aonang Travel and Tour, 43 Moo 2, Ao Nang Beach, T075-637152, www.aonang travel.co.th. Specializes in half- and 1-day kayaking and island boat tours.
AP Travel & Tour, Beachfront Rd, T075-637 342, www.aptravelkrabi.com. Offers a range of tours to various islands, temples and short 'jungle tours' – very helpful and friendly though not terribly exciting.

Koh Boda and Koh Gai *p101*
Canoeing and sea kayaking
Although the trips to areas like Koh Hong with its coral reefs are appealing, in some ways the trips to the limestone karst and mangroves along the mainland are more exotic and interesting. It's also worth remembering that coral reefs are only really wonderful when you snorkel and are thus able to catch the sealife spectacle just inches below the water.

Phra Nang and Rai Leh *p101*
Rock climbing
Hot Rock Climbing School, East Railay (between Yaya resort and Bhu Nga Thani resort, www.railayadventure.com, T075-662 245. Courses for climbers of all levels.

○ **Transport**

Ao Nang, Nopparat Thara and Khlong Muang *p99, map p99*
Boat
Regular long-tailed boats to **Rai Leh** during high season (Nov-Apr), from the beach opposite Sea Canoe, 15 mins, approx ฿150-250 depending on number of passengers. The *Ao Nang Princess* links Ao Nang with Rai Leh and **Koh Phi Phi** daily during high season. The boat departs from Ao Nang at 0900 returning at 1630. This is subject to change and depends on the number of travellers. In high season, Nov-Mar, there are at least 2 daily ferry trips direct to Phuket and one to Koh Lanta. Arrange a ticket through your guesthouse.

Jeep and motorbike hire
Jeep hire (฿900-1200 per day) and motorbike hire (฿250 per day) are available from travel agents and guesthouses.

Songthaew
Regular white *songthaew* connections with **Krabi**, 30 mins, ฿40, or ฿80 after dark. For Krabi, *songthaews* leave from the eastern end of the beach road, opposite Sea Canoe. The service runs regularly 0600-1800.

Phra Nang and Rai Leh *p101*
Boat
Aonang Travel and Tour (see Tour operators, above) runs a daily boat to **Phi Phi** and **Phuket** during the high season, leaving from Haad Nopparat Thara and stopping on the way to Phi Phi in the bay in front of Rai Leh West, where long-tails ferry guests out to the boat from the beach.

Islands south of Krabi

For most arrivals on Koh Phi Phi it seems like you've reached paradise. Anvil-shaped and fringed by sheer limestone cliffs and golden beaches, Koh Phi Phi – the setting for the Leonardo Di Caprio film *The Beach* – is stunning. However, a quick walk along the beach, heaving with masses of pink, roasting flesh, or through Ton Sai village, which is filled with persistent touts and standardized tourist facilities, soon shatters the illusion of Nirvana; the endless stream of boats spewing diesel into the sea doesn't help either. Ostensibly Phi Phi should be protected by its national park status but this seems to cut little ice with the developers who appear to be doing more irretrievable damage than the Asian tsunami that devastated the island on 26 December 2004. Whether Phi Phi can encourage enough sustainable tourism to survive the future is debatable; what is certain is that it has very quickly reached the same levels of development that existed pre-tsunami.

Koh Phi Phi → *For listings, see pages 115-119.*

Kho Phi Phi was one of the sites worst-hit by the tsunami – there is a aerial photograph on display in the **Amico** restaurant in Ton Sai village which shows the apocalyptic dimensions of the devastation. Both Ton Sai and Loh Dalem Bay were almost wiped out by the impact of the killer waves overlapping simultaneously on either side of this thin stretch of island. Today, Phi Phi is back to rude health. Tourists are streaming in and the dive shops, hotels, restaurants, shops and bars are now fully up and running. It should also be pointed out that large parts of the island were completely unaffected by the tsunami.

Phi Phi Le is a national park, entirely girdled by sheer cliffs, where swiftlets nest (see box, page 112). It found fame as the location for the film *The Beach* starring Leonardo Di Caprio and Tilda Swinton. It is not possible to stay on Phi Phi Le but it can be visited by boat. The best snorkelling off Phi Phi is at **Hat Yao** (Long Beach) or nearby Bamboo Island and most boat excursions include a visit to the **Viking Cave**, which contains prehistoric paintings of what look like Viking longboats, and the cliffs where birds' nests are harvested for bird's nest soup.

Getting there Phi Phi lies between Krabi and Phuket and can be reached from both, but the only way to get there is by boat. There are daily connections with Krabi, taking one hour on an express boat and 1½ hours on the normal service. Boats also run from the beaches of Ao Nang and Rai Leh close to Krabi (two hours). There are daily boats from Koh Lanta (one hour) and from various spots on Phuket (one to 1½ hours). The quickest way of

4 Koh Phi Phi

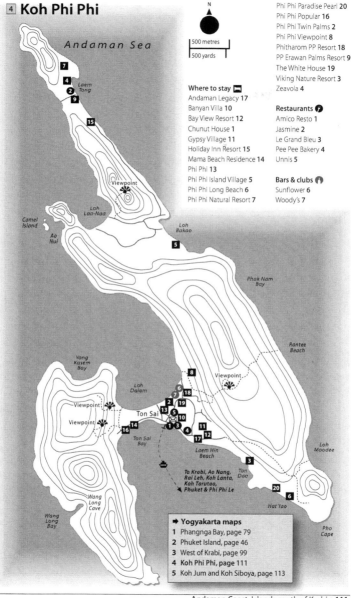

Andaman Sea

N

500 metres
500 yards

Phi Phi Paradise Pearl 20
Phi Phi Popular 16
Phi Phi Twin Palms 2
Phi Phi Viewpoint 8
Phitharom PP Resort 18
PP Erawan Palms Resort 9
The White House 19
Viking Nature Resort 3
Zeavola 4

Where to stay 🛏
Andaman Legacy 17
Banyan Villa 10
Bay View Resort 12
Chunut House 1
Gypsy Village 11
Holiday Inn Resort 15
Mama Beach Residence 14
Phi Phi 13
Phi Phi Island Village 5
Phi Phi Long Beach 6
Phi Phi Natural Resort 7

Restaurants 🍴
Amico Resto 1
Jasmine 2
Le Grand Bleu 3
Pee Pee Bakery 4
Unnis 5

Bars & clubs 🍸
Sunflower 6
Woody's 7

Laem Tong
Camel Island
Ao Nui
Loh Laa-Naa
Viewpoint
Loh Bakao
Phak Nam Bay
Rantee Beach
Vong Kasem Bay
Loh Dalam
Viewpoint
Viewpoint
Ton Sai
Ton Sai Bay
Laem Hin Beach
Ton Dao
Wang Long Cave
Wang Long Bay
Loh Moodee
Hat Yao
Pho Cape

To Krabi, Ao Nang,
Rai Leh, Koh Lanta,
Koh Tarutao,
Phuket & Phi Phi Le

➡ **Yogyakarta maps**

Bird's nest soup

The tiny nests of the brown-rumped swift (Collocalia esculenta), also known as the edible-nest swiftlet or sea swallow, are collected for bird's nest soup, a Chinese delicacy, throughout Southeast Asia.

The semi-oval nests are made of silk-like strands of saliva secreted by the birds which, when cooked in broth, softens and becomes a little like noodles. Like so many Chinese delicacies, the nests are believed to be an aphrodisiac and the soup has even been suggested as a cure for Aids.

The red nests are the most valued and the Vietnamese emperor Minh Mang (1820-1840) is said to have owed his extraordinary vitality to his inordinate consumption of bird's nest soup. This may explain why restaurants serving it in Southern Thailand are usually also associated with massage parlours.

Collecting the nests is a precarious business and is only officially allowed twice a year – between February and April and in September. The collectors climb flimsy bamboo poles into total darkness, with candles strapped to their heads. In Hong Kong 1 kg of nests may sell for US$2000 and nest concessions in Thailand are vigorously protected.

---

getting to Phi Phi from Bangkok is to fly to Phuket and catch a boat from there. Note that all arriving visitors must pay a A20 'cleaning fee' at the pier – this charge is not included in the ferry ticket price. ▸▸ *See Transport, page 119, for further information.*

Best time to visit It is possible to travel to Koh Phi Phi all year round but during the rainy season (May to October), the boat trip can be very rough and not for the faint-hearted. December to February are the driest months, but hotel rates are ridiculously high and it can be difficult to find an available room.

Beaches
Koh Phi Phi's beaches include **Loh Dalam**, which faces north and is on the opposite side to **Ton Sai Bay**, so is still under recovery. **Laem Hin** next to Ton Sai Bay, has beautiful fine sand. **Ton Dao** beach is a small and relatively peaceful stretch to the east of Laem Hin, hemmed in with the usual craggy rocks and vegetation.

Hat Yao (Long Beach), post-tsunami, has become a day-trippers' destination as curious folk from the mainland resorts hit Koh Phi Phi to see where everything happened. However, it is gradually starting to attract overnighters. There are other reasons to stay here; the beach has excellent snorkelling offshore. Even before the tsunami, it was touted as having the cleanest water in Koh Phi Phi. Early in the morning (the best time being before 0930) black-tip sharks are a regular fixture here, before they swim further out to sea as the temperature rises. A walk to Hat Yao along the beach from the former Ton Sai Village takes about 30 minutes. You can also get a boat for around ฿100.

Loh Bakao is one of the larger of the minor beaches dotted around this island. **Phi Phi Island Village** is the only resort on this stretch of wide golden sand. **Laem Tong** (Cape of God) boasts a wonderful sweep of white sandy beach that's relatively quiet and empty. There are only a few upper range resorts here, where many guests prefer poolside sunbathing, or the privacy of their own verandas, to the beach. The resorts also offer day trips, diving, snorkelling and cave-exploring expeditions. Increasingly, resorts are also conducting cultural workshops in skills such as Thai cookery, batik-painting and language courses.

Around the island

Hire a long-tailed boat to take a trip around the island. A six-hour tour costs ฿3000 per boat, maximum four passengers; three-hour tours ฿1500. A day trip snorkelling is well worthwhile (฿600 per person, including lunch, snorkels and fins), with Bamboo Island, Hat Yao and, on Phi Phi Le, Loh Samah and Maya Bay, being particularly good spots. Diving is also possible, with a chance of seeing white-tip sharks. Areas of interest include the Bida Islands, south of Phi Phi Le, where the variety of coral is impressive. There is a 50-m underwater tunnel here for more experienced divers. Wrecks can be found behind Mosquito Island – so-named for its mosquitoes, so do take repellent. The best visibility (25-40 m) is from December to April.

Trips can be taken to see the cliff formations at **Phi Phi Le**, the **Viking Cave**, **Lo Samah Bay** and **Maya Bay** (about ฿300 per person). Maya Bay was used in the filming of *The Beach* starring Leonardo Di Caprio.

5 Koh Jum & Koh Siboya

2 km
2 miles

Where to stay 🛏
Andaman Beach Resort **1**
Bodaeng Beach Resort **5**
Joy Bungalows **2**
Oon Lee Bungalows **3**
Siboya Bungalow **4**
Woodland Lodge **6**

Koh Jum, Koh Bubu and Koh Siboya → For listings, see pages 115-119.

These islands, south of Krabi, are places to escape the crowd. The beaches are not as divine as other Andaman Sea spots but they are quiet and somewhat away from the *farang* trail.

Koh Jum (Jam)

ⓘ *The boat from Krabi to Koh Lanta goes via Koh Jum, 1½ hrs, ฿350. There are also connections with Koh Phi Phi and with Laem Kruat, on the mainland.*

The island itself, with its beige-yellow beach and shallow waters, is not one of the most beautiful in the Andaman Sea, although it does have a magnificent pair of sea eagles who make regular appearances on the village side. Its main attraction is as an escape from the crowds on other islands, a slightly rough-hewn edge and enough variety in accommodation and restaurants to keep things interesting. Recently, the island, which only has around a couple of hundred residents – mostly Chao Le and Muslim fishing families – has seen a flourishing of cheap bungalows and there are now over 20 places to choose from. There is a fear that the resort side of the island is quickly running out of space, thus seriously hampering the privacy and quiet that travellers find here. Additionally, there are concerns that high-level developers will step in to create hermetically sealed resorts and drive out the smaller set-ups. But this still seems unlikely as the beach is not particularly attractive and there are no sites of note on the island to visit.

There is also still a sense of being in the jungle, with pythons making slithering debuts in resort kitchens from time to time. Mains electricity has now reached the island but a number of places still remain off the grid, adding a touch of romantic escapism to the experience. The island also has a undeniable quirky charm, both in terms of the locals and expats who have set up semi-permanent base here. There is a working fishing village with a mosque on the other side of the island from the resorts, which protects Koh Jum from being a toy island like the voluptuous Koh Ngai. The village has a superb restaurant with sophisticated seafood dishes that would not be out of place in a metropolis, general stores and clothes shops selling ubiquitous backpacker tat – fishermen trousers, hippy Alice bands and multi-coloured ashram muslin shirts. You can also watch fishermen at work here or have a cool beer away from the resorts. Finally, if you find that Koh Jum is not isolated enough for you, then take a day trip to Koh Bubu or Koh Siboya (see below).

Koh Siboya

① In high season Nov-Apr, the easiest way to get here is by booking accommodation in advance and catching a Krabi–Lanta ferry. The ferry will stop offshore and the resort will send a long-tail out to pick you up; you'll have to pay full fare, however. Otherwise, take the local bus from Krabi south to Laem Hin Pier (฿100, one hour), then catch a long-tail ferry for the 10-minute trip. The cost is ฿20-40 and boats depart whenever they're deemed full enough, until about 1500. Long-tail ferry boats also depart infrequently from the pier at Laem Kruad, about 30 km south of Krabi Town. To get to the pier, take the local bus from Krabi Town through Neua Klong town. Or take a private long-tail from Koh Jum.

Koh Siboya is a speck of an island with a population of about 1000 people, most of whom are Muslim and involved in rubber or fisheries. The beach is really just mud-flats that stretch for an astonishing length and bake and crack in the midday heat. However, it is the isolation of Koh Siboya that attracts returnee visitors – a mixture of hardcore travellers and middle-aged hippies. You will also find expats here who came for a couple weeks years ago and who have stayed on living in idiosyncratic and charming bungalows. There is not a lot to do and, from our reports, the main attraction/activity for visitors remains watching monkeys catch crabs on the beach, and freeform meditation.

Islands south of Krabi listings

For hotel and restaurant price codes and other relevant information, see pages 12-16.

⊖ Where to stay

Koh Phi Phi *p110, map p111*
$$$$ Banyan Villa, 129 Moo 7 Ton Sai, T075-611233, www.ppbanyanvilla.com. Right in the centre of Ton Sai though its large gardens and pool create a secluded feel. Well run, though nothing too exciting, each room is en suite, with a/c and TV. Fitness centre.
$$$$ Bay View Resort, 43/19 Moo 5, Laem Hin, T075-601127-31, www.phiphibayview. com. Split-level bungalows on a hill with views of Tonsai Cliffs and Phi Phi Ley. Pool, beach club and restaurant on the sand.
$$$$ Holiday Inn Resort, Laem Tong, T075-627300, www.phiphi.holidayinn. com. 79 mostly low-rise bungalow-style buildings and 47 studio rooms in 8 ha of garden setting right on the beach. Rooms are somewhat antiseptic and frumpy in the Holiday Inn way, though they do have wooden floors. 2 restaurants, 2 bars. Lots of activities on offer such as learning Thai cookery, batik painting, etc. Swimming pools, jacuzzi, spa. Even provides picnic hampers for guests who wish to explore. One of the better equipped resorts on Phi Phi. Lovely stretch of turquoise sea, very quiet beaches.
$$$$ Mama Beach Residence, Ton Sai Bay, T075-601365, www.mama-beach.com. Chic French-run 2-level bungalows, all a/c, in a bright, modern style with private balconies, some with sea views. Rather swish-looking wooden platforms with built-in sunbeds for guests on the beach. No pool, but good range of services and tasty breakfasts. Recommended.
$$$$ Phi Phi Island Village, Loh Bakao, T075-628900-99, www.ppisland.com. Set alone to the north of the island this is the only resort on this stretch of beach. 100 traditional Thai bungalows and 12 private pool villas set in immaculately tended gardens with a view of the beach. The rooms are extremely pleasant, with a/c, satellite TV, minibar, wooden flooring set off by bamboo and whitewashed walls and muted colours used for en suite bathrooms. Decent-sized verandas. There's a nearby diving centre, a pool and a resort speed-boat for quick journeys. Attached spa.
$$$$ Phi Phi Natural Resort, Laem Tong, T075-819030, www.phiphinatural.com. There's nothing natural about the huge signage outside this resort nor the endless stream of boats that bring day-trippers to eat in their very average restaurant. It's a shame because the location on the northern stretch of Laem Tong beach is gorgeous. Around 70 wood bungalows. Swimming pool with children's section, beachside bar, coffee house and diving centre.
$$$$ Phi Phi Paradise Pearl, Hat Yao (Long Beach), T075-618050, phiphiparadise pearl.com. 35 a/c bungalows with a range of clean rooms, some have sea view. Big, overpriced restaurant and Thai-style massage cabanas. Organizes tours to Phi Phi Le, and kayaks, snorkels and fins are available for hire.
$$$$ PP Erawan Palms Resort, Moo 8 Laem Tong, T075-627500-23, www.pp erawanpalms.com. Decent-sized wooden bungalows and standard rooms with freshwater swimming pool on the northern tip. Set in well-manicured paths. Beachside restaurant and nightly performances of Thai classical music, although not necessarily very good ones. Still entertaining and at times, edifying.
$$$$ Zeavola, Laem Tong, T075-627000, www.zeavola.com. Set on the beachfront, close to the swimming pool or on the hillside among gardens of the flowering plant after which the resort is named (*Scaevola taccada*, in Thai the flower's name means Love the Sea). Some of the beautifully furnished wooden suites have outside showers and bathrooms with coloured ceramic sinks.

Outside living areas with chairs and minibars are also a feature, although the mosquitoes can be horrific. The food is decidedly average though you can dine on the beach by candle-light or under the fabulous striped awning at the **Tacada** restaurant or enjoy Thai cuisine at **Baxil**, the covered restaurant. Excellent spa. There's a PADI dive centre and excursions are arranged. Staff are friendly, helpful and courteous.

$$$$-$$$ Andaman Legacy, 1 Moo 7, T075-601106, www.phiphiandamanlegacy. com. Concrete bungalows arranged around a garden area with a swimming pool at its centre. Rooms are basic but well maintained and clean. Only a short walk from the beach. The '24-hour' Hippies bar nearby might be a worry for noise.

$$$$-$$$ Phi Phi Viewpoint, 107 Moo 7, T075-601200. Around 60 airy a/c bungalows on stilts, surrounded by coconut trees. Big verandas. Small seafront pool. Not all bungalows have good views and they are rather too close together. With the bar scene moving to Loh Dalum, the peaceful nights that could once be enjoyed here are now but a memory.

$$$$-$$ Chunut House, on the road between the mosque and water reservoir, T075-601227, www.phiphichunuthouse. com. Bright, modern, airy and clean rooms in wooden huts arranged in a well-kept garden. About a 10-min walk to Ton Sai Bay and Loh Dalum Bay.

$$$ Phi Phi Popular Beach Resort, Ton Sai Bay, T08-4744 7665 (mob), www.phiphi popularbeach.com. Double and triple a/c rooms, most with sea views. Rather dramatic setting right up against the karst at the far end of Ton Sai past the hospital. Popular with families.

$$$ Phi Phi Twin Palms, Loh Dalum Bay, T075-601285, www.phiphitwinpalms.com. Simple bamboo huts, with fan, very near to the beach. Mosquito net, bathroom and balcony. Friendly smiling staff. Set just behind the blasting Woody's bar, so sleepless nights are assured.

$$$ The White & The White 2, 125/100 Moo 7, T075-601300, www.whitephiphi. com. Rooms in this modern building are, you've guessed it, white, cool and relaxing. All come with a/c, hot water, cable TV. decor. Close proximity to the bars and restaurants might mean it's too noisy for some. Free Wi-Fi for guests. The newer White 2 offers similar room styles and rates.

$$$-$$ Phi Phi Long Beach, Hat Yao, T08-9973 6425 (mob). Very basic huts, some with sea view. Good food, some private bathrooms, saltwater showers in dry season.

$$$-$$ Viking Nature Resort, T075-819399, www.vikingnaturesresort.com. These huts have been individually designed with Balinese influences. Most sit on the cliff-side with sea views, all have bags of character. Now operating together with neighbouring Maphrao bungalows, it has direct access to 2 very quiet and secluded sandy beaches between Ton Sai Bay and Hat Yao. Recommended.

$$ Gypsy Village (also called Gypsy Bungalow), Ton Sai Bay, T075-601045. Just inland from the mosque towards Loh Dalum. Bungalows are arranged around an open area. Big verandas. Quiet, but very tired looking. One of the cheapest options on the island.

Koh Jum (Jam) *p113, map p113*
The website www.kohjumonline.com gives a pretty thorough, though perhaps dated overview of accommodation on Koh Jum. There are around 20 bungalow operations on the tiny island. Prices vary according to the season but Koh Jum is generally very reasonably priced compared with some other island destinations although many of the bungalows shut down for 6 months of the year so you do need to check. Accommodation is simple bamboo bungalows or other basic A-frame bungalows although more upmarket regimental set-ups are appearing. They are evenly spread along the beach.

$$$$-$$ OonLee Bungalows, T08-7200 8053 (mob), kohjumoonleebungalows.com. Built and run by a Frenchwoman and her Thai husband. Well crafted wooden bungalows on stilts with sea views. Good restaurant and loads of comfortable lounging space.

$$$-$ Joy Bungalows, T075-618199, kohjum-joybungalow.com. Best known and most established resort; still the most imaginative in terms of variety, with wooden family beachfront chalets, bamboo huts on stilts, wooden bungalows and treehouses: 36 rooms in all. Tour counter and an average restaurant. The bungalows at the back are not particularly well-kept and are too close together. There is a path that will take you to the Muslim and Chao Le village. Recommended.

$$$-$ Andaman Beach Resort, T08-9724 1544 (mob). Around 20 modern A-frame chalets that look like pathological Wendy houses in mauve. They even have a fake balcony and 2nd floor. All are set facing each other in a square U-shaped plan on a rather bare site. These are different in ambience and style from other resorts and, one hopes, not a precursor to the homogenized bungalow barracks set-up seen on islands like Koh Lanta. Fan or a/c chalets have attached bathrooms with hot-water showers. This set-up is usually patronized by members of the Thai military or police when they need to stay on Koh Jum.

$$-$ Woodland Lodge, next to Bodaeng Beach Resort, T08-1893 5330 (mob), www.woodland-koh-jum.com. Run by Englishman Ray and his Thai wife Sao, reliable set-up with only 5 family and double bungalows. Helpful staff. What makes this place stand out is its marooned Gilligan's Island feel, as it acts as a meeting spot for expats on the island. One other thing, the establishment is next door to the Chao Le graveyard, apparently anathema to thieves. Open year-round. Recommended.

$ Bodaeng Beach Resort, between Woodland Lodge and the Andaman Beach Resort. These are basic solar-powered bamboo huts on stilts with shared bathroom. Remains steadfastly backpacker-orientated, while most resorts on the island move upmarket. Attracts hardcore travellers and those seeking spiritual solace in physical discomfort. Excellent restaurant, however, the best of all the resorts. Entertaining owner with a roguish twinkle in her eyes and an outrageously contagious giggle. Do check the bills, however, as her maths needs a bit of work.

Koh Siboya *p114, map p113*

There are only 3 resorts on the island. Private houses can also be rented but it seems that most people who rent them are so attached to them that they stay for months and months. Friendly staff, good food and interesting residents.

$$$$-$$ Thai West Resort, www.thai-west.com. Offers a range of accommodation, from basic bungalows to houses, a/c or fan. Restaurant, and kayaks and mountain bikes for hire. Can also arrange tours.

$$-$ Siboya Bungalows, around 500 m south of Lang Koh Village on the west coast of Koh Siboya, T075-618026, T08-1979 3344 (mob), www.siboyabungalows.com. If you do plan on staying it is best to make arrangements for transportation after contacting their office in Krabi town or on the island. A choice of 20 simple bungalows or 20 private houses, all with attached toilets and fans, set in spacious gardens near the sea. Restaurant with Wi-Fi.

⊘ Restaurants

Koh Phi Phi *p110, map p111*

Nearly all the food on the island is aimed at tourists and so few of the culinary delights found in the rest of the country are available here. There are some good Western restaurants though, and Ton Sai is packed with bakeries and all manner of seafood.

$$$ Le Grand Bleu, Ton Sai. French- and Thai-run restaurant near the pier. Excellent

wine list and seafood make this one of the best places to eat on the island. Good atmosphere and friendly service.
$$$-$$ Amico Resto, Ton Sai. Great little pizza and pasta place near the pier. Perfect pit-stop if you're jumping on the ferry. Friendly, with good, efficient service.
$$ Unni's, Phi Phi Don Village. Tex-Mex restaurant popular with the expat divers.
$$-$ Jasmine, Laem Tong beach. A tiny little Thai eatery next to the sea gypsy village. Tak (translates as grasshopper), the owner, is a friendly character who serves up excellent Thai seafood. The beachside tables are romantic. Highly recommended.
$$-$ Papaya, in front of Rolling Stoned bar, Ton Sai. Bare-bones eatery popular for its more authentic Thai flavours and generous portions. Harsh neon lighting lends no ambience though. Opens about 1700. Good value for Phi Phi.
$$-$ Pee Pee Bakery, Ton Sai. In the heart of Ton Sai this awesome little bakery and coffee house sells donuts, choc-chip cookies and anything else you need for a sugar rush. If too crowded, Pacharee bakery just across the road, is worth checking out.
$ No-name corner sandwich shop, opposite Pichamon Tour, Ton Sai. Does a roaring trade in the morning, especially for its fresh baguettes, smoothies and espressos. Great place to grab a takeaway meal.

Koh Jum *p113, map p113*
$$ Koh Jum Seafood, on a mini pier next to the actual working pier. Choose fine fresh seafood directly from traps. Cooked to perfection with a sophisticated range of ingredients – do not be surprised to find them cooking the shellfish in a broth of around 15 different ingredients. Having anything simply steamed would be a waste of their talents. Sweet views too – you can watch the birds following the boats for fish and all the activities of a working pier while taking in the islands opposite. It may seem expensive after the resorts but it is worth it.

$ Bodaeng Beach Resort, see Where to stay, above. Excellent fare from the owner here, especially the salads and soups. But take a mosquito coil or repellent as the restaurant is open and set in a little from the beach. The best you will find among the resorts and the best price too. Recommended.

Foodstalls
You can also get simple noodle, chicken and rice dishes in the local food market – particularly at **Mamas**. There is only 1 tiny street – the prices are slightly cheaper than the resorts with little difference in preparation or taste although more atmosphere.

Bars and clubs

Koh Phi Phi *p110, map p111*
The fireshow, drink-bucket and DJ music scene has moved from Ton Sai Bay to the northern part of the Loh Dalum beachfront in recent years, with Woody's, Slinky's, Stones and the Moken Beach bars among the busiest – and unbearably loudest.
Banana Bar, between the village centre and Loh Dalum. Rooftop open-air bar that throbs with DJ music and wild dancing till the wee hours.
Carlito's Bar, east from Ton Sai Bay, www.carlitosbar.net. Became a hub for volunteers and humanitarian aid groups as well as residents after the tsunami. Now offers rooftop yoga classes by day, DJs, cocktail buckets and fireshows by night. Well worth visiting.
Sunflower Bar, at the northern end of Loh Dalum Bay. This bar, made from flotsam and other debris, is a good place to chill out and enjoy a few cocktails. BBQ and live music. Some rooms for rent here, too.

What to do

Koh Phi Phi *p110, map p111*
As well as the activities listed below, kayaking can be arranged through resorts

or tour operators for about ฿700 per day; paddle boats can be rented for ฿150 per hr from the northern shore, where waterskiing is also possible; snorkelling is popular too, and snorkels and fins can be hired from most resorts and bungalows for ฿150 per day.

Cookery courses
Pum Cooking School, 125/40 Moo 7 (near the village market), T08-1521 8904. Cheap and cheerful Thai cookery courses for as little as ฿399 for a one-dish lesson. Longer courses that include a market tour and cookbook also available.

Diving
There are currently around 15 dive shops operating on Koh Phi Phi. Most of the dive shops charge the same, with 2 local fun dives coming in at around ฿2500. Open Water courses start from ฿13,800. Alternatively, you can book with one of the many dive centres on Phuket (see page 72). One of the oldest and the best local outfits is PP Aquanauts, T075-601213, www.ppaquanauts.com. You could also try Phi Phi Scuba Diving Center, main street in Ton Sai, T075-601 148, www. ppscuba.com; The Adventure Club, T08-1895 1334, phi-phi-adventures.com; Moskito Diving, a few branches in Ton Sai, T075-601154, www.moskitodiving.com, or Visa Diving, main street in Ton Sai, T076-01157, www.visa diving.com.

Fishing
Arisa Big Game Fishing, T08-1894 7269/ 5069 6157. Locally run half-day, full-day and night squid fishing tours on a Thai fishing vessel. ฿6000-9000 for up to 8 passengers. Sak Fishing, T08-5167 1802 (mob). Offers half-day trips on long-tail boats, ฿4000 total for up to 4 passengers.

Rock climbing
The limestone cliffs here are known internationally, and post-tsunami rebolting efforts have expanded the number of available routes in recent years.

Spidermonkey Climbing, near Tonsai Bay, T075-819 384, www.spidermonkeyclimbing. com. Has several years of Phi Phi experience under its safety belt.

Therapies
Zeavola Spa, Zeavola, T075-627000. Open 0900-2100. It is definitely worth stopping here for some wonderful treatments. The signature massage is the Zeavola Body Brush Massage – a full-body brushing followed by a head massage then full-body massage with rice oil and lemongrass, kaffir lime and essential oils.

Koh Jum p113, map p113
Tour operators
Koh Jum Center Tour, shop on the opposite side of Koh Jum Seafood and the pier at 161 Moo 3. Native Koh Jumian Wasana Laemkoh provides tickets for planes, trains, buses and boats. She will also change money, make overseas calls, and arrange 1-day boat trips. Her husband is a local fisherman so you may end up going with him. You can also rent motorbikes here. Honest and reliable.
Wildside Tours, along the road opposite Koh Jum Village School (signposted). This set-up, operated by a German lady, offers kayaking and snorkelling expeditions, and some trekking.

⊕ Transport

Koh Phi Phi p110, map p111
Boat
To Krabi, 4 services a day at 0900, 1030, 1400 and 1530, 1hr 45 mins, ฿350. Some of the resorts also offer private boat connections with Krabi.
Daily connections to Ao Nang, 1530, 2 hrs, ฿390; and Rai Leh, 1 hr 45 mins, ฿390 on the Ao Nang Princess. Connections with Phuket, 0900 and 1430, 1½ hrs, ฿350. There's a daily seasonal service to Koh Lanta, departing at 1130, 1400 and 1500, Oct-Apr, ฿350.

Koh Lanta

It's not that long ago that Koh Lanta provided a genuine opportunity to get away from it all and have an authentic encounter with a unique local culture. There were no telephones, no electricity and the road that ran the length of the island was unpaved. Step off the boat at Sala Dan Pier today and into the arms of the resort ambushers with their private van service to one of more than 100 resorts and you can see that the island is in the grips of real estate mania.

Not only are new resorts sprouting up, many existing players are busily upgrading and adding swimming pools – hotel pools, we're told, are key in the effort to make Lanta a year-round destination. But while three- to five-star resorts are pushing out bargain shoppers, there are still ฿300 backpacker bungalows towards the national park end of the island. Koh Lanta, with its 85% Muslim population increasingly attracts families and pensioners, mainly here for R&R although superb diving, including the world-famous Hin Daeng (Red Rock) and Hin Muong (Purple Rock), also pull in swashbuckling hardcore divers.

In contrast, Koh Lanta's east coast is still underdeveloped, with villagers dependent on wells and young people rejecting the traditional economy of rubber, cashew and fishing for the tourist industry. And, while it is worth a motorbike ride to see the east coast's rough and tumble hills with giant umbrella trees and the rare python sunning itself in the middle of the unfinished road, there are scant architectural gems apart from the Old Town, site of trade routes for China in the early 1900s and home to an Urak Lawoi (sea gypsy) village. The island was also affected by the tsunami of 2004 when several resorts were swamped and some tourists lost their lives – signs along the main road point to tsunami evacuation routes, though even these have been misplaced, often resulting in conflicting directions.

Arriving on Koh Lanta

Getting there

The main access point to Koh Lanta is from Klong Jirad, around 5 km out of Krabi Town to Sala Dan, via Koh Jum (two hours). The island largely shuts its tourist industry down during the wet season when unpredictable large waves make it too dangerous to cross (May to October). At this time of year, a minibus takes visitors via two short car ferry crossings from Lanta Noi to Sala Dan (two hours). There are boat connections with Ban Hua Hin at the southern end of Koh Klang, and *songthaews* from Krabi to Ban Hua Hin. Minibuses also run from Trang and, during the high-season (November to March), boats run to and from Phi Phi. ▶▶ See Transport, page 134, for further information.

Getting around

Not one bay area accessible from the road has not been developed. To get to the resorts and bungalows, there is a road that stretches the length of the island from Sala Dan Pier to the national park end. It is now fully sealed making exploration of the island easy. However the roads leading to resort land are seriously potholed, steep and after periods of dry weather covered with plumes of chronic red dust. Further down this road, as it approaches the national park and the sealed tarmac ends, accidents are common, it therefore makes sense to wear long trousers and sturdy footwear.

Songthaews are the main form of public transport around the island, though they are few and far between. Motorbikes and mountain bikes are available for hire from guesthouses, some shops and tour companies. Although the rental situation has improved greatly with most places renting out nearly new motorbikes, it is advisable to check the tyres, the brakes and the tank before you set off as most of the rental places expect you to sign a contract before you set off agreeing to pay for any damages incurred. A more reliable solution is to rent a jeep but these are considerably more expensive and there are still only small operators here with no credit-card facilities; thus, you'll be asked to turn over your passport as security. Long-tailed boats can be chartered for coastal trips. There are also a smattering of tuk-tuks in Sala Dan but prices are high – even for the shortest 2-km hop.

Background

Koh Lanta is packed with bungalows and resorts. Some of these set-ups are replete with internet, minimarts, souvenir shops, spas, restaurants, pools and bars so that guests need never leave. Meanwhile, on the main road, there is almost a total absence of cultural outposts like libraries, bookshops or music stores. Instead, the road is dominated by restaurants in shacks, garages, the occasional massage and tattoo parlour and general grocery shops along with *farang*-tailored bars that promise the latest football results and pub dinners. Still, in the evening when the fairylights are switched on and the dust clouds expand with Saharan girth, it is bearable – briefly.

There is a sizeable Urak Lawoi (sea gypsy, or Chao Le) village in the southeast of the island. The village comprises shacks – some awash with the flotsam and jetsam of a fishing life – from broken equipment to torn nets mixed in with today's ecologically nightmarish household rubbish. Swedish researcher Lotta Granbom, who has been studying the effects of tourism on Lanta's Urak Lawoi since 2003, paints a fairly bleak picture of their situation. In one report she concludes that, "Even if economic gain [from tourism] is realised, the relationship between hosts and guests has obvious colonial overtones. If the plight of the

Urak Lawoi is not heard, most of them will live in miserable slum villages as poor Thai people in the near future." Post-tsunami there has been a parade of journalists, NGO groups, students and curious visitors coming with a range of goals and activities in mind, which Ms Granbom says has created some added stress amongst the villagers. Walking through the chaotic layout of their living space, it is impossible not to intrude and, while

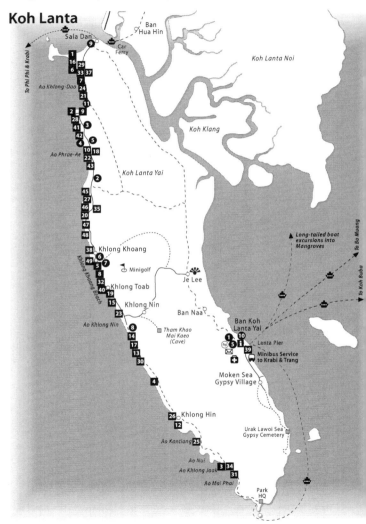

Koh Lanta

the Chao Le are remarkably patient and gracious, it is perhaps better to resist curiosity about the 'indigenous lifestyle' unless invited. Yet local tour operators on the island and further afield are now including this village in their itineraries. It's a good idea to check with tour operators about the extent to which the visits benefit and show respect towards the Chao Le people, although, of course, you can't guarantee an entirely honest response.

1 km
1 mile

Where to stay 🛏
Anda Lanta Resort **3**
Andaman Lanta Resort **2**
Banana Garden Home **7**
Bee Bee Bungalows **8**
Blue Sky Resort &
  Restaurant **42**
Chaba Bungalows &
  Art Gallery **24**
Chaw Ka Cher Lanta
  Tropicana Resort **35**
Costa Lanta **1**
Dream Team Beach
  Resort **4**
D R Lanta Bay Resort **29**
Fisherman's Cottage **5**
Freedom Estate **18**
Golden Bay Cottage **6**
Hans Restaurant &
  Bungalows **29**
Holiday Villa **2**
Houben **26**
Khlong Jark Bungalows **34**
La Lanta Hideaway
  Resort **31**
Lanta Emerald Resort **47**
Lanta Garden Home
  Resort **9**
Lanta Marina Resort **11**
Lanta Marine Park
  Resort **12**
Lanta Mermaid Boutique
  House **37**
Lanta Miami **13**
Lanta Nature Beach
  Resort **14**
Lanta New Coconut
  Bungalows **32**
Lanta Palace **15**
Lanta Palm Beach Resort **42**
Lanta Paradise **17**
Lanta River Sand **19**
Lanta Riviera Resort **20**
Lanta Sand Resort & Spa **2**
Lanta Sea House **21**
Lanta Sunny House **22**
Lanta Thip House **38**
Mango House **39**
Mook Lanta **45**
Nakara Long Beach
  Resort **10**
Narima Bungalow
  Resort **23**
Nice & Easy **48**
Pimalai Resort **25**
Rawi Warin Resort & Spa **40**
Relax Bay **27**
Royal Lanta **16**
Sayang Beach **28**
Sea Culture House **46**
Somewhere Else **41**
Southern Lanta Resort **33**
Sri Lanta **30**
Sun, Fun & Sea Resort **29**
Thai House Beach Resort **43**
Where Else Resort **49**

Restaurants 🍴
Bulan Lanta **7**
Cook Kai **8**
Danny's **3**
Faïm de Loup **5**
Frog **9**
Green Leaf Café **6**
Krue Lanta Yai **1**
Mango House **10**
Mr Wee Pizzeria **4**
Retro **2**
Rom Thai **5**
Time for Lime **11**

Around the island → For listings, see pages 127-135.

Sala Dan

This dusty two-street town on the northern tip of the island is most arrivees' introduction to Koh Lanta, as the majority of ferries and boats dock here. During the high season it can resemble the Village of the Damned with throngs of blond, blue-eyed Scandinavians mingling with the grumpy locals most of whom seem keen to fleece every dumb *farang* that passes through. To cut to the chase, Sala Dan is geared to emptying the pockets of tourists as quickly as possible. It does provide numerous facilities, including banks, ATMs, internet, bars and restaurants, though most are excessively overpriced, filled with *farang* and serving up weak examples of Thai food.

Ban Koh Lanta Yai

Blink and you miss it; Ban Koh Lanta Yai, the old administrative centre and port on Koh Lanta, usually called 'Old Town' in the brochures, is developing its own tourism niche. With stunning views across to the islands of Koh Bubu, Koh Po, Ko Kum and Koh Tala Beng, and most of its original old wooden shophouse/fishing houses still standing, this micro-town, which is actually only a couple of streets, has buckets of charm. Here, local entrepreneurs have opened galleries and souvenir shops, there are bed and breakfasts and the closest thing to family stays available on the island (see Where to stay, page 127). Ban Koh Lanta really comprises one main street that doesn't even go on for that long. The end of this road is indicated by an extraordinary ancient tree rather like a banyan and a tiny canal rivulet. There is a distinct Thai-Chinese ambience with rows of busy shophouses, each replete with its own exotically plumed bird in a wooden cage. Trade on this main street is largely fishing tackle shops and general goods stores, indicating the locals' overruling occupations. There are excellent restaurants offering either good working man's fare or more sophisticated seafood dishes.

Koh Bubu
Koh Bubu is a tiny uninhabited island in the Lanta group of Koh Lanta Yai which takes a mere 15 minutes to walk around. There is one resort, see Where to stay, page 127. People who have stayed here return to the mainland completely relaxed and detached from the world they left behind. There is a very pleasant walk around the island and lots of birdwatching opportunities.

Ao Khlong Dao
Ao Khlong Dao, which starts on the edge of Sala Dan, was one of the first bays to open to tourism in Koh Lanta and as little as eight years ago had only about six small bungalow resorts and a couple of independent restaurants, not to mention the occasional buffalo family going for a paddle in the sea. While it is a lovely bay with soft sand and pleasant views over to Deer Neck Cape, development here has been rapid and unplanned. The bay is now heavily developed with most resorts encroaching onto the beach, some separated by high walls. Khlong Dao itself is a relatively safe place to swim and good for families and with the number of 'proper' hotels, it is often booked via travel agencies offering package tours to Lanta.

Ao Phra-Ae (Long Beach)
Ao Phra-Ae, also known as Long Beach, is a lovely beach to stroll on with soft white sand and a very long, gently sloping stretch that allows for safe swimming at both low and high tides. In the late evening, as you splash your feet in the waves close to the shore, a magical phospheresence appears as if you are walking on a thin surface of stars. This beach is catering increasingly to well-heeled retirees and families, particularly the Scandinavians, although there are still remnants of its earlier days as a backpacker haven with restaurants and bars like the **Ozone**, which holds big DJ bashes every Thursday. While great for those who like to party all night and sleep all day, the new style of tourists have complained about the noise, although everyone seems to like the by-now standard fire shows. The resorts here are no longer owned by local families and the bungalow resorts make their most lucrative profits through restaurant and bar sales. To encourage their guests to 'stay at home', many of the resorts have created barriers that extend right down to the beach and may use barbed wire or natural borders like strategically planted palms to keep the tourists in. This has resulted in more independently minded travellers feeling trapped and resentful, and has generated an atmosphere of comically poisonous competition between the resorts.

Hat Khlong Khoang
Hat Khlong Khoang is advertised by some as the 'most beautiful beach on Lanta'. But the beach is fairly steep down to the sea and the sand not as fine as that at Long Beach. The views along the bay are pleasant, but not spectacular. Behind many bungalow resorts is a canal which is treated as a dump for all sorts of waste from construction debris to coconut husks. In many parts of the beach it smells and is a mosquito trap and consequently best avoided if you are offered a room anywhere near. That said, there are a handful of

establishments with real character and charm and, offshore, there are coral reefs that are increasingly attracting snorkellers and divers.

Khlong Toab

Khlong Toab, just beyond the Fisherman's Cottage and close to Khlong Toab village, supports two resorts in marked contrast to each other. It is a quiet area and the beach shelves gently and the swimming is safe, so is particularly suitable for families.

Ao Khlong Nin

Ao Khlong Nin is a bit of a mixed bag in terms of accommodation, ranging from basic backpacker places through to the top-of-the-range resorts. There is, as they say, just about something for everyone. The beach itself is picturesque with rocks dotted about and not just a single sweep of sand; the sand is white and fine. The downside is that this means that swimming, in places, can be tricky. Usually, though, it is possible to find a safe place to swim.

Ao Kantiang

Ao Kantiang was once the cheap and secluded hideaway for many Europeans and Scandinavians who spent months resting in bungalows overlooking the bay. With golden sand, steeply sloping hillsides and only a small village, the only accommodation was locally owned and operated and set well back from the local community. All that has changed with the arrival of the **Pimalai Resort**. This luxury resort has completely altered the feel of this bay. Speedboats send guests off to a floating jetty (thus avoiding putting any money into local coffers through the ferry and avoiding the road which was substantially torn up by the construction vehicles building the resort). The Scandinvians still frequent this beach, as do wealthy European retirees.

Ao Khlong Jaak

Ao Khlong Jaak used to be one of the most peaceful bays on Koh Lanta, a relatively small bay with sloping hills to the north and south and coconut plantations and grassland in the middle. However, there is rampant land speculation in this area now, as with all the beaches. In the bay area there is an elephant trekking station (up to the waterfall), and the big beasts are often brought to sea in the late afternoon for a bath. It is important to remember that during the dry season the waterfall turns to a trickle, as this is one of the main selling points of Klong Jark. However, it is still possible to find cheap accommodation and more independently minded tourists here.

Ao Mai Phai

Ao Mai Phai is the last bay before the national park and one of the few on the west coast of Lanta with good snorkelling opportunities. Again, it is a relatively small bay with steeply sloping hills leading down to the bay on the north and south and with a more extensive area of flatter land in the middle.

Moo Koh Lanta Marine National Park

① ฿400.

The park covers much of the southern part of the island and extends over numerous islands in the area including Koh Rok, Hin Muang and Hin Daeng. The national park headquarters is at Laem Tanod and involves either a boat trip or a long and painful drive. The road to the park is in very bad condition and practically impassable during the rainy season. The peninsula is named after the tanod trees (a type of sugar palm) that grow throughout the area and give it an almost prehistoric atmosphere. There are two bays and in the middle is the lighthouse (navy controlled but the peninsula is accessible to the public). One bay has fine soft sand and is great for swimming. The other, which faces west, bears the full brunt of the monsoons and is rocky and a good place to explore if you like rock pools. Beyond the visitor centre and the toilet and shower block, is a lily pond and the park headquarters. Just beyond this, is a nature trail which takes you up a fairly precipitous path into the forest and then along a contour around the back of the offices in a half loop ending at the road entering the park. It's a well-designed trail though not suitable for children or the elderly because the path is very steep in the early parts and can be slippery. Take plenty of water and some snacks with you. The bay is surrounded by forested hills and filled with forest sounds and the gentle or not so gentle sound of waves crashing on to the rocks or beach (depending on the season). It is a beautiful spot to spend a day swimming and walking, and then watching the sunset from the viewpoint on Laem Tanod.

Koh Lanta Noi

If you take the car ferry route to Lanta Yai, Lanta Noi is the island you cross between the two ferry crossings. Undeveloped for tourism, this island is dominated by mangrove forest and paperbark forest. Few tourists visit the island, but it is worth making a quick visit from Sala Dan using the small long-tailed boats. This will take you to the pier used for the district office (now located on Lanta Noi but once based in Ban Koh Lanta Yai). From here you can walk for at least a couple of hours along a stretch of beach complete with casuarina trees and paperbark forest. With good views to the coast and across to islands, this is a pleasant place from which to escape the noise and dust of the main island. Also on Lanta Noi, but on the main road and in the only village passed en route to Koh Lanta, is a women's group shop that sells the woven matting bags, mats, etc that you may see in souvenir shops on Lanta Yai. Prices here are not much lower than what you'd pay in the shops, but at least all of the money goes to the makers. The quality of the weaving here is very high.

Had Thung Thale Non-Hunting Area, Koh Klang

ⓘ *There are few organized tours to this area, but you can self-drive. Signs are reasonably well marked – it's about 17 km off the main road down a couple of turn-offs and through some small villages and plantations.*

Had Thung Thale Non-Hunting Area is on Koh Klang, but you'll have a hard time spotting that fact even if you do drive over to Lanta Yai and take the car ferries. Koh Klang is joined to the mainland by a bridge. The non-hunting area comprises several hundred hectares of beautiful paperbark forest (*pa samet*), coastal grasslands and casuarina forest, and is bordered with some beautiful long stretches of grey/white beaches. Rarely visited, occasionally it is taken over completely with local school trips for their scouting activities and government groups on corporate bonding sessions – the same sort that go to Tarutao. There are several conservation projects sponsored by the king. The paper-bark forests have a bleak but beautiful aspect, are fragrant and present relatively easy walking opportunities.

Koh Lanta listings

For hotel and restaurant price codes and other relevant information, see pages 12-16.

● Where to stay

Most bungalow operations are scattered down the west coast of Koh Lanta Yai and usually offer free pick-ups from the pier at Sala Dan. Even if you do not have a place sorted out, you will be inundated with reps on the boats traversing between the various islands, most with photo albums showing pics – though not very reliable ones – of their resorts and promising discounts because they like you. You might find the hail-fellow-well-met routine unravels once they hand over the key to your room but it is still best to stay on good terms, as there is considerable communication between the various touts. Travel agents and tour companies in Krabi and Ao Nang advertise accommodation on Koh Lanta so it is possible to get a pretty good idea of the various places before arriving. The choice is basically between simple concrete bungalows (some with a/c), bamboo or wood bungalows (usually fan), luxury resorts one step away from a theme song, and chic spa boutique resorts that offer total comfort and brand T-shirts. Some resorts have been nicknamed 'chicken farms' for their unimaginative and overcrowded lay-out and there are more and more of these turning up, erected in cleared land that has been scraped clean of trees and foliage. Further south along the coast, there are some new and more interesting resorts and the whole area is much less crowded and has a peaceful atmosphere (although there are regular parties during the high season). There is considerable variation between high season (Nov-May) and low season (Jun-Oct) rates, with a low-season rate being roughly half that of the high season rate.

Ban Koh Lanta Yai *p123, map p122*
The tiny old town of Lanta keenly displays the charm of a non-segregated version of tourism as opposed to the Thai-corp style where tourists stay in one place and residents stay in another. It must be said that there are very few places to stay here – a good sign as the village is reliant on other forms of income and hasn't succumbed to the draw of the tourist dollar.
$$$ Mango House, middle of the main street, T075-697181, www.mangohouses. com. Restored old wooden house overlooking the sea. Was once, allegedly, a government-run opium den. Rooms are nicely decorated, with hardwood floors, kitchenettes and seafront decks. Limited a/c. The owners also have a number of villas for rent (**$$$$**). One of the most original places to stay on the island. Rates halve during the low season (May-Oct). Highly recommended.

Koh Bubu *p124*
$$ Bubu Island Resort, T075-618066. Restaurant and little else, except sea and solitude. The electricity goes off after 2200 and you are left to the sound of the waves and the moonlight. That said, the beds are rather uncomfortable and the beach is difficult to swim off during low tide because of the sea urchins. Closed in low season.

Ao Khlong Dao *p124, map p122*
$$$$ Costa Lanta, Moo 3, T02-6623550, www.costalanta.com. Modernism may not be to everyone's taste, but this exclusive resort has succeeded in creating an ambience somewhere between modern urban living and beach hideaway. Designed by Thai architect Duangrit Bunnag, the concrete and wood cabana rooms have huge retractable teak doors that completely open 2 sides to the elements, flooding them with natural light.

$$$$ Lanta Sand Resort and Spa,
Ao Khlong Dao edging to Ao Phra-Ae,
T075-684633, www.lantasand.com.
Spacious rooms, amazing bathrooms
with glass walls – the monkeys can peer
in while you take a bath. Good service,
fine food. Recommended.

$$$$ Royal Lanta, 222 Moo 3, Khlong
Dao Beach, Sala Dan, T075-684361,
www.royallanta.com. Aiming for the
family market with children's pool and
playground. Also offers spa, minimart,
internet and good coffee shop selling tasty
cakes. Impersonal large restaurant, rather
bare rooms. Over 50 cottages with red
steeply pitched roofs.

$$$$-$$$ Andaman Lanta Resort,
142 Moo 3, Khlong Dao Beach, T075-
684200-2, www.andamanlantaresort.
com. Towards the south, this was the first
real hotel on Koh Lanta, which is used as
a selling point. The 2-storey building of
69 rooms is nothing special and, although
there is a pool, these rooms are overpriced
for what they are. The blue-roofed
bungalow rooms are better value and nicer.
Perhaps because of increased competition,
good discounts are offered even in peak
season without too much prompting.

**$$$$-$$$ Cha-Ba Bungalows & Art
Gallery**, 20 Moo 3, Khlong Dao beach,
T075-684118, www.krabidir.com/
chababungalows. Walk along Khlong
Dao beach and you'll eventually come
across a series of giant, brightly coloured,
amorphous sea creature sculptures. The
rooms and bungalows are not as inspired
as the artwork, but it is very friendly. The art
gallery holds various exhibitions differing in
quality. Good food. Recommended

$$$$-$$$ DR Lanta Bay Resort, 206 Moo
3, T075-668383, www.drlantaresort.com.
Typical resort-style accommodation ranging
from rooms to bungalows. All rooms come
with TV, fridge, a/c, safety deposit box and
hot water. New rooms at the back near the
2nd pool offer the best value. A bit pricey,
especially since breakfast is not included.

$$$$-$$$ Golden Bay Cottage, 22 Moo 3,
T075-684161, www.goldenbaycottagelanta.
com. There are 4 styles of room, all with
TV, fridge, a/c and hot water. Hotel room
ambience. Friendly, helpful owners and an
easy place to get to. Awesome restaurant
serving some of the best Thai and Isaan
food on the beach.

$$$$-$$$ Holiday Villa, 220 Moo 3, Sala
Dan, T075-684370, www.holidayvillalanta.
com. A large 42-room hotel at the
southern end of the beach. Big concrete
suite bungalows and a pool. Rooms are
spacious but rather dark. The 2 waterslides
keep the kids entertained.

**$$$$-$$$ Lanta Mermaid Boutique
House**, 333 Moo 3 Khlong Dao Beach,
T075-684364, www.lantamermaid.com.
Well-designed and contemporary small
hotel set on the main road 200 m from the
beach. Rooms are all a/c and en suite with
balconies and cable TV – the ones at the
back are both quieter and cheaper.

$$$$-$$$ Sayang Beach, situated just
south of the **Lanta Villa** between Khlong
Dao and Ao Phra-Ae, T08-1476 6357
(mob), www.say angbeachlanta.com.
This operation is run by a local family that
took care to protect the environment
while constructing their bungalows (unlike
many), leaving trees to provide necessary
shade and ambience. Excellent food cooked
by one of the daughters, with fresh fish
nightly. The bungalows are large; the ones
towards the beachfront are better quality,
while the others at the back are rather too
close together.

$$$$-$$$ Southern Lanta Resort,
105 Moo 3, T075-684175, www.southern
lanta.com. Concrete bungalows, clean if
a tad boring. Price varies with location.
All rooms have a/c, TV, fridge. There is a
restaurant, swimming pool, playground,
shop and internet. Staff are friendly, helpful
and speak very good English. Pool can get a
bit murky. Loads of kids here.

$$$$-$$ Lanta Garden Home Resort,
18 Moo 3, T075-684084, www.krabidir.com/

lantagardenhome. This resort offers a variety of accommodation. The cheapest rooms have fan and shared facilities; the most expensive have hot water, a/c and beachside location. Small swimming pool.

$$$ Banana Garden Home, 20/2 Moo 3, T08-1634 8799 (mob), www.bananagarden home.com. Wooden bungalows with a/c, rather tightly packed together but well crafted with natural materials. The manager really goes the extra mile for her guests. Decent restaurant and cushioned beachfront lounging area. No pool but still good value for this location. Recommended.

$$$ Lanta Sea House, 15 Moo 3, Sala Dan, T075-684073-4, www.lantaseahouseresort. com. A/c bungalows and beachfront pool. Consistently well-kept establishment. Chilled-out and cheerful. A range of room types, all are clean and well supplied; the more expensive have spacious balconies and their own bathroom. Very good value in the low season.

$$$-$ Hans Restaurant & Bungalows, next to Fun, Sun & Sea, T075-684152. Basic wooden bugalows with cold water bathrooms. Fresh coffee available. Looking neglected and dirty in places. Ripe for a renovation.

$$ Sun, Fun & Sea Resort, 240 Moo 3, T075-684025. Both fan and a/c rooms have hot water but all are dated and the beds are uncomfortably old. Good location but still overpriced.

Ao Phra-Ae (Long Beach) p124, map p122

$$$$-$$$ Chaw Ka Cher Lanta Tropicana Resort, 352 Moo 2, T075-667122, www.lantatropicanaresort.com. Set on a hill just off main road at the far southern end of Ao Phra-Ae, this is a friendly and beautifully laid out resort. The gorgeous bungalows have open-air bathrooms. There's a pool, excellent restaurant, free internet and a huge library. 500 m from the beach; owners supply bicycles to get you there. Recommended.

$$$$-$$$ Lanta Palm Beach Resort, 47 Moo 3, T075-684603, www.lantapalm beachresort.com. Recently upgraded to all a/c bungalows. It's clean, and the staff are helpful. Next to a hippy-like village, situated on the beach, which is full of bars and restaurants. PADI dive centre on site.

$$$$-$$$ Nakara Long Beach Resort, 172 Moo 3, T075-684198, www.lantalong beach.com. Recently renovated and rebranded, this collection of a/c bungalows now has the feel of a package tour resort. A bit overpriced for what's offered, but excellent location and 2 pools.

$$$$-$$ Mook Lanta, 343 Moo 2, T075-684638, www.mooklanta.com. These bungalows have been built with considerable attention to detail. All rooms, even fan, come with hot water and Wi-Fi access. Beautifully designed with nice finishes, such as silk throws, mood lighting and curtains. The management go out of their way to be helpful. Highly recommended.

$$$$-$$ Relax Bay, 111 Moo 2, T075-684194, www.relaxbay.com. 37 large rustic bungalows, some basic, some VIP, raised high off the ground and scattered through a beachside grove. They have unusually angled roofs, comfortable verandas, glass and/or mosquito panels in the windows, fans and showers. Some tented beachfront cabanas are also available. Decent beach bar, restaurant and pool. Recommended.

$$$ Freedom Estate, 157 Moo 2, T075-684251, www.lanta-servicedapartments. com. At the back of Ao Phra-Ae and up Lanta hill, overlooking the beach. 6 self-contained and serviced fan units with gas-oven kitchens, good for families who tire of eating out all the time, but you would need access to transport into the markets in Sala Dan or the old town. You could also try buying fish directly off the Chao Le fishermen in the Old Town. Balcony. Excellent value in the low season. Recommended.

$$$-$$ Lanta Sunny House, 42 Moo 2, Ao Phra-Ae, T075-684347. Fan or a/c rooms. Tired looking guesthouse which has seen better days. The beach is a short walk down an alleyway. Pool, restaurant and internet.

$$$-$$ Thai House Beach Resort, 38/2 Moo 2, T075-684289, www.thaihousebeach resort. net. This resort is on the beach and offers a range of rooms, including some spacious bungalows, a/c and fan. Friendly management offers discounts for long-term stays.

$$ Blue Sky Resort & Restaurant, 238 Moo 3, T075-684871, www.blueskylanta. com. Bamboo huts, very clean and surprisingly spacious. Super-friendly staff. Recommended for its beachfront location.

$$ Somewhere Else, next to Lanta Sand Resort, T09-731 1312. The bamboo huts with decorative woven walls are rather dark inside but have fan and mosquito net and pretty bathrooms with cold water. All huts have verandas and hammocks. Great cabanas right on the beach. Closed in low season.

$$-$ Lanta Marina Resort, 147 Moo 2, T075-684168, www.lantamarina.com. Bamboo bungalows on stilts which look a bit like haystacks but are comfortably, if basically, furnished with mattresses on the floor and mosquito nets, some with bathrooms attached. Good access to beach with swimming and snorkelling.

$ Sea Culture House, 317 Moo 3, T075-684541. Next to Relax Bay on a very quiet stretch of beach with soft sand – the sea here is good for swimming. Basic wooden bungalows which are sturdier than they look. Bathroom inside. Owner also rents out tents for ฿100. Occasional beach parties with live reggae music. For this price and location, recommended.

Hat Khlong Khoang p124, map p122
$$$-$$ Lanta Emerald Resort, 154 Moo 2, T075-667037. Bamboo fan bungalows at the back and concrete a/c rooms nearer the beach. Family atmosphere and a laid-back vibe with many people returning year after year. Swimming pool, internet and restaurant.
$$$ Nice and Easy, 315 Moo 2, T06-891 2764, www.niceandeasylanta.com.

It's easy to spot this resort as the owner's art deco house-cum-spaceship, fronts onto the beach. The solid teak, a/c bungalows resemble very quaint Swiss cottages inside. There is a small pool and the staff are friendly.

$$$-$$ Lanta New Coconut Bungalow, 22 Moo 2, T75 667107. Sturdy wooden fan and a/c bungalows with TV. Hot-water showers in the large but dim bathrooms. Big restaurant. Swimming pool. Great location on the beach. Chilled-out vibe.

$$$-$$ Lanta Riviera Resort, 121 Moo 1, Sala Dan, T075-667044, www.lantariviera resort.com. Bungalows with fan or a/c and attached shower, quiet and relaxed atmosphere. Bar, restaurant, internet and swimming pool.

$$$-$ Where Else Resort, 149 Moo 2, T075-667024, www.lanta-where-else. com. Bags of character at this budget resort featuring well-designed bamboo and driftwood bungalows half hidden in the coconut grove. All have semi-outdoor bathrooms, mosquito screens and hammocks. The ones at the back are a little cramped together. Recommended.

$$ Fisherman's Cottage, 190 Moo 2, Klong Khong Beach, T08-1476 1529 (mob), www.fishermanscottage.biz. Collection of 9 concrete bungalows, all with sea views, thatched roofs and a funky style. The bohemian staff are very family friendly – so is the beach, a safe place to swim. Good music at the bar. Recommended.

$$ Lanta Thip House, 361 Khlong Khoang Beach, T075-684-888, www.lantathip house.com. Small hotel set on the main road about 200 m from the northern end of the beach. Rooms are all a/c, en suite and have a contemporary, modern feel. Friendly owners and excellent food and coffee.

$$-$ Bee Bee Bungalows, T081-537 9932 (mob), www.diigii.de/sugarbeebee. A village-like set-up of unusual-looking bamboo bungalows set just back from the beach in a coconut plantation. Some with 2 levels and all with bamboo bathrooms.

Charming and different. Closed during the low season. Recommended.

Khlong Toab *p125, map p122*
$$$$ Rawi Warin Resort and Spa, 139 Moo 8, T075-607400, www.rawi warin.com. The most luxurious and most expensive resort on the island. This is a massive development of stunning pool villas (US$2000 a night), with incredible facilities including a floating swimming pool and a private cinema. There's even a music room featuring a US$150,000 stereo system built by the hi-fi-obsessed Chinese owner. Service and food quality might not quite match the prices charged, however.

$$$ Lanta Palace, 29 Moo 8, T075-662571, www.lantapalace.com. Looks like something straight out of a European seaside resort, with concrete cottages in a small garden. The bungalows are a bit too close together, but this is a quiet part of the coastline, comfortable and popular with families. Don't bother with the cheaper rooms at the back – they are in a bland concrete building set behind the car park with no views.

$$ Lanta River Sand, T075-662660, www.lantariversand.com. This is actually between Khlong Toab and Klong Nin beaches. Touted as being made from 'ecological materials grown locally' (or trees), these 15 simple bamboo bungalows are set around a brackish water lagoon and in amongst trees with lots of mosquitos. It is also the sister resort of **Lanta Marina**. Interesting and in a more secluded location, even if a little dark. Also a reasonable-ish price for these parts.

Ao Khlong Nin *p125, map p122*
$$$$ The Houben, 272 Moo 5, T075-665144, www.thehouben.com. Modern, delightfully bizarre cliffside resort with big rooms and fantastic sea views. Looking more like a UFO making a pit stop on Planet Lanta, the design couldn't be more incongruous to its surroundings, but it's fun

all the same. Red-tiled swimming pool. Full range of facilities including en suite double jacuzzis. No beach though. Popular with honeymooners.

$$$$ Narima Bungalow Resort, 98 Moo 5, Klong Nin, T075-662668, www.narima-lanta.com. Large family-run bungalows with wooden floors overlooking a quiet part of beach. Good Thai food. Pool, exercise bicycle, DVDs, CDs and a mini-library. Good discounts if you stay for 7 or 14 nights. Recommended.

$$$$-$$$ Lanta Paradise Beach Resort, 67 Moo 6, T075-662569, lantaparadisebeach resort.com. All beds have mosquito nets and fans, some have a/c. Big beachfront restaurant and pool but the beach isn't the best. Both the staff and surroundings could use a bit of an uplift.

$$$$-$$$ Sri Lanta, T075-662688, www.srilanta.com. This fairly upmarket resort stars spacious, well-designed bamboo-and-wood bungalows with a/c (but sadly no mosquito screening or ceiling fans) and hot showers. Beautiful spot with access to a sandy beach, massage pavilions and a stylish pool. Recommended.

$$$ Dream Team Beach Resort, 38 Moo 5, T075-662551, www.dreamteambeach resort.com. Good restaurant that uses the resort's own home-grown produce. Concrete bungalows with fan or a/c, nothing special but in a nice garden setting, some with sea views. Swimming pool.

$$$-$$ Lanta Miami Resort, 13 Moo 6, T075-662559, www.lantamiami.com. A/c and fan bungalows have recently been refurbished with attractive wood panelling and a contemporary interior style. Some rooms have bathtubs. Now has a pool and is open year-round. Tour desk, internet, massage. Helpful staff. Recommended.

$$$-$ Lanta Nature Beach Resort, 54 Moo 6, T075-662560, www.lanta naturebeachresort.com. Decent fan and a/c bungalows, friendly and helpful management. Also has very basic but cheap fan bungalows across the main road.

Nice big lounging platforms on the beach and a laid-back traveller feel. Closed during the rainy months.

Ao Kantiang *p125, map p122*
$$$$ Pimalai Resort, 99 Moo 5, Ba Kaiang Beach, T075-607999, www.pimalai.com. Huge and very pricey resort; beautifully designed rooms, although there's an awful lot of concrete used in the gardens. The resort also encroaches on the beach – something that undoes its avowed eco-aims in one fell swoop. Extensive facilities.
$$$-$$ Lanta Marine Park View Resort, 58 Moo 5, www.lantamarinepark.com. Set up high on the hill overlooking Ao Kantiang with great views of the bay from the bungalows in front. Several styles of bungalow: the small bamboo ones set back from the view are the cheapest; the larger concrete ones with views from the balconies are the most expensive. Rooms are spacious and comfortable. The walk up to the bungalows will keep you fit. Cleaning and maintenance could be better.

Ao Khlong Jaak *p125, map p122*
$$$$ Andalanta Resort, T075-665018, www.andalanta.com. Well-run, friendly resort set amid trees and by the beach. Variety of wood and concrete bungalows, good facilities. Free kayaks. Boat trips are organized to nearby islands and other places of interest. Shuts down in the rainy season.
$ Khlong Jark Bungalows. Simple bamboo bungalows. Frogs in the room can be very pleasant to hear late at night. Good slap-dash atmosphere. Closed in low season.

Ao Mai Phai *p125, map p122*
There are several bungalow resorts in this bay from **Bamboo Bay Resort** to **Last Resort**. All offer roughly the same style accommodation in **$$-$** range, with simple bamboo bungalows and varying degrees of access to the sea/views, etc. All seem

friendly. It's difficult to get to in the rainy season given the bad state of the road, but a good escape from the more built-up resort areas on Koh Lanta and within easy reach of the national park.
$$$$ La-Laanta Hideaway Resort, T075 665066, www.lalaanta.com. A new and decidedly upmarket addition to Mai Phai, La-Laanta has well designed a/c bungalows with a cool rustic-meets-modern design, artistic touches and good facilities including a pool. 4 room types, each with TV/DVDs and Wi-Fi.

Restaurants

All the guesthouses and hotels provide restaurants with similar menus.

Sala Dan *p123, map p122*
In Sala Dan there are some small cafés, **Swiss Bakery** and **Santos**, good pastries and coffee.
$$$-$$ The Frog Wine & Grill, T075-668325, has a mostly Western menu, including tasty burgers and, for those pining for some wine, it has more than 60 selections to choose from.
$ Seaview 1 (aka **Monkey in the Back**), offers slow service, good, cheap seafood, no electricity. **$ Seaview 2**, has a larger menu of Thai and seafood; it's friendly and cheap, and the enormous scones are tasty and filling. Both overlook the bay between Lanta Noi and Lanta Yai (rather windy).

Ban Koh Lanta Yai *p123, map p122*
$$$-$ Mango House Restaurant, below **Mango House** guesthouse. Decent Thai and Western food in this 70-year-old wooden shophouse turned atmospheric little hang-out spot. Bar serves cocktails, wines and various whiskies.
$$ Krue Lanta Yai Restaurant, at the end of 'town', T075-697062. Hours variable. A restaurant on the pier along a walkway filled with plants. Good selection of fresh seafood nicely prepared. Recommended.

$ Rom Thai, on the pier. Downmarket; also sells seafood but it's not as sophisticated as Krue Lanta Yai.

Ao Khlong Dao *p124, map p122*

$$$ Sayang Beach Resort Restaurant, Khlong Dao Beach by Lanta Sand Resort and Spa. Excellent Malay-Thai fusion cuisine here – among the best along the west coast cooked with real flair and precision. Recommended.

$$$ Time for Lime, 72/2 Moo 3, Klong Dao Beach, T075-684590, www.timeforlime.net. Popular offshoot restaurant from the Thai fusion cooking school of the same name (see What to do, below). Profits go to the owner's local animal welfare centre.

$$$-$$ Costa Lanta Restaurant, northern stretch of the beach. Lunch and dinner, served in exquisite surroundings. This spacious building mixes concrete, wood and fabrics to create a very special ambience. Delicious Thai food and a decent wine list. The bar is perfect to relax with a drink, after a hard day on the beach; this isn't the place to lounge about in a bikini or Speedos. Recommended.

$$$-$$ Golden Bay, see Where to stay, above. Beachside restaurant in the bungalow operation of the same name. Excellent Thai and Isaan food on sale here. They also BBQ a fresh catch of seafood daily and offer discounts in low season. Reasonably priced in comparison to other places.

$$$-$$ Picasso Restaurant, Chaba Bungalows & Art Gallery, 20 Moo 3, Khlong Dao beach, T075-684118. Eclectic array of good Mexican-, Thai- and Mediterranean-inspired food in this funky restaurant.

Ao Phra-Ae (Long Beach) *p124, map p122*

$$ Faim de Loup, on the main road opposite Mr Wee pizza. Modern French bakery that's become a haven for sandwich and coffee lovers. Great desserts, too.

$$ Retro Restaurant & Bar, on the main road, located behind Red Snapper.

Rustic restaurant made from natural local materials, touches most bases on the culinary spectrum: Thai, pizza, pasta and the usual, other European fare.

Hat Khlong Khoang *p124, map p122*

$$-$ Bulan Lanta, opposite Sonya Homestay. Impressive range of Thai food to satisfy your taste buds. Some Western food, such as chips and burgers. Also open for breakfast. Check out the specials board. Free Wi-Fi.

Ao Khlong Nin *p125, map p122*

$$-$ Cook Kai, just across the road from the beach. This family-run restaurant serves a great range of Thai dishes including a comprehensive selection of vegetarian food. Food is served in a traditional Thai building with ornamental seashell chandeliers that tinkle in the sea breeze, making it a beautiful setting to enjoy lunch or dinner Recommended.

$ Green Leaf Café, on the main road, opposite the entrance to the **Where Else Resort**. A warm welcome awaits at this comfy café, which has a rather homely feel. The English and Thai owners offer up real coffees, generous baguettes, served on fresh multi grain bread and healthy salads. For a *farang* food fix, highly recommended.

⚙ Shopping

Koh Lanta *p120, map p122*

Basic supplies are available in Sala Dan and Ban Koh Lanta Yai. Numerous mini-marts are springing up along the main road.

Hammocks

Hammock House, main street, Ban Koh Lanta Yai. A great little shop in an old wooden house. The owner is very friendly and provides visitors with a 'Lanta Biker Map' as well as trying to sell well-made hammocks and art.

Handicrafts.
A Little Handmade Shop, main road, Ao Kantiang, www.littlehandmadeshop. com. Cute, friendly place selling eco-aware items including clothing, notebooks and toys made locally.

What to do

Koh Lanta *p120, map p122*
Cookery classes
Time for Lime, T075-684590/08-9967 5017 (mob), www.timeforlime.net. Contact Junie Kovacs. Learn Thai cookery beside Klong Dao beach.

Diving and snorkelling
There are several schools in Sala Dan (some with German spoken); check equipment before signing on. Snorkelling is known locally as 'snorking'. Most guesthouses hire out equipment for about ฿100 per day, although the quality varies.

Try **Blue Planet Divers**, 3 Moo 1, Ban Saladan, T075-668165, www.blue planetdivers.net; or **Scuba Fish**, Narima Resort, Klong Nin Beach, T075-665095, www.scuba-fish.com.

Horse riding
Mr Yat Riding School, Ao Phra-Ae. Riding along the beach and in the forest.

Tour operators
Most bungalows can make travel arrangements and offer day trips to Trang's Andaman Islands (see page 136), ฿950-1400 per person (depending on the type of boat), including lunch and snorkelling gear. (Note that it is a long trip – 3 hrs each way – and some people find the noise unbearable for just 1 or 2 hrs' snorkelling.) You can also organize trips from Ban Koh Lanta Yai. For long-tailed boat trips from Ban Koh Lanta, including fishing and camping tours, contact **Sun Island Tours**, 9/1 Sri Raya Rd (main waterfront), Lanta Old Town, T08-7891 6619 (mob), www.lantalongtail.com.

Boats leaving from this side of the island can save a couple of hours from the return trip to Koh Ngai and will take you to explore some of the islands on the east side. There are a couple of small tour shops running these businesses in the old town, and **Khrua Lanta Yai** also runs boat trips. **Freedom Adventures**, T08-4910 9132 (mob), www. freedom-adventures.net, organize various day trips (from ฿1400) and camping adventures (from ฿2600). Encourage your boatman to buoy, rather than use an anchor which damages the coral. Comprehensive island tours are offered by a number of tour agencies based in Sala Dan. **Opal Travel**, www.opalspeedboat.com, has reasonably priced tours and excellent service. Lanta Paddlesports, at the Noble House Resort, Ao Khlong Dao, www.lantapaddlesports. com, offers guided paddleboard tours, plus rentals and lessons for surfing and stand-up paddleboarding.

Hire long-tailed boats from bungalows for ฿1200 per person, based on 4 people per trip, per day. This price includes all snorkelling gear and food.

Transport

Koh Lanta *p120, map p122*
Bicycles
The laterite roads are rough. Mountain bikes can be hired from bungalows for ฿150 per day, motorbikes for ฿250 per day. Alternatively, go to Sala Dan.

Boat
Boats leave from Sala Dan on the northern tip of the island and from Lanta Pier on the southeast coast. To **Phi Phi**, there are 2 departures a day, 0800 and 1300, ฿350. Includes transfer from resort to the pier. To **Phuket** boats leave daily, 0800 and 1300, ฿750, and connect with a minivan, ฿196. To **Krabi**, there's 1 ferry daily (high season only) at 0800, 2 hrs, ฿350. To Ao Nang and Railay, 1 ferry a day (high season only), 1330, 2 hrs, ฿350.

Koh Lanta is a stop along the route of Tigerline high-speed ferry that runs a daily service departing from Lanta at 1030 and arriving at Langkawi, Malaysia, at 1000, with stops at Koh Ngai, Koh Kradan, Koh Mook, Had Yao Pier in Trang and Koh Lipe. To Phuket, the ferry departs Lanta at 1600 with a brief stop at Phi Phi. Also runs a service to Ao Nang with stops at Krabi and Koh Jum. You can do some island-hopping and book any leg of these routes separately. Prices and schedule on www.tigerlinetravel.com. Operates Nov-Apr only.

For a quick but rough ride, take the speedboat trip by Satun Pakbara Speedboat Club, www.tarutaolipeisland.com, which has daily transfer services to Phuket, Phi Phi and Koh Lipe.

Minivan
Minivans to **Trang** leave on the hour 0700-1500, ฿250; to **Krabi**, every hour from 0600-1500, ฿200, or ฿300 to the airport.

Pick-up trucks
Some ply the island, but can be horrendously expensive, others serve individual bungalows.

Trang and its islands

On first sight, Trang looks like a somewhat drab but industrious Chinese-Thai town, filled with temples and decent schools – in other words – a good place to raise your children. Everything shuts down at around 2230 in the evening and even the traffic signals seem to go to sleep while early morning is filled with bustling tradespeople, eager to make their fortunes and provide for their families. But there is an underlying cranky charm and no-nonsense energy to this town which is famous for its char-grilled pork, sweet cakes and as the birthplace of former Prime Minister Chuan Leekpai. Its unique entertainments include bullfights (bull to bull) and bird-singing competitions (bird to bird) while the people are hugely friendly and exceptionally helpful the minute they realize that you like Trang too.

Finally, Trang has a nine-day Vegetarian Festival in October, similar to that celebrated in Phuket. Vegetarian patriots, dressed all in white, parade the street, dancing through clouds of exploding fireworks, with the revered few shoving various objects through their cheeks. Trang is also an excellent jumping-off point for Koh Lanta, Krabi and the exotic coral islands just off the coast.

Arriving in Trang

Getting there and around
Trang has an airport, 20 minutes from town, and an air-conditioned minibus costs ฿100 and drops you outside the train station. It is possible to charter a tuk-tuk for ฿150, but this depends very much on your bartering skills. Buses arrive at the Thanon Huay Yod terminal, including buses from Satun, which used to arrive at Thanon Ratsada. To visit the islands you need to arrange minibuses to Pak meng pier. There are also two overnight trains from Bangkok which stop at the station on the western end of Thanon Rama VI. ▸▸ See Transport, page 146, for further information.

Best time to visit
The best time to visit is between January and April, out of the monsoon season. In the low season, some of the island resorts close down, so you do need to check availability.

Background

The town was established as a trading centre in the first century AD and flourished between the seventh and 12th centuries. Its importance rested on its role as a relay point for communications between the east coast of Thailand and Palembang (Srivijaya) in Sumatra. It was then known as Krung Thani and later as Trangkhapura, the 'City of Waves'. The name was shortened in the 19th century to Trang. During the Ayutthaya period, the town was located at the mouth of the river and was a popular port of entry for Western visitors continuing north to Ayutthaya. Later, during King Mongkut's reign, the town was moved inland because of frequent flooding.

The arrival of the Teochew (Chinese) community in the latter half of the 19th century was a boon to the local economy which, until the introduction of rubber from Malaysia, was reliant on tin mining. Trang's rubber plantations were the first in Thailand (the first tree

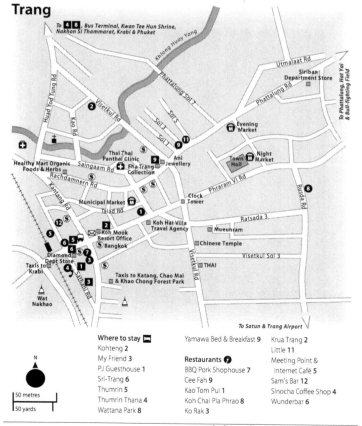

Trang

Where to stay
Kohteng 2
My Friend 3
PJ Guesthouse 1
Sri-Trang 6
Thumrin 5
Thumrin Thana 4
Wattana Park 8

Yamawa Bed & Breakfast 9

Restaurants
BBQ Pork Shophouse 7
Cee Fah 9
Kao Tom Pui 1
Koh Chai Pla Phrao 8
Ko Rak 3

Krua Trang 2
Little 11
Meeting Point &
  Internet Café 5
Sam's Bar 12
Sinocha Coffee Shop 4
Wunderbar 6

was planted just south of the city) and its former ruler, Phraya Rasdanupradit Mahitsara Phakdi, is credited with encouraging the spread of its cultivation. He also built the twisting road from Trang across the Banthat Range to Phattalung. There is a statue of him 1 km out of town on the Phattalung road.

Trang → *For listings, see pages 141-147.*

Trang has retained the atmosphere of a Chinese immigrant community, many of whom would be descendents of those who fled the corrupt and oppressive Manchu government. There are good Chinese restaurants and several Chinese shrines dotted throughout the town that hold individual festivals. The **Kwan Tee Hun shrine**, dedicated to a bearded war god, is in Ban Bang Rok, 3 km north of Trang on Route 4. The Vegetarian Festival centres around the **Kiw Ong Eia Chinese Temple** and **Muean Ram**. There is also the **Rajamangkala Aquarium** ① *T075-248201-5, open daily during 'official hours'*, which lies 30 km from the city on the road to Pakmeng and is housed in the Fishery Faculty of the Rajamangkala Institute of Technology. The aquarium has 61 tanks of freshwater and marine life. Former **Prime Minister Chuan Leekpai's house** (ask locally for directions) has also become a pilgrimage spot of sorts and is open to visitors.

Beaches around Trang
Trang's embryonic tourism industry has so far escaped the hard sell of Phuket and Pattaya – excellent news for nature lovers, reef divers and explorers. The strip of coast running south from Pakmeng (38 km west from Trang) round to Kantang, boasts some of the south's best beaches. Unfortunately, it is also a relatively expensive place to stay with frankly exorbitant rates charged at some of the more popular beaches and islands and very ordinary food. **Pakmeng and Chang Lang** beaches are the most accessible – 40 km west of Trang town. The sea is poor here for swimming but it's a nice place to walk, although scarcely as scenic as the beaches of Koh Lanta or Krabi.

To the north, down the road from Sikao, is **Hua Hin** which has a good beach and is famed for its *hoi tapao* – sweet-fleshed oysters. Unfortunately the oyster season climaxes in November – the peak of the wet season. Hua Hin Bay is dotted with limestone outcrop islets. Other beaches to the south include **Hat San**, **Hat Yong Ling**, **Hat Yao** and **Hat Chao Mai**; private ventures are not permitted at any of the beaches within the national park (ie Hat Chao Mai, Hat Yong Ling and Hat San).

Parks around Trang
Hat Chao Mai National Park has some impressive caves near the village, known for their layered curtain stalactites. The beaches and many of the offshore islands fall under the jurisdiction of the 230-sq-km Hat Chao Mai National Park. Accommodation is available at park headquarters (6 km outside Chao Mai). See Where to stay, page 142. To get to the park, you need to take a minibus from the minibus station on Thaklang Road (฿100).

Khao Chong Forest Park, 20 km from town, off the Trang–Phattalung road, supports one of the few remaining areas of tropical forest in the area and has two waterfalls, Nam Tok Ton Yai and Nam Tok Ton Noi. Government resthouses are available here. To reach the park, you can take a local bus (from the bus station on Huay Yod Road), bound for Phattalung or Hat Yai, ฿15 or a *songthaew* from near the old market on Ratchadumnuen Road, ฿25.

Trang's Andaman Islands → For listings, see pages 141-147.

Trang's Andaman Islands number 47 in total and spread out to the south of Koh Lanta. More tourists are visiting the islands, and the beauty, rich birdlife and the clear waters that surround them make more upmarket development highly likely. The islands can be reached from several small ports and fishing villages along the Trang coast, the main ones being Pakmeng (take a minibus from Thaklang Road, ฿60) and Kantang, 24 km from Trang. It is also possible to charter boats with the Muslim fishermen who live on the islands. The best time to visit the area is between January and April. The weather is unsuitable for island-hopping from May to December and although it is sometimes still possible to charter boats out of season, it can be expensive and risky: the seas are rough, the water is cloudy and you may be stranded by a squall or equally by the boatmen's incompetency

Trang's Andaman Islands

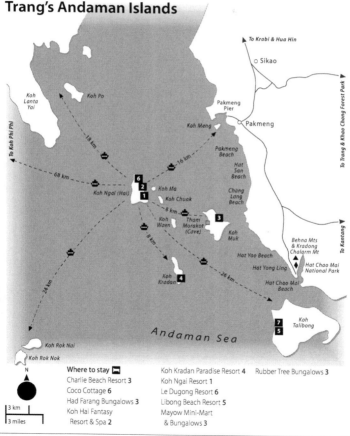

Where to stay
Charlie Beach Resort **3**
Coco Cottage **6**
Had Farang Bungalows **3**
Koh Hai Fantasy
  Resort & Spa **2**
Koh Kradan Paradise Resort **4**
Koh Ngai Resort **1**
Le Dugong Resort **6**
Libong Beach Resort **5**
Mayow Mini-Mart
  & Bungalows **3**
Rubber Tree Bungalows **3**

3 km
3 miles

and a vessel which was never seaworthy in the first place. There is a also a tendency to overbook these boats and consequent delays as the operators wait for further customers.
▸▸ *See Where to stay, page 142, for accommodation on the islands.*

Koh Ngai (Hai)

This 5-sq-km island is cloaked in jungle and fringed with glorious beaches. It also enjoys fabulous views of the limestone stacks that pepper the sea around it. A coral reef sweeps down the eastern side, ending in two big rocks, between which rips a strong current – but the coral around these rocks is magnificent. Koh Ngai is the clichéd resort island retreat where you wake up, eat and sleep at the same place. There are just a handful of resorts on this island and no local community. If you like this sort of intense group intimacy, Koh Ngai is perfect but guests have complained of cabin fever setting in after a week. It is more suited to honeymooners or those who will stay here as a base and do day trips to other islands. Although Koh Ngai forms the southernmost part of Krabi province and is most easily reached from Pakmeng in Trang province, 16 km away, it is also possible to get there from Koh Phi Phi and Koh Lanta. Tourists also stop here on island-hopping day trips to eat at one of the resorts and to snorkel in the magnificently clear waters which are rich with marine life.

Koh Chuak and **Koh Waen** (between Koh Hai and Koh Muk) are also snorkellers' havens – the latter is the best reef for seafan corals.

Koh Muk (Mook)

On the western side of Koh Muk is the **Emerald Cave** (Tham Morakot) – known locally as Tham Nam – which can only be entered by boat (or fearless swimmers) at low tide, through a narrow opening. After the blackness of the 80-m-long passage it opens into daylight again at an inland beach straight out of Jurassic Park – emerald water ringed with powdery white sand and a backdrop of precipitous cliffs that look as if they are made of black lava frozen over the centuries. The cave was only discovered during a helicopter survey not very long ago and is thought to have been a pirates' lair. **Be warned**, you can only leave the pool at low tide. Unfortunately this is being oversold and there have been groups of Southeast Asian tourists who combine the swimming into the cave with positive reinforcement songs that can be heard up to a mile away as everyone shouts in unison – 'we can do this' and 'we will succeed, onward, onward'. Unless you are in with the crowd, this is unfailingly depressing and destroys the mystique of this one-off place. The only way around the group scene is to hire a long-tailed boat privately and try to go at an early hour although the tide does dictate when it is safe to swim in.

The island's west coast has white beaches backed by high cliffs where swallows nest. There are also beautiful beaches on the east coast facing the craggy mainland.

Koh Kradan

Koh Kradan, most of which falls within the bounds of the Chao Mai National Park, is regarded as the most beautiful of Trang's islands, with splendid beaches and fine coral, on the east side. Two Japanese warships sunk during the Second World War lie off the shore and are popular dive spots. The area not encompassed by the national park is a mixture of rubber smallholdings and coconut groves. The island – bar the park area – is privately owned, having been bought by tycoon Mon Sakunmethanon in 1985 for ฿5 million. There are just a handful of places to stay here, see Where to stay, page 143.

Koh Talibong (Libong)

Koh Talibong (Libong), which is part of the Petra Islands group to the south, is renowned for its oysters and birdlife. The Juhoi Cape and the eastern third of the island is a major stopping-off point for migratory birds, and in March and April the island is an ornithologist's El Dorado. Typical visitors, on their way back to northern latitudes, include brown-headed gulls, crab plovers, four species of terns, waders, curlews, godwits, redshanks, greenshanks, reef egrets and black-necked storks. From October to March the island is famed for its unique Hoi Chakteen oysters. The rare manatee (*Manatus senegalensis*) and the green turtle also inhabit the waters off the island. The best coral reef is off the southwest coast, directly opposite the **Libong Beach Resort**. Snorkelling equipment is available from the resort, which also provides fishing gear. Libong's main town is Ban Hin Kao, where the daily ferry from Kantang docks. Motorcycle taxis take visitors along rough trails to the island's beaches and villages. Just 4 bungalow resorts operate here. The population is almost exclusively Muslim, and alcohol is not widely available, so you would need to stock up in Trang.

Koh Sukorn (Muu), Koh Petra, Koh Lao Lieng (Nua and Tai)

Koh Sukorn, Koh Petra, Koh Lao Lieng (Nua and Tai) are also part of the Petra Islands group, off Palien, 47 km south of Trang, and can be reached from there or Kantang. Koh Sukorn (locally known as Koh Muu – or Pig Island) is inhabited by Muslims, who do not seem to mind the name. Apart from its golden powdery beaches, its main claim to fame are the mouth-watering watermelons that are grown here (March/April).

Koh Petra and **Koh Lao Lieng** have sheer cliffs which are the domain of the birds' nest collectors who risk life and limb for swiftlet saliva (see box, page 112). The islands have excellent sandy beaches on their east coasts and impressive reefs which are exposed at low tide. Dolphins can often be seen offshore.

Trang and its islands listings

For hotel and restaurant price codes and other relevant information, see pages 12-16.

🛏 Where to stay

Trang *p138, map p137*
Trang makes a good base if you want to explore the south; most places are handily situated between the clock tower and the railway station.
$$$$-$$ Wattana Park, 315/7 Huay Yod Rd, T075-216216, www.wattanaparkhotel. com. A little way out from the town centre on the road in from Krabi. A modern hotel with good rooms and friendly service – probably the best value business-class hotel in Trang. No pool. Recommended
$$$-$$ Thumrin Thana, 69/8 Huay Yod Rd, T075-223223, www.thumrin-thana.com.

This is a couple of kilometres from the town centre, so not an ideal choice if you arrive on the sleeper train from Bangkok. All 285 rooms are en suite, a/c and with colour TVs. There is a pool.
$$$-$ Thumrin, Phraram VI Rd, T075-211011, www.thumrin.com. Downmarket sister hotel to the Thumrin Thana, though the a/c en suite rooms are decent enough, service is fine and location good. Often used as a stopover point for long-distance buses from Malaysia and can be booked out.
$$-$ Sri-Trang Hotel, 22-26 Station Rd (right in front of the station), T075-218122, www.sritranghotel.com. The art deco-styled lobby and atmospheric wooden clapboard exterior ooze character but, while the location is also excellent (though a bit noisy), the rooms here are very average and

a bit overpriced. Mix of fan, a/c, some with private facilities, others without. A good bet if everywhere else is full.

$ Kohteng, 77-79 Phraram VI Rd, T075-218622. Very basic rooms – the a/c options represent best value. No hot water. Staff can be rude and unfriendly.

$ My Friend, 25/17 Sathani Rd, T075-255447, www.myfriend-trang.com. All rooms in this clean, well-run guesthouse are en suite with TV and a/c. Convenient location near the station – they'll let you check-in early, if they have availability, which is good news for those arriving on the sleeper train from Bangkok. Internet, lots of local information, staff are helpful but don't speak much English. Free hot drinks.

$ PJ Guesthouse, 25/12 Sathani Rd, T075-217500. Home-like set-up with traveller ambience and attention to detail. Rooms are small but not too dark and very clean. Shared shower and toilet per floor. Tour service downstairs. Motorbike rental, Wi-Fi. Joy and Pong are helpful owners and both speak good English. Good location about 100 m from the station. Recommended for those on a tight budget.

$ Yamawa Bed and Breakfast, 94 Visetkul Rd, T075-216617. Clean, comfortable fan or a/c rooms in a shophouse. Good price and helpful staff. The rooms at the top are not as dark but avoid the noisy street front. Free Wi-Fi. Recommended at this price.

Beaches around Trang *p138*
$$$$ Anantara Si Kao Resort (formerly the Amari Trang Beach Resort), 198-199 Moo 5, Had Pak Meng, Changlang Beach, T075-205 888, www.sikao.anantara.com. Luxury resort with 139 rooms, suites and pool suites, spa, 5 restaurants, swimming pools, kids' club and a private beach club on Koh Kradan. Aimed at the Scandinavian family market, so couples may be left wanting here. It's set on the beach, but the water and sands here are not especially inviting.

$$$$-$ Lay Trang Resort, 54/22 Moo 4, Pakmeng, T075-274 227-8, www.laytrang. com. A bungalow resort just up from the pier. Good seafood restaurant, well-built and well-equipped resort. Sea canoes and guides for hire. The resort will also arrange camping on the nearby islands, complete with tents, picnic and mobile phone.

$$$-$$ Pakmeng Resort, 60/1 Moo 4, Pakmeng, T075-274 112, www.pakmeng resort.com. Turn left after reaching the main seafront and continue on towards the national park. The resort is on the left and is well marked. Wooden bungalows with attached bathroom and fan and some a/c. The resort backs onto the main khlong leading to the river. Good restaurant. Motorbikes (฿350 per day) and bicycles (฿100 per day) for rent.

$$-$ Haadyao Nature Resort, Chao Mai Marine Park, Hadyao, T08-1894 6936 (mob), nature-haadyao.weebly.com/index.html. Eco-resort with simple a/c bungalows and dorm rooms. Popular spot for student groups. Staff here are well versed about the sights and activities in the area and they arrange tours such as dugong tracking and bird watching. Recommended.

Parks around Trang *p138*
$ Hat Chao Mai National Park Bungalows. There's no restaurant here; you can buy food from a very small shop in Chao Mai village.

Koh Ngai (Hai) *p140*
$$$$-$$$ Coco Cottage, T08-1542 9757/9724 9225, www.coco-cottage.com. Set on Kradan's northeastern side, Coco offers 5 types of a/c bungalows designed to give a real jungle-island feel, with coconut-trunk walls and wood and bamboo-leaf roofs. Some bungalows have verandas that extend over a canal. Decent restaurant and beach bar. Possibly overpriced.

$$$$-$$$ Koh Hai Fantasy Resort and Spa, next door to Koh Ngai Villa, T075-210317, www.kohhai.com. A/c bungalows and family suites. Obscured in the foliage of this idyllic island. Pool. Stately rooms. Has been upgraded since its early days and now has decent food.

$$$$-$$$ Koh Ngai Resort, 142/1 Moo 4, T075-206951, www.kohngairesort.com. In the southeastern corner of the island, with its own magnificent private beach, this is a massive development, with around 60 suites, cottages, villas and bungalows, fan and a/c with private balconies. Overpriced, but the service is friendly and the food has improved. Dominates the beachfront.

Koh Muk (Mook) *p140*

The majority of the accommodation here shuts for 6 months of the year due to navigational difficulties and drought. Nevertheless, Koh Muk has seen a bit of a boom in accommodation; there are now around 20 resorts, which is perhaps surprising for an island with a single 1-km beach with rocks both ends. The other side of the island also has accommodation options, but none are recommended as the village is fairly unsightly, the beach is filthy and the pools of stagnant water are likely to encourage dengue fever.

$$$$-$$ Charlie Beach Resort, T075-203281, reservations T076-356032, www.kohmook.com. Smack bang in the centre of the beach. The bungalows are faultlessly clean and the restaurant and bar serve reasonable food. Swimming pool. Staff can be surly and unfriendly. Very conscious of its monopoly and is overpriced.

$$$-$$ Pawapi, on Sivalai Beach, T08-9669 1980, 08-6889 2112, www.pawapi.com. New, small resort with 10 thatched-roof bungalows on stilts right on the narrow beach. Big, bright and nicely designed, with balconies, private bathrooms but no a/c.

$$$-$$ Rubber Tree Bungalows, T075-215972, www.mookrubbertree.com. Up a long wooden staircase cut into the hill are these marvellous, family-run bungalows with attached toilet and bathroom. Set in a working rubber tree plantation, so you may be woken early in the morning by the lanterns of the rubber tree tappers. You

are welcome to observe them at work. The attached restaurant has easily the best food on the island, cooked by a northern Thai native. Let her choose what to cook if you can't decide. This is a magical place to have an evening drink, with dozens of twinkling lights providing a dreamy backdrop.

$$-$ Had Farang Bunglaows, near Mayow on the hilly part, T08-7884 4785. There are 17 bamboo bungalows with attached bathroom and toilet, some with a/c. It doesn't get much light, as it's in the foliage, but it is close to the beach. Open Nov-Apr only.

$ Mayow Mini-Mart and Bungalows, over a little wooden walkway to the right of Sawadee. 5 bungalows with showers and toilet outside. Mayow (or Meow) is the name of the female owner and she also has a café/kitchen which does good fried fish and banana fritters along with Thai curries. It also operates Dugong Dugong Travel, which arranges snorkelling and diving.

$ Mookies, down the lane/dirt path towards the sea gypsy village (there is only one path on from Rubber Tree), T08-72756533 (mob), mookiebrian@yahoo.com. Open all year. Cross over a wooden bridge and follow the disco music to Mookie's Bar, where you are likely to find Aussie Mookie reading pulp fiction and drinking in the mid-afternoon. This is a completely eccentric set-up. Rooms are large with spring mattresses and 24-hr electricity with light and fan inside. While the toilet and shower is shared, they are kept clean to military standards. The shower outside also has hot water. Highly recommended. See also Restaurants, below.

Koh Kradan *p140*

$$$ Koh Kradan Paradise Resort, book through Trang office, 25/36 Sathani Rd, T075-211391. The Trang office also runs a daily boat service to the island. Expensive, concrete bungalows that have been painted to look like wooden bungalows, and are failing miserably. Friendly staff but overpriced. Visitors regularly complain that the restaurant is one of the poorest in Thailand. Open year-round but only daytime electricity through low season (May-Oct). **$$$-$$ Kalume Village**, T08-9650 3283, www.kalumekradan.com. Small bamboo and wooden bungalows with restaurant and beach bar. Friendly place. Fairly good value for Koh Kradan. Only direct bookings with the resort available.

Koh Talibong (Libong) *p141*
$$$-$$ Libong Beach Resort, Ban Lan Khao, T075-225205, www.libong beachresort.com. Large open-fronted restaurant with about 15 basic bungalows set in a coconut grove facing onto a sandy beach. Overpriced, as is most of Trang's island accommodation.
$$-$ Le Dugong Resort, T08-7972 7228, www.libongresort.com. Simple but rather stylish fan bamboo bungalows with attached bathrooms on stilts sprinkled along the beach. Small restaurant. A bit of a divers' haven with an adjacent dive shop.

Koh Sukhorn (Muu), Koh Petra, Koh Lao Lieng (Nua and Tai) *p141*
Koh Sukorn (Muu)
$$$ Sukorn Cabana Resort, T075-225894, www.sukorncabana.com. Bungalows, all with a/c, are set in coconut trees with attached bathrooms. There's a restaurant on site but there have been complaints about the food quality.
$$$-$$ Sukhorn Beach Bungalows, T075-207707/203301, www.sukorn-island-trang.com. Owned by a Dutchman, some individual bungalows, some attached, with fan and a/c. Excellent restaurant, private beach frontage, bikes for rent, tours arranged. Open year-round.

🍴 Restaurants

Trang *p138, map p137*
Trang's moo yang (BBQ pork) is delicious and one of the town's few claims to national

fame. It is made from a traditional recipe brought here by the town's immigrant Chinese community and is usually served with rice. It's the speciality of several Chinese restaurants, many of which also serve excellent dim sum, and it can also be bought from street vendors, usually only 0900-1500ish. Adventurous foodies should also hit the night market to sample curries and broths ladled over kanom jeen (fermented rice noodles) and topped with raw vegetables, among other exotic local treats.

Opposite the **Meeting Point** are stalls and a **Roti Bread Place** as well as **M & P Bakery**. There is an excellent small night market, selling everything from seasonal fruit through to Isaan food, just off of Phraram VI Rd past the town hall. Open every night 1800-2100. You can also find a few night stalls in the square in front of the railway station. During the day, the municipal market near Rachdamnern Rd is great for fresh fruit and a huge assortment of other munchies. There is a local evening market on the corner of Ruenrom Rd and Pattalung Rd, perfect if you fancy experimenting with local delicacies.

There are several restaurants on Visetkul Rd offering excellent Thai food, and a couple of coffee shops catering to more Western tastes. This area appears to be a hub for tourism development, with souvenir shops on the corner opposite the clock tower and on the road itself.
$$ Koh Chai Pla Phrao, Rusda Rd. Look for a bright yellow sign (Thai only) and a big open-plan eatery for one of the most popular places in Trang. Don't be fooled by the cheap plastic furniture, the Thai food here is awesome. House speciality is grilled fish – so fresh it will be staring back at you – or steamed fish with a mood altering chilli and lime sauce. Highly recommended.
$$ Krua Trang, Visetkul Rd. Excellent Thai food and draft Carlsberg beer. The stuffed steamed seabass is a specialty and is delicious, filleted, stuffed with shrimp and vegetables and then steamed. The entire

range of food is impressive. Staff are friendly and helpful at recommending dishes.

$ BBQ Pork Shophouse, corner of a small *soi* on Kantang Rd. This tiny Chinese place is often packed to the rafters with families queuing for either takeaway or a table. Only really sells one dish – BBQ pork smothered in a sweet gravy with leafy green vegetables on rice. You can also get chicken satay if you ask nicely. Highly recommended.

$ Cee Fah, Pattalung Rd Soi 5. Deliciously cheap and healthy vegetarian Thai food.

$ Kao Tom Pui Restaurant, 111 Phraram IV Rd, T075-210127. Since 1967. Family restaurant, very popular with the locals, an unpretentious café setting with Sino-Portugese feel. Does cauldrons of seafood soup, excellent seafood dishes, including steamed bass. Good vegetables – morning glory with garlic especially nice. Regulars include local gangsters and their girls and large families. Recommended.

$ Ko Rak (also called **Somrak**), 158-160 Kantang Rd. Friendly shophouse-style eatery surrounded by a throng of stalls which sell tender duck and pork rice and noodles. The family who runs this packed place is originally from the Chinese island of Hainan and first came to Trang over 70 years ago. Full of bustle and good grub.

$ Little Restaurant, a stones throw further up Pattalung Rd from from the **Cee Fah** restaurant. Serves both Western and local food, popular with the small expat community.

$ Meeting Point Restaurant and Internet Café, right along from the railway station. This does a good breakfast, decent coffees in an airy café with tiled ceramic floor and wooden benches. For some reason there are pictures of Native Americans on the wall. Also has a little bar. Recommended.

$ Pong O Cha, where Wisekul Rd meets Huai Yod Rd. Popular with locals for tasty traditional Thai breakfasts, cakes and coffee. Opens very early.

$ Sam's Bar, opposite the railway station. Happy hour 1600-1800. Also does fantastic salads and sandwiches. The baguettes are loaded with fresh salad from the deli and are recommended if you are craving some *farang* food.

$ Sinocha Coffee Shop, next to train station. Does a good selection of coffees and decent pastries, tasty Thai food and ice cream. Popular hang-out with tuk-tuk drivers and locals.

$ Wunderbar, 24 Sathani Rd. Western cuisine in small dark wooden café. Good selection of magazines and papers. Decent breakfast and excellent place to pick up information. Also does cheeses if you have a hankering for dairy products. Comforting drinking hole in the evening.

Beaches around Trang *p138*
$ Hat Yao Seafood, Hat Yao. A very good restaurant which is open-fronted and looks out onto the beach.

Koh Muk (Mook) *p140*
$ Mookies Bar. Does spare ribs, hamburgers, grilled chicken, but you need to order ahead of time so he can get the supplies from the mainland. The entertainment here is provided through the colourful tales of Russell who first came to Thailand in 1969.

✱ Festivals

Trang *p138, map p137*
Oct **Vegetarian Festival** (movable). 9-day festival in which a strict vegetarian diet is observed to purify the body. Mediums pierce their cheeks and tongues with spears and walk on hot coals. On the 6th day a procession makes its way around town, in which everyone dresses in traditional costumes. The same event occurs in Phuket, see page 151.

❂ Shopping

Trang *p138, map p137*
Best buys in Trang include locally woven cotton and wickerwork and sponge cake.

Thaklang and Municipal markets are next door to each other in the centre of town, off Rachdamnern Rd.

Ani, T08-1397 4574 (mob), original shop on junction of Visetkul and Pattalung rds, open 0900-1700; new shop on Radchadamnoen Rd near train station, open 0900-2100. Huge range of jewellery, much of it made on the premises.

Charonemwit Bookstore, 88-88/1 Phraram VI Rd and Kantang Rd. For English-language magazines and books. Family-run and very helpful staff.

Fha Trang Collection, 283 Radchadamnoen Rd, T075-217004. Posh and pretty souvenirs reasonably priced. Embroidered shoes, scarves, artistic mobiles and folk craft. There is also a second-hand bookshop next door.

Trang Sura Thip Whiskey Shop, 69/1 Phraram VI, near the clocktower. This tobacco and whiskey shop looks like a log cabin on the inside. Good selection of whiskies and liquors.

⚫ What to do

Trang *p138, map p137*
Bull fighting
Fights between bulls take place at random, depending on whether the farmers have a suitable bull. The only way to find out about whether they are taking place is to ask around. But be warned – this is a very much a local entertainment and you might get some curious looks when you ask, particularly if you are a woman. Scarcely any women attend these events. The fights are usually held during the week and only in the daytime. They occur in a field off Trang-Pattalung Rd near the Praya Ratsadanupradit Monument. The best way to get there is by tuk-tuk, which takes about 20 mins from the railway station. They are always packed by an excitable betting crowd screaming with dismay or joy and there are plenty of stalls about selling drinks and foods, including noodles and fruit. Dusty and hot but exciting.

Snorkelling
Trang Travel, Thumrin Sq. Equipment for hire.

Therapies
Ministry of Health Spa, Panthai Clinic, 32-34-36 Saingam Rd. This superb spa does everything from ear candles to moxibusiton (Gwyneth Paltrow is a great fan of this detoxification process which involves hot suction caps). You can get acupuncture here and Chinese remedies, as well as Thai massage. Reasonable prices in beautiful surroundings. Highly professional.

Yamawa Bed and Breakfast, see Where to stay, above. There is a well-run spa in the guesthouse, offering foot massage and Thai massage at reasonable rates. A cut above the usual offerings with this walk-in shophouse.

Tour operators
Chao Mai Tour Ltd, 15 Satanee Rd, contact Jongkoolnee Usaha, T075-216380, www.chaomai-tour-trang.com, jongkolneetrang@hotmail.com. Reliable, trustworthy and go out of their way to help. Can make hotel reservations, offer information, airport reservations, a/c bus/van transport and tours. English spoken. Recommended.

Underwater weddings
Trang Underwater Weddings. These occur in Feb. For information contact the Trang Chamber of Commerce, T075-5225353, www.underwaterwedding.com.

Koh Ngai (Hai) *p140*
Diving
Rainbow Divers, Koh Ngai Fantasy Resort & Spa, T075-206962. www.rainbow-diver.com. Run by a German couple, who offer PADI courses and excursions, Nov-end Apr.

⊖ Transport

Trang *p138, map p137*
Air
Currently only budget domestic carriers fly to and from Trang Airport, with 4

departures daily to **Bangkok**, with Nok Air, www.nokair.com, at 0920 and 1700; AirAsia, www.airasia.com, at 1125, and Orient Thai, www.flyorientthai.com, at 0910.

Boat

Boats leave from **Pakmeng**, about 25 km west of Trang. Boats from Pakmeng to **Koh Hai**, 45 mins, **Koh Muk**, 1 hr, **Koh Kradan**, 1½ hrs, same price ฿1000-1500 one way, for all destinations. To Ko Muk and Koh Kradan, take a boat from Kuantungku pier, minibuses leave every 30 mins from the minibus station, ฿100. To **Koh Libong**, take a minibus to Hat Yao pier, ฿80, then a long-tailed boat, 0700-1600, ฿80 per person.

To **Koh Tarutao** (Nov-May), take a ferry from Ban Pak Bara pier, 0900, 1100, 1330 and an irregular service at 1630, 1½ hrs. You must buy a National Park ticket, ฿400.

To **Langkawi**, a minivan from your hotel to Tammalang Pier in **Satun**, 2hrs, ฿300, then a ferry boat, ฿400.

Kradan Island Resort operates a boat, minimum 4 people, ฿400 one way, including minivan from Trang. For **Koh Talibong** (Libong) take a taxi from Trang to **Kantang**, ฿350, for the taxi. From there a ferry leaves daily at 1200 for Koh Talibong's (Libong's) 'capital' of Ban Hin Khao and motorcycles take visitors the 5 km to the only hotel, the Libong Beach Resort. **Trang Travel**, opposite the Thumrin Hotel in Trang, also operates a boat which can be chartered to any of the islands. For those with less time on their hands, they offer day excursions.

Trang's Had Yao pier is a stop along the route of Tigerline high-speed ferry that runs a daily service departing Had Yao at 1230 and arriving in Langkawi, Malaysia, at 1700, with a stop at Koh Lipe. To Phuket, the ferry departs at 1300, stopping at Mook, Kradan, Ngai, Lanta and Phi Phi islands along the way. Also runs a service to Ao Nang with stops at Krabi and Koh Jum. You can do some island-hopping and book any leg of these routes

separately. Prices and schedule on www.tigerlinetravel.com. Operates Nov-Apr only.

Bus

Buses to **Bangkok** leave from the bus station on Ploenpitak Rd. Normal a/c at 1630 and 1730, ฿671. VIP at 1730, ฿781. Super VIP at 1700 and 1730, ฿1040. To **Phuket**, regular services from Ploenpitak Rd, from 0600-1800, normal a/c ฿290, VIP ฿340. These buses also stop at **Krabi**. To **Saturn**, non a/c ฿150, from the bus terminal on Huai Yod Rd. To **Phattalung**, a non a/c bus runs from Ploenpitak Rd, 1½ hrs, ฿50.

Minibuses to **Koh Lanta** leave from outside KK Travel, opposite the train station, every hour from 0930-1630, ฿250, 2½ hrs. This is by far the easiest way to get to the island, the minivan drops you off at your resort so you avoid the touts at Sala Dan. Minivan to **Hat Yai** from Huai Yod Rd, every hour 0600-1700, 2 hrs, ฿100. To **Phattalung**, 1 hr, A100; to **Nakhon Si Thammarat**, from Wisekul Rd, every hour from 0600-1700, 2½ hrs, ฿200. To **Ban Pak Bara**, organize a minivan from your hotel, or book through agency, 2 hrs, ฿300. To **Surat Thani**, minivan from Thaklang Rd, near the fruit market, 3 hrs, ฿170.

Motorbike

Available from a number of agencies and hotels, ฿250 per day.

Songthaew

Shared taxi to **Satun**, 6 people, ฿200 each, from Ratsada Rd. To **Ban Pak Bara**, take a *songthaew* from Satun, ฿20. To **Hat Yai**, 6 people, from 0600-1700, leaves when full, ฿120 each.

Train

Overnight trains to **Bangkok** leave twice daily at 1325 and 1720. For an a/c sleeper carriage, an upper bed is ฿761, a lower bed is ฿831.

Tarutao National Park and the far south

While some say that Tarutao is merely a mispronunciation of the Malay words *ta lo trao*, meaning 'plenty of bay', when first spying this ominous humped island rising out of the sea, it is far easier to believe a second interpretation. That is, that Tarutao comes from the Malay word for old, mysterious and primitive. Resonating with a murky history of pirates, prisoners and ancient curses, it is no wonder the island was picked for the reality television series *Survivor* in 2002. Despite dynamite fishing in some areas, the island waters still have reasonable coral, and provide some of the best dive sites in Thailand – particularly around the stone arch on Koh Khai. Adang Island has magnificent coral reefs. These are part of Thailand's best-preserved marine park, where turtles, leopard sharks, whales and dolphins can be spotted.

Inland, over half of Koh Tarutao is dense dark rainforest with only a single 12-km road cutting through the length of the island and scant paths leading into a potentially lethal jungle filled with poisonous snakes and volatile beasts like the wild boar. Created in 1974, the marine national park comprises 51 islands – the main ones being Tarutao, Adang, Rawi, Lipe, Klang, Dong and Lek. Tarutao Park itself is divided into two main sections– the Tarutao archipelago and the Adang-Rawi archipelago.

In the far south, there is the Muslim town of Satun with its preserved shophouses and the Thale Ban National Park.

Arriving in Tarutao National Park

Getting there

Koh Tarutao lies off the coast 30 km south of Pak Bara; Koh Adang, Rawi and Lipe are another 40 km out into the Andaman Sea, while Koh Bulon-Leh is 20 km due west of Pak Bara. Beware of travelling to any of these islands during bad weather; it is dangerous and a number of boats have foundered.

Getting to Tarutao National Park requires some planning. For much of the year, it is not advisable to take a boat to these beautiful islands. Ferries run from October to June, but speedboats or privately hired long-tailed boats can be chartered at other times of year. If you are based on Koh Lipe or Koh Bulon-Leh then hiring private long-tails to other islands is advised as you will otherwise be facing a roundabout route from Satun or **Ban Pak Bara**, thus adding hours to your journey. Ferries depart from Ban Pak Bara and also from Satun's Thammalang pier. ▸▸ *See Transport, page 161, for further information.*

Getting around

Rented bicycles provide an adequate means of traversing Tarutao's main road which is a gruelling route of steep curves occupied at times by cobras and pythons sunning themselves. The only other road on the island is around 6 km long and was built by the prisoners to link the two jails.

Best time to visit

November to April are the best months; the coolest are November and December. The park is officially closed from the end of May to 15 October, but it is still possible to get there. Services run providing the weather is alright. Koh Bulon-Leh is accessible year

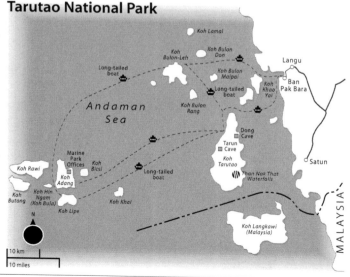

Tarutao National Park

round, although most resorts are closed for six months of the year so it is wise to ring ahead. The annual Tarutao-Adang Fishing Cup Festival takes place in March.

Tourist information

With limited electricity, basic beach restaurants, simple accommodation and few concessions to mainstream tourism, most of the islands attract hardier, more bohemian travellers in search of an unspoilt paradise. Koh Lipe, however, is rapidly transforming into a mini Koh Phi Phi with most of the area's resorts. Bring plenty of cash, as there are no banks on the islands, and only a few dive shops and resorts accept credit cards. Bring food to Koh Tarutao as the park shop has little choice so you might want to stock up on the basics – including alcohol and even fruit. The entrance fee to Tarutao is ฿200 for adults, ฿100 for children under 14. This charge is not enforced on the other islands. The **national park headquarters** ① *close to the ferry port at Pak Bara, T074-781285*, provides information and books accommodation on Tarutao and Adang (messages are radioed to the islands). There can be a shortage in high season. Camping spaces are usually available. On Koh Tarutao and Koh Adang the accommodation is Forestry Department (ie government) run; Koh Lipe and Koh Bulon-Leh are the only islands where the private sector has a presence, meaning the resorts are better and activities more varied.

Background

Koh Tarutao boasts the remains of the prison that held around 10,000 criminals and political prisoners, some of whom became pirates during the Second World War to stave off starvation. Island rumour also has it that somewhere on Koh Tarutao a tonne of gold dust looted from a French ship still remains buried along with the murdered pirates that attacked the unfortunate vessel. Not all of the prisoners on this island were pirates. Indeed the translator of the English/Thai dictionary – Sor Settabut – completed the T section of the book at Tarutao. Another scholar – Prince Sithiporn Kridaka – continued his study of crop diversification that helped modernize Thailand's agriculture. The prince, who was educated largely in England and was a lifelong Anglophile, had been interned for his involvement in attempts to send railway cars to jam tracks on which tanks were being brought to defend Bangkok during widespread insurrections in 1932. The prince was also known for having invented Thailand's first shorthand – still used today – and for forming a boy scout troop among the youths at a government opium factory that he was sent to manage. Imprisoned for 11 years, the prince fell prey to life-threatening dysentery. Yet, it is now believed that the political prisoners received the best of the treatment on Koh Tarutao, where the general criminals may even have served them. Certainly the two groups did not mix, with the criminals held in the eastern part at the present-day Taloh Wow Cove and the political prisoners detained at Udang Cove in the southern tip. But all suffered during the Second World War when the island was completely cut off – along with essential food supplies. In cahoots with the guards, prisoners took to ambushing passing ships, originally for food and then for anything of value. This only came to an end in 1947 when the British, who had retaken Malaya, sent in the Royal Navy to quell the pirates. Afterwards, the island was left in total isolation with the prison gradually reduced to the remains of the prison director's house on top of a dune along with a sawmill below and a mysterious hole indicating a torture cellar. Legend has it that, centuries ago, a princess of Langkawi who had been accused of misdeeds declared that the island would never be discovered. Certainly much of Koh Tarutao holds on to its mystery with its brooding interior and inaccessibility throughout the rainy season.

Koh Tarutao

The mountainous island of Tarutao is the largest of the islands, 26 km long and 11 km wide and covering 151 sq km. A mountainous spine runs north–south down the centre of the island, with its highest point reaching 708 m. The interior remains largely forested, cloaked in dense semi-evergreen rainforest. The main beaches are **Ao Moh Lai**, **Hin Ngam**, **Ao Phante**, **Ao Chak** and **Ao Sone**, mostly on the west of the island which has long sweeps of sand punctuated by headlands and mangrove. Ao Sone, for example, is a 3 km-long stretch of sand fringed with casuarina trees. (Much of the mangrove was cut for charcoal during the early 1960s before the national park was finally gazetted in 1974.) Notorious as the beach where a lone pirate killed a camping tourist in the 1980s, this eerie strip has quite a physical presence, unlike any of the other beaches along the west coast. The water is aggressive and choppy while Tarutao looms out from the water. This haunting beach, while it does have refreshments at one end, is not as busy as the others. Well worth the visit to Tarutao for the feeling that not everything has been tamed. You can also spot the delightfully electric kingfisher here.

Tae Bu cliff, just behind the park headquarters on Ao Phante, has good sunset views. You climb up an imaginative route which includes a path cut into the hill, rickety wooden plank steps and extraordinary rock formations, all the while hearing the sound of monkeys, mouse deer, hornbills and perhaps wild boar. Finally you reach the top and a lookout point over the beach and surrounding forest, which is not as satisfying as the walk itself. You may also find it taken over by groups of young park staff – especially in the early morning.

The prison at Ao Talo U-Dang, in the south, was established in 1939 and was once used as a concentration camp for Thailand's political prisoners; the graveyard, charcoal furnaces and a fish fermentation plant are still there. The other main camp, at Ao Talo Wao on the east side of the island, was used for high-security criminals. During the Second World War, when communications were slow and difficult, the remoteness of the island meant it was cut off from supplies of food. After 700 out of the 3000 prisoners died, the desperate inmates and some of the guards became pirates to stay alive. The prisons have been partially restored as historical monuments. Today the only people living on the island are the park wardens and other staff.

Coconut plantations still exist on Tarutao but the forests have barely been touched, providing a habitat for flying lizards, wild cats, lemur, wild boar, macaques, mouse deer and fishing cows, believed to have bred when the prisoners were taken from the island. Crocodiles once inhabited Khlong Phante and there is a large cave on the Choraka (crocodile) water system known as **Crocodile Cave** (bring a torch). The best way to see wildlife on Koh Tarutao is to walk down the 12-km road during the dry season when animals come out in search of water. There are also many species of bird on the islands including colonies of swiftlets found in the numerous limestone caves – mainly on **Koh Lo Tong** (to the south of Tarutao) and **Koh Ta Kieng** (to the northeast). Large tracts of mangrove forest are found here, especially along Khlong Phante Malacca, on Tarutao. The islands are also known for their trilobite fossils, 400 to 500 million years old, found not just on Tarutao but all over the national park.

While the waters around Tarutao are home to four species of turtle (the Pacific Ridleys, green, hawksbill and leatherback), whales and dolphins are also occasionally seen; the sea is clearer further west in the waters of the Adang-Rawi archipelago (see below).

Koh Bulon-Leh

① *Numerous resorts and fishermen operate boat tours around the area, costing about ฿800 for a half-day of swimming, snorkelling and sometimes fishing. Whales, dolphins and turtles are common.*

While Koh Lipe has had an Urak Lawoi (sea gypsy, or Chao Le) population for perhaps centuries, only in the past 50 years or so has Koh Bulon-Leh had year-round residents: a Muslim population of around 50. The reason for this is down to the superstition of the sea gypsy fisher people, who believed the island was cursed and that everyone who lived there met an untimely death. This kept the island uninhabited until after the Second World War; since then it was discovered that the high mortality rate was due to tuberculosis.

The lifestyle here is exceedingly laid-back and in the more expensive resorts – boho-chic. One of the perks to having had few tourists and a rather isolated position, is that visitors will often join simple pleasures like the evening rugby games by the school or fishing trips with the locals. The island has attracted many returnees – many from Italy and France – and of a wide age range. More upmarket than Koh Lipe, it does offer greater comfort to the well-heeled who sometimes stay for months at a time.

Development is still relatively low-key but land speculation has been going on since the 1990s and investors are no doubt hoping that Koh Bulon-Leh will develop, especially as it is relatively near the pier at Pak Bara. Koh Bulon-Leh is less than 20 km north of Koh Tarutao and about the same distance west of Ban Pak Bara. While it is part of the same archipelago as Tarutao, the island is outside the boundaries of the national park. Furthermore, it has two caves of interest: **Bat Cave**, which houses a small colony of fruit bats, and **Nose Cave**, where it's possible to dive in from one side, swim under the rocks and among thousands of little fish (but beware the moray eel) and come up on the other side.

Adang-Rawi archipelago → *For listings, see pages 155-162.*

Koh Adang and Koh Rawi

Adang and Rawi lie 43 km west of Tarutao and are the main islands in the archipelago of the same name. They offer a stark contrast to Tarutao. While Tarutao is composed of limestone and sandstone, the rugged hills of Adang and Rawi are granite. Adang's highest mountain rises to 703 m while Rawi's is 463 m in height. Koh Adang is almost entirely forested and there is a trail that leads up to the summit, Chado Cliff, for good views over Koh Lipe and the Andaman Sea. There are also a handful of trails through the dense vegetation; to spot the shy inhabitants – including a variety of squirrels, mouse deer and wild pigs – it is best to wait half an hour or so in silence. The main beaches on Adang are Khai, Laem Son, Ao Lo Lae Lae and Lo Lipa, and Sai Khao on Rawi.

Koh Lipe

Koh Lipe, the main tourist destination in this archipelago, is a tropical idyll that is somehow outside the jurisdiction of Tarutao national park despite being located within its bounds. Over the past few years, word of its 600-strong Urak Lawoi sea gypsy populace, its excellent diving and snorkelling in some of the clearest waters in the Andaman Sea, its blindingly white sand beaches and its terrific seafood has spread, particularly among European families with kids in tow. Net result: much of the tiny island, especially the main beach, Pattaya, is now densely populated by bungalows, restaurants and bars, and prices have shot up dramatically. The onslaught hasn't quite reached Koh Lanta or Koh Phi Phi proportions, but signs of environmental strain are everywhere, most glaringly in the form of the smelly barge, overflowing with bags of garbage, that now sits in the middle of Pattaya Beach. Many locals openly lament this rapid development, and its effects were all too obvious on our last visit, when shoddily erected shops were popping up almost overnight along the island's Walking St. While certain resorts have a surface aura of cleanliness and order, this is quickly dispelled by the smell of burning plastic, since rubbish disposal here is largely accomplished on a chaotic and sporadic basis. A rush to push the island upmarket has seen the addition of more energy-sucking amenities, including air-conditioning and swimming pools. Still, though clearly under environmental stress, and pricey, Lipe remains a startlingly beautiful and very mellow island that attracts many returnees.

The Urak Lawoi, who live in a village beside the island's eastern Sunrise Beach, also manage, just, to keep their culture and language intact and hold a traditional ceremony called *pla juk* twice a year. For this, a miniature boat is built out of *rakam* and *teenped* wood by the villagers. Once the boat is completed, offerings are placed in it, and the Chao Le dance until dawn and then launch the boat out to sea, loaded with the village's communal bad luck.

Rampant bungalow expansion on this tiny island means that the resident sea gypsies are hemmed in on both sides by tourist resorts that intrude on their privacy. Some resorts even back directly onto villages, with the unfortunate effect that tourists in bikinis can all too easily stroll into a communal shower occupied by the modest Chao Le, few of whose homes have running water and bathrooms. The Chao Le areas are still at shanty town level, which makes one wonder what benefits they are receiving from unchecked tourism. Indeed, it was only in 1940 that Koh Lipe officially became Thai territory; up to then it was unclear whether the Chao Le here were Malay or Thai. Locals maintain that the Thai authorities encouraged them to plant coconut trees to show that they had settled, presumably on the basis that occupation is as good as ownership.

It's getting harder to do so, but try to seek out and patronize Chao Le-owned businesses wherever possible. More information and tips on being a more eco-conscious visitor are at www.kohlipe.net. Also, bring plenty of cash; as of writing there are still no ATMs on the island, and the resorts and tour desks charge 5-10% for cash advances.

Other islands

Koh Hin Ngam (Koh Bula) is southwest of Adang. The name means 'beautiful rocks', and this striking beach is covered in smooth oval stones that appear to have been polished by hand and that twinkle as the waves wash over them. According to legend, these stones should never be removed or the ghost of Hin Ngami will curse you with bad luck. There is excellent snorkelling. **Koh Khai** has the famous stone arch depicted on many postcards, white powdery sand beaches and some excellent diving. *Khai* means 'egg' in Thai, as this island was a popular turtle nesting site in the past. **Chabang**'s sunken reef is home to hundreds of soft corals of many different colours that make for wonderfully rewarding snorkelling.

The far south → *For listings, see pages 155-162.*

Approached through towering karst peaks and bordered by limestone hills, Satun is a pleasant town with friendly, mostly Muslim inhabitants. Its only real tourist attraction is old town and the Kuden Mansion – a good example of British colonial architecture built by Penang artisans – which can be seen in a day. Most people use the town as a stopover en route to boats for Koh Tarutao, Koh Lipe and Malaysia. Thale Ban National Park, filled with birds and animals and forest trails is 37 km from Satun.

Satun province, which borders Malaysia on the west coast near the Straits of Malacca in the Indian Ocean, is a relatively peaceful place but it has the misfortune of having some troubled neighbours. The deep south provinces of Narathiwat, Yala and Pattani are hotbeds of an ongoing insurgency that has killed more than 4000 since flaring up in the early 2000s. Blanket travel advisories on the far south have meant that Satun is viewed as a danger zone for terrorist activity, particularly following bombings and attacks over the years in some tourist and transport sites in nearby Hat Yai. Having said that, Satun's majority Muslim population is well integrated with the larger Thai society and has remained largely free of violence.

Satun

Surrounded by mountains, Satun is cut off from the Malaysian Peninsula and the eastern side of the Kra Isthmus. Few towns in Thailand, particularly provincial capitals, have escaped thoughtless redevelopment. Satun, though, has done better than most. It has an attractive, low-key centre with preserved shophouses and is Malay in feel; 85% of the population are thought to be Muslim. Few tourists include Satun on their itinerary. Instead, they make a beeline for Ban Pak Bara, 60 km or so north of town and catch a boat to the Tarutao islands (see page 149). But perhaps Satun deserves a few more visitors.

The province seems to have spent the last century searching for an identity separate from that of its neighbours. In the early years of the last century it was administered as part of Kedah, in Malaysia. In 1909, following a treaty between Thailand and Britain, it came under the authority of Phuket. Fifteen years later it found itself being administered from Nakhon Si Thammarat, and it was not until 1932 that it managed to carve out an independent niche for itself when it was awarded provincial status by Bangkok.

The town's main mosque, the **Mesjid Bombang**, was built in 1979 after the previous mosque – also in the shape of a pyramid – fell prey to rot and was torn down. The mosque is on Satunthani Road. More interesting perhaps are the preserved **Chinese shophouses** on Buriwanit Road. They are thought to be around 150 years old; fortunately the town's authorities issued a preservation order on the buildings before they could be torn down and replaced by something hideous. **Ku Den's Mansion**, on Satunthani Road, dates from the 1870s. It was originally the governor's residence. The windows and doors share a Roman motif while the two-storey roof is in Thai Panyi style.

Thale Ban National Park

① *Thale Ban National Park Office, Amphoe Khuan Don, Satun Province, T074-797073. Open daily during daylight hours. Take Highway 4, 406 and 4184 to the park. By public transport catch a songthaew from Samantha Prasit Rd (by the pier) to Wang Prajan. From here there are occasional songthaews the last few kilometres, or take a motorcycle taxi.*

Bordering Malaysia, the Thale Ban National Park was gazetted in 1980 after four years of wrangling and threats from local so-called *ithiphon muut*, or 'dark influences'. It is a small park, covering just over 100 sq km, 37 km from Satun and 90 km from Hat Yai. How it got its name is the source of some dispute. Some people believe it is derived from the Malay words *loet roe ban*, meaning sinking ground; others that it comes from the Thai word *thale*, meaning sea.

The best time to visit Thale Ban is between December and April, when rainfall in this wet area (2662 mm per year) is at its minimum.

At the core of the park is a lake that covers some 30 ha, between the mountains Khao Chin to the east at 720 m and Khao Wangpra to the west. The park has a large bird population: hawks, **hornbills**, falcons and many migratory birds. Animals include dusky-leaf monkeys, white-handed gibbon, lesser mousedeer, wild boar and, it is said, the **Sumatran rhinoceros**. Forest trails lead from the headquarters and it is not unusual to see hornbills, langurs, macaques or even wild pigs. The round trip takes about four hours.

A hiking trail leads from the park headquarters to the summit of **Khao Chin** where it is possible to camp. There are also waterfalls and caves; the most frequently visited waterfall is **Ya Roi**, 5 km north of the park headquarters and accessible by vehicles. The falls plunge through nine levels; at the fifth is a good pool for swimming. En route to Ya Roi is a modest cave: **Ton Din**.

Tarutao National Park and the far south listings

For hotel and restaurant price codes and other relevant information, see pages 12-16.

◯ Where to stay

Tarutao National Park *p148, map p149*
Ban Pak Bara
$$ Bara Resort, 205 La Ngu-Pak Bara Rd (on the beach), T074-783333-4. A/c bungalows with hot water. Nice view but noisy and dusty from traffic.
$$-$ Best House Resort, T074-783058, www.besthouseresort.com. Close to the pier and arranged around a pond, 10 a/c and clean bungalows with comfortable beds, friendly owners and a good restaurant. Recommended.

Koh Tarutao
$$-$ Diamond Beach, T074-783138. Fan and a/c bungalows with sea views.

Koh Tarutao *p151*
Book through the National Park office in Bangkok, T02-579052, or the Pak Bara office located next to the pier, T074-783485. Accommodation is in the north and west of Tarutao. There are 3 choices: multi-occupancy bungalows that can accommodate families or groups, longhouses and tents. The 3 main beaches, Ao Pante, Ao Molae and Ao Sone, all offer some or all of these types, with Ao Pante, the one closest to the pier where the park warden offices are, offering the most selection. The rooms may have shared

outside toilets. The bungalows are sparsely furnished wooden structures, set along the side of the road against the cliffs. At all beaches the rates are the same: a small, 2-person bungalow costs ฿600, and the larger 4-person, ฿1000. There are big dormitory-type buildings, too, that are usually hired out to large Thai families or students. Tents are on the beach with a public shower and toilet. Check your tent for size and condition, and, if you intend to stay for more than 2 nights, seriously consider buying a tent from the mainland; it will pay for itself and be clean, in good condition and odour-free. Hired tents cost ฿100-200; camping in your own tent costs ฿60. Note that the treatment given to tent visitors varies. Best spots for camping are on Ao Jak and Ao Sone. You can also camp on the beach close to the national park bungalows (฿30 per night per person, as in other Thai national parks).

Koh Bulon-Leh *p152*
If you want to camp, **Charan Tour** can rent tents (see Satun tour operators, page 161.
$$$ Pansand Resort, T08-16933667 (mob), www.pansand-resort.com. Well-maintained and welcoming bungalows with attached bathrooms and dormitories. The views are good and the garden pleasant. Watersports, camping, snorkelling and boat trips. Has an evening internet service. Set in from main beach but this is a plus as it makes it feel more exclusive. Recommended. Closed Jul-Sep.

$$$-$$ Bulone Resort, T08-1897 9084 (mob), www.bulone-resort.com. Well positioned where the boats dock overlooking a beautiful beach. A wide range of bungalows from pleasant, spacious, almost colonial options to the more basic, single rooms with spotless shared bathrooms. All in good shape and run by friendly and helpful management. Electricity 1800-0200. Good restaurant and the island's best breakfast. Recommended.

$$ Bulon Viewpoint Resort and Tours, T074-728005. Some bungalows get little light and have poor views, others have great views, spotless bathrooms and plenty of sunshine. These are some of the most secure bungalows in Bulon-Leh. Good landscaping; the manager loves birds and insects. From the drop-off point on the beach you have a 15 to 20-min walk up a dirt path that becomes paved. Offers internet and has a good bar on the beach.

$$ Panka Bay Resort, T08-9466 8957 (mob). Up the hill and down on the Panka Bay side of the island, this is the only resort here. There are 21 bungalows at this Muslim Malay/Thai family-run establishment. They are arranged along the beach and in tiers up a hill, with handmade stone and sand steps built by the family. The beach is not great, as it has a rocky shore, but you can walk to the other beach in 20 mins and see some amazing bird and lizard life on the way. Excellent service: they offer a free pickup from the **Bulon-Le Resort**. Another perk is electricity until 0500. Huge restaurant with superb Thai-Malay fusion food. Recommended.

$$-$ Ban Sulaida Bungalows, near Panka Noi Bay. Pleasant, clean rooms set in carefully tended gardens, with friendly owner who gives discounts for longer stays. 5 mins from the beach, but this is not the white-sand idyll of the eastern coast, although it's good for snorkelling. Small, airy restaurant is decorated with shells, hanging bird nests and plants, serving good seafood. Closed in low season.

$$-$ Marina Bungalows, T074-728032, www.marina-kobulon.com. These log bungalows set into the hill going up towards Panka Bay are charming and romantic but overpriced. They are more treehouse than bungalow – you can see the ground through the spaces in the log floor and there is no glass in the windows. But, even if snakes and palm rats can clamber through the logs at night, there are perks like comfortable double beds, clean linen, fans and large verandas big enough for hammocks. For those who don't mind roughing it.

$ Chaolae Food and Bungalows, up hill further on from **Bulon Viewpoint Resort** (also called Chao Le Homestay). Run by a Chao Le family. 8 raised brick and bamboo bungalows – all adorable. It has sunken bathrooms with squat toilet and shower. Tucked away, so you might miss it, but it is well worth the hunt. Plenty of personal touches. Sweet restaurant with shell mobiles and lined with cacti and brightly hued flowers in pots. You can choose your fish from the daily catch for beautiful cooking with herbs and spices. Recommended.

Koh Adang and Koh Rawi *p152*

Accommodation is all on the southern swathe of Adang island, with longhouses offering **$$$-$$** rates, where some rooms accommodate up to 10 people. Tents are available for Adang at ฿200, own tent ฿30 at Laem Son. There is a simple restaurant. The island essentially closes down during the rainy season (mid May-mid Nov). The bungalows here differ in terms of the perks offered, such as hot showers.

Laem Son, ฿600 for 2-person bungalow, big tents (8-10 people), ฿300, medium/ middle tents (3-5 people), ฿300, small tents (2 people), ฿150.

Rawi Long House, ฿400. 4 people per room. Toilet outside.

Koh Lipe p152

Accommodation on Lipe is expanding and moving upmarket in rapid order. A few years ago, the Chao Le mainly operated the guesthouses, but more commercially astute outsiders have muscled in on the tourism industry. Electricity is sometimes only available from dusk onwards, mosquito nets are provided but not all places have fans or a/c that work, and, during the dry season, the water pressure can be low or non-existent. Free Wi-Fi is becoming more widely available. The bungalows are either concrete or bamboo and quite basic for the prices charged. Most of the action is on Pattaya Beach, which has powder-soft white sand and crystal-blue water that's unfortunately getting crowded with numerous long-tail and speed boats, adding noise and fumes and squeezing out safe areas to swim. On the opposite side of the island is the smaller, slightly less dazzling Sunset Beach, with a more artsy-hippy scene. Sunrise Beach lines the east side of the island; the beach here is beautiful and peaceful, with water clear and blue enough to hurt your eyes, although it is shallow for some distance making it better for paddling than swimming.

$$$$ Serendipity Beach Resort, southern tip of Sunrise Beach, T08-8395 5158/9794 4803, www.serendipityresort-kohlipe. com. Stylish wood a/c and fan bungalows perched on the rocks. Bar and restaurant. Its many stairs can be tiring to navigate. Among the new swish resorts popping up on Lipe, this is the only one we found that has a detailed 'green plan', which it publishes on its website.

$$$$-$$$ Andaman Resort, Sunrise Beach, T074-728017, www.andaman resortkohlipe.com. Next door to Mountain Resort sits this mix of 40 concrete, log and bamboo bungalows generously spaced around Sunrise Beach's pretty northern curve and well shaded by pine trees. The best rooms are the white-and-blue concrete row on the beach near the restaurant, although they lack some of the other huts' character. Clean, quiet, bright rooms popular with families. Run by a Chao Le-Chinese-Thai family. Recommended.

$$$$-$$$ Castaway Beach Resort, Sunrise Beach, T08-31387 472 (mob), www.castaway-resorts.com. Castaway's bungalows are pricier than most of the competition, but also heaps more stylish: thatched, 2-storey, Swiss Family Robinson-style treehouses with ethnic touches, slick bathrooms, balconies and hammocks. No a/c but Sunrise Beach's often strong northeasterly winds mean that most guests don't miss it. The beachfront bar with cushion-strewn wood decking is a popular spot for sundown tipples, even luring in guests from nearby resorts, but the food is overpriced even for Lipe. The resort's diveshop, Castaway Divers, is one of the friendliest and most professional on the island, albeit not the cheapest. Recommended.

$$$$-$$$ Lipe Resort, Pattaya Beach, T074-724 336, T074-750291, www. liperesort.com. A/c bungalows of varying sizes, set in part among the pine trees and all fairly clean with lino/tile floors and attached toilets, and 1 beachfront pool villa. The more expensive white wooden bungalows at the front are better value and have large verandas, while others sit over an unattractively crowded and waterlogged inlet. There are also cheaper longhouses at the back, and a new row of bungalows on stilts are under construction. The large, airy restaurant faces onto the beach. The staff go out of their way to be helpful but guests have complained of intimidation from the unpleasant owner.

$$$$-$$ Mountain Resort, bay to west of Sunrise Beach, T074-750452, www. mountainresortkohlipe.com. Well spaced corrugated-roof bungalows dot a steep, shaded hillside, many with idyllic views across the channel between Koh Lipe and Koh Adang. The fan or a/c rooms have 24-hr electricity, large verandas and basic tiled bathrooms. Steep cliff steps from the large wooden restaurant lead down to a gorgeous beach flanked by a row of pricier deluxe bungalows. Recommended.

$$$ Blue Tribes, Pattaya Beach, T08-1802 0077, www.bluetribeslipe.com. 2-level wooden fan bungalows and a happy traveller's vibe. Restaurant serves Italian. Popular.

$$$ Pooh Bungalows, Walking St (in the middle of the island), T074-750345/T089-463 5099 (mob), www.poohlipe.com. Has 6 clean fan bungalows set in an excellent, friendly, family-run complex of bar, internet, restaurant, travel agency and dive shop. Nice enough bungalows but they are not on the beach. Breakfast, free water refills and 20 mins of daily internet use are included. Convenient for early morning coffee and everything else at this 1-stop operation run by the affable Mr Pooh ('crab' in English). Recommended.

$$$ Ricci House, central part of island, just north of Walking St, T074-750457, www.riccihouse.com. Clean, spacious, well-crafted wooden a/c bungalows in a pleasant garden setting. Friendly service. The location's neither here nor there but easy enough to get around, and they'll meet you at the beach on arrival, if you book ahead.

$$$-$$ Green View Beach Resort, Pattaya Beach, T08-2830 3843, www.greenviewkohlipe.com. Fan bungalows in a shady area with tropical gardens. Care has been taken to protect the environment. No restaurant and reception closes in the evening, but there's a large and comfy beachfront lounging area. Bamboo walls offer good ventilation but also can be noisy. A bit pricey but pleasant.

$$$-$ Varin Beach Resort, Pattaya Beach, T074-750447/T081-598 2225 (mob), www.varinbeachresort.com. 109 clean bungalows, suites and villas set in a fairly cramped and regimental layout facing each other. The operation is run by a Muslim Thai/Malay family. Extremely busy in the peak season

with a bit of a churning guest-factory feel. The restaurant is a little characterless but service is excellent and attentive. Recommended.

$$ Pattaya Song (Two), Pattaya Beach, T074-728034/T08-6960 0418 (mob). These 39 fan bungalows are set in the hillside overlooking the water with an ideal view. Unfortunately, you have to navigate a rickety wooden staircase just above the rocks. The rooms are only partly clean and the whole set-up feels a bit like a squat. Too bad because the restaurant does good Italian meals and the views are marvellous. Aim for the more sturdy concrete bungalows at the front rather than the bamboo shacks out back. Run by Stefano from Bologna, a larger-than-life character and avid fisherman who set up in Koh Lipe years ago.

$$ Viewpoint Resort, south end of Sunrise Beach, T08-6961 5967 (mob). 15 basic and rickety bungalows on a pretty but small beach, studded with boulders and overlooking the nearby islands. Built on a hill so plenty of step climbing is needed to get to each bungalow. Quiet and secluded. Restaurant attached.

$$-$ Daya Resort, Pattaya Beach, T074-728030. Offers 48 concrete and bamboo bungalows with attached Western toilets and some rooms set in gardens. The bungalows are rather dirty and run-down, and also far too cramped, but the resort boasts the island's most popular seafood restaurant.

$$-$ Porn Resort, Sunset Beach, T08-9464 5765 (mob). This Chao-Le operation headed by Mr Gradtai (Rabbit) dominates quiet Sunset beach, which usually does live up to its title. A fairly self-contained resort with a mix of concrete and simple woven bamboo huts, it's incredibly popular with return visitors, especially families with small children. The restaurant is a bit overpriced but the menu at the nearby Flour Power bakery is an excellent alternative (see Restaurants, below).

Satun p154

$$$-$$ Pinnacle Satun Wangmai Hotel,
43 Satunthani Rd, T074-711607-8,
www.pinnaclehotels.com/satun/index.
html. White 5-storey dated, slightly musty
place with good facilities and clean a/c and
fan rooms, plus a restaurant. Decent level of
comfort and well priced.

$$-$ Ang Yee's House, 21/23 Trasatit
Rd, T08-0534 0057 (mob), T074-723844,
angyeeshouse.com. Colourful place with
only 6 a/c and fan rooms with shared
bathrooms, centrally located. Bar-restaurant
in small garden area on the ground floor.
Best to get a room at the back or be
content with the street noise and early-
morning blasts from the nearby community
announcement loudspeaker.

$ Rain Tong, Samantha Prasit Rd, at the
western end, by the river. Cheap, dank
flophouse with attached dirty bathrooms
and cold-water showers.

Thale Ban National Park p154

There are 10 bungalows for rent around the
lake, sleeping between 8 and 15. There is
also a restaurant and an information centre
at the park headquarters. Tents are available
for hire from the park headquarters. Advance
booking available on the Department of
National Park website, www.dnp.go.th.

Restaurants

Koh Tarutao p151

Each cluster of bungalows has its own basic
National Park-run Thai restaurant selling
average Thai food at reasonable prices;
there is also a shop selling some snacks
near the pier by the park entrance.

Koh Bulon-Leh p152

$ Orchid, near Ban Sulaida Bungalows,
see Where to stay, above. A good,
cheap restaurant.

Koh Lipe p152

Excellent simple seafood is served along the
main Pattaya Beach where tables and chairs
are laid out at night. You can choose the cut
and fish. **Varin Resort** also does marvellous
salads and baked potatoes with the fish. For
cheap eats, there are several stands along
Walking St selling fried and satay chicken,
sausage on a stick and roti.

$$ Pattaya Song restaurant, west end of
Pattaya Beach, next to Daya. Italian pasta
dishes and pizza as well as Thai food. Nice
setting at the base of the steep hill.

$$ Pooh's Restaurant, near the Sunrise
Beach end of Walking St, T074-750345.
Usually the busiest place, offering music,
a good bar and tasty meals in a relaxed
al fresco setting. The bakery next door is
also decent.

$ Banana Tree Restaurant, in the Walking
St village near Pooh's. A popular spot with
an extensive Thai menu and acclaimed
burgers, it shows movies in the evenings.

$ Flour Power Bakery, Sunset Beach,
behind Sabye Sports. As well as its staple
fruit pies, brownies, fresh bread and
cinnamon rolls, it also offers a mouth-
watering selection of Thai and Western
dishes, such as lemon chicken. The
vegetarian selection is good and all meals
are served with fresh bread or baked
potatoes and salad.

$ Khonlay Restaurant, 2 branches along
Walking St. Grilled seafood and the usual
Thai fare, popular with families.

$ Papaya Mom, Walking St. Friendly
no-nonsense place with bamboo tables
and lounging platforms, serving authentic
Isaan (Northeastern Thai) food, including
som tam papaya salad, and a decent range
of Thai dishes.

$ Pee Pee Bakery, Walking St, about 50 m
from Pattaya Beach. In the battle for Koh
Lipe's best bakery, this one is a serious
contender, partly due to its good location
but mostly due to its excellent fresh breads,
croissants, cakes and decent coffee.

$ Sunrise Beach Restaurant, Sunrise Beach, next to Varin 2 bungalows. Enjoy decent Thai and European food, and a friendly welcome, at this driftwood shack with sheltered seating planted in the sand.
$ Thai Pancake Shop, opposite the massage centre. A popular spot serving pancakes, sandwiches, burgers, breakfasts, simple Thai dishes, lassis, shakes and excellent cocktails.

Satun *p154*
Pretty much opposite the **Sinkiat Thani** are several small restaurants serving Malay food and a *roti* shop selling banana, egg and plain *rotis* in the mornings.
$$-$ Banburee, Buriwanit Rd. 1 of 2 places with English signs. Modern establishment behind the **Sinkiat Thani**.
$$-$ Kualuang, Sa*tuntanee Phiman. Best in a group of small restaurants.
$ The Baker's, Sa*tuntanee Phiman, main street into town. Pastries, ice cream and soft drinks.
$ Smile, round the corner from **Wangmai Hotel** on Sa*tuntanee Phiman Rd. Fast food, budget prices.
$ Suhana, 16/7 Buriniwet Rd. The other English-signed place on this road behind the mosque. Muslim food.

Foodstalls
Night market with stalls serving Thai and Malay dishes on Satun Thani Soi 3. There are plenty of roadside food vendors – particularly on Samantha Prasit Rd. All serve cheap rice and noodles.

Bars and clubs

Koh Lipe *p152*
As the volume of tourist trade picks up, more of these are springing up. On Pattaya Beach there's **Time to Chill** probably the pick of the bunch due to the super-friendly dreadlocked owner Mut and a lovely laid-back atmosphere; **Monkey Bar, Moon Light Bar, Barracuda** and **Peace and Love Bar**, all

of which are relaxed with mats and candles on the beach.
The Box, Walking St. Trendy spot serving tapas and cocktails. Brings in a big flashpacker crowd.
Jack's Jungle Bar, up in the hills (follow the signs from the village). Has a more upbeat feel and is popular with the diving crowd. Make sure you bring a torch for the trek home.
Karma beach bar, on the charming bay below the **Mountain Resort**. A popular bar. The owners are friendly and it normally has a great island-idyll atmosphere.
Pooh's remains a favourite watering hole and is rather more upmarket than the beach bars, with a stage for live bands.

What to do

Tarutao National Park *p148, map p149*
Diving and snorkelling
Some of the best areas for coral are in the waters northwest of Koh Rang Nok, northwest of Tarutao, southeast of Koh Rawi, around Koh Klang between Tarutao and Adang, and off Koh Kra off Koh Lipe's east coast. Equipment is for hire on Adang and Lipe.

Kayaking
There are a few kayak rental shops on each beach and some resorts have free kayaks for guests. These are all sit-on-top crafts, suitable for short excursions only.

Tour operators
For tours to Tarutao, see also Satun, below.
Tarutao Travel, in La-Ngu town (on the way to Pak Bara Pier), T074-722 150.
Udom Tour, Ban Pak Bara, just before the port, T08-1897 4765 (mob).

Koh Lipe *p152*
Diving
Castaway Divers, Sunrise Beach, Castaway Resort (see Where to stay), T08-7478 1516, www.kohlipedivers.com. Very professional but approachable outfit.

Forra Dive Centre, opposite Varin Resort on Walking St; also on Sunrise Beach near Gypsy Resort, T08-0545 5012, www.forradiving.com.
Lotus Dive (Pooh's), T08-3642 4821, www.lotusdive.com.
Sabye Sports, T08-9464 5884 (mob), www.sabye-sports.com. The island's first scuba-diving and sports centre, next to **Porn Bungalows**, offers diving and rents canoes and snorkelling equipment.

Tour operators
Heading further west from Lipe, there are countless islands and coral reefs teeming with a staggering variety of fish – the locals know all the good spots. The best locations, only 1 or 2 hrs away, include Koh Dong, Koh Pung and Koh Tong, Koh Hin Son, Koh Hin Ngam and Koh Chabang.
Dang Dee, next to Sunrise Beach at the end of Walking St, T074-750402, www.dang deeservice.com. A friendly family-run outfit that arranges all-day snorkelling tours for around ฿2200-2800 per boat for 6 people, as well as boats off the island, visa runs, etc.
KohLipeThailand.com. Well organized tour agency with 2 shops along Walking St. Arranges snorkelling trips, transport and accommodation, and publishes a handy map. The larger shop has an internet café and books for sale. There are many more scattered around.

Satun *p154*
Tour operators
Charan Tour, 19/6 Satunthani Rd, T074-711453. Runs daily boat tours to the islands Oct-May. Lunch and snorkelling equipment are provided. Has a good reputation.

⊖ Transport

Tarutao National Park *p148, map p149*
Boat
Koh Tarutao lies off the coast 30 km south of Pak Bara; Koh Adang, Rawi and Lipe are another 40 km out into the Andaman Sea. Koh Bulon-Leh is 20 km due west of Pak

Bara. Beware of travelling to any of these islands during bad weather; it is dangerous and a number of boats have foundered.
   Speedboats to **Pak Bara** or **Koh Lipe** depart 5-6 times a day during high season (Nov–May), 3 times a day during low season. One operator, Satun Pakbara Speedboat Club, posts its schedule for this and other transfer routes between Phuket and Langkawi on its website www.tarutaolipeisland.com. Long-tail boats can also be chartered.

Bus
There are regular buses from **Ban Pak Bara** to **Trang** and **Satun**, 60 km south. Connections to **Hat Yai**, 1½ hrs. Hat Yai is 158 km east of Pak Bara (1½hrs).

Koh Bulon-Leh *p152*
Boat
Note that all arriving and departing passengers must take a long-tail boat to and from shore, ฿50, which is not included in the ferry ticket price. There is now only speedboat service from Pak Bara, departing at 1230 daily, returning at 0930 (฿400 each way, 30 mins). To Koh Lipe there are 2 trips a day (1330 and 1530), returning daily 0900 (฿600 each way). There is also a daily speedboat service to Phuket (฿3100), departing at 1000 with stops at Koh Mook (฿900), Koh Kradan (฿900), Koh Ngai (฿1050) and Koh Lanta (฿1600) on the way. Long-tail boats can be chartered from Pak Bara to Bulon-Leh for about ฿1500.

Koh Lipe *p152*
Boat
Koh Lipe boat transfers have increased significantly in recent years. There are new boats and routes being added all the time. Watch for overcrowding, though. Speedboats connect Koh Lipe to the mainland pier of Pak Bara, stopping briefly at Koh Tarutao to drop off and pick up passengers. They depart the floating offshore pier at Pattaya beach at intervals

0930-1330 and can be booked at travel agents all over the island (try Dang Dee; see Tour operators, above). They run less frequently during low season. Journey time is roughly 1½ hrs.

The last speedboat to Lipe from Pak Bara currently leaves at 1400, so if coming via Hat Yai aim to arrive no later than 1100, as the minibus from the airport or train station takes about 1½ hrs. Late Oct–mid May, there is also a daily speedboat service from Malaysia's Langkawi.

Koh Lipe is a stop along the route of Tigerline high-speed ferry that runs a daily service departing Lipe at 1600 and arriving in Langkawi, Malaysia, at 1830. To Phuket, the ferry departs at 1100, stopping at Hat Yao in Trang, and Mook, Kradan, Ngai, Lanta and Phi Phi islands along the way. Also runs a service to Ao Nang with stops at Krabi and Koh Jum. You can island-hop and book any leg of these routes separately. Prices and schedule on www.tigerlinetravel.com. Operates Nov–Apr only.

Note that all arriving and departing passengers must take a long-tail boat to and from shore, ฿50, which is not included in the ferry ticket price.

Satun *p154*
Air
Hat Yai airport offers several daily connecting flights to Bangkok with **Air Asia**, THAI, **Nok Air** and **Orient Thai Airlines**. There is also 1 daily direct flight to Chiang Mai and Kuala Lumpur on AirAsia and to Singapore on Tiger Airways.

Boat
There is 1 boat a day from Tammalang Pier (Satun) to the islands (**Tarutao** and **Lipe**) at 1230, ฿650 one way. It is also possible to charter a boat from Satun, but it is a lot cheaper catch an early bus to **Pak Bara** and take 1 of the regular boats from there (see above).

Bus
Overnight connections with **Bangkok**, 15 hrs. Buses for Bangkok leave from Sarit Phuminaraot Rd. Regular connections with **Hat Yai** and **Trang** from opposite the wat on Buriwanit Rd. To **Pak Bara**, buses leave from Plaza Market. The buses connect with ferries.

Taxi
To **Hat Yai** from Bureevanith Rd; to **Trang**, from taxi rank next to Chinese temple.

Contents

Footnotes

Index

Titles available in the Footprint *Focus* range

Latin America	UK RRP	US RRP
Bahia & Salvador	£7.99	$11.95
Brazilian Amazon	£7.99	$11.95
Brazilian Pantanal	£6.99	$9.95
Buenos Aires & Pampas	£7.99	$11.95
Cartagena & Caribbean Coast	£7.99	$11.95
Costa Rica	£8.99	$12.95
Cuzco, La Paz & Lake Titicaca	£8.99	$12.95
El Salvador	£5.99	$8.95
Guadalajara & Pacific Coast	£6.99	$9.95
Guatemala	£8.99	$12.95
Guyana, Guyane & Suriname	£5.99	$8.95
Havana	£6.99	$9.95
Honduras	£7.99	$11.95
Nicaragua	£7.99	$11.95
Northeast Argentina & Uruguay	£8.99	$12.95
Paraguay	£5.99	$8.95
Quito & Galápagos Islands	£7.99	$11.95
Recife & Northeast Brazil	£7.99	$11.95
Rio de Janeiro	£8.99	$12.95
São Paulo	£5.99	$8.95
Uruguay	£6.99	$9.95
Venezuela	£8.99	$12.95
Yucatán Peninsula	£6.99	$9.95

Asia	UK RRP	US RRP
Angkor Wat	£5.99	$8.95
Bali & Lombok	£8.99	$12.95
Chennai & Tamil Nadu	£8.99	$12.95
Chiang Mai & Northern Thailand	£7.99	$11.95
Goa	£6.99	$9.95
Gulf of Thailand	£8.99	$12.95
Hanoi & Northern Vietnam	£8.99	$12.95
Ho Chi Minh City & Mekong Delta	£7.99	$11.95
Java	£7.99	$11.95
Kerala	£7.99	$11.95
Kolkata & West Bengal	£5.99	$8.95
Mumbai & Gujarat	£8.99	$12.95

Africa & Middle East	UK RRP	US RRP
Beirut	£6.99	$9.95
Cairo & Nile Delta	£8.99	$12.95
Damascus	£5.99	$8.95
Durban & KwaZulu Natal	£8.99	$12.95
Fès & Northern Morocco	£8.99	$12.95
Jerusalem	£8.99	$12.95
Johannesburg & Kruger National Park	£7.99	$11.95
Kenya's Beaches	£8.99	$12.95
Kilimanjaro & Northern Tanzania	£8.99	$12.95
Luxor to Aswan	£8.99	$12.95
Nairobi & Rift Valley	£7.99	$11.95
Red Sea & Sinai	£7.99	$11.95
Zanzibar & Pemba	£7.99	$11.95

Europe	UK RRP	US RRP
Bilbao & Basque Region	£6.99	$9.95
Brittany West Coast	£7.99	$11.95
Cádiz & Costa de la Luz	£6.99	$9.95
Granada & Sierra Nevada	£6.99	$9.95
Languedoc: Carcassonne to Montpellier	£7.99	$11.95
Málaga	£5.99	$8.95
Marseille & Western Provence	£7.99	$11.95
Orkney & Shetland Islands	£5.99	$8.95
Santander & Picos de Europa	£7.99	$11.95
Sardinia: Alghero & the North	£7.99	$11.95
Sardinia: Cagliari & the South	£7.99	$11.95
Seville	£5.99	$8.95
Sicily: Palermo & the Northwest	£7.99	$11.95
Sicily: Catania & the Southeast	£7.99	$11.95
Siena & Southern Tuscany	£7.99	$11.95
Sorrento, Capri & Amalfi Coast	£6.99	$9.95
Skye & Outer Hebrides	£6.99	$9.95
Verona & Lake Garda	£7.99	$11.95

North America	UK RRP	US RRP
Vancouver & Rockies	£8.99	$12.95

Australasia	UK RRP	US RRP
Brisbane & Queensland	£8.99	$12.95
Perth	£7.99	$11.95

For the latest books, e-books and a wealth of travel information, visit us at:
www.footprinttravelguides.com.

footprinttravelguides.com

Join us on facebook for the latest travel news, product releases, offers and amazing competitions:
www.facebook.com/footprintbooks.